ON STONE OR SAND

PLEROMA
PRESS

ON STONE OR SAND

The Ethics of Christianity, Capitalism, & Socialism

by
MICHAEL KELLEY

Address all orders, correspondence, and queries to:

Pleroma Press
Box 242
Carson, ND 58529

Pleroma Press and Publishing Company is a branch of Beth-El Institute for the Arts and Sciences, Carson, North Dakota.

Library of Congress Catalogue Card Number: 93-083942

ISBN:0-9636834-0-3

First Printing, June, 1993

10 9 8 7 6 5 4 3 2 1

Printed in the United States of America

To Dick Remick

Amicus et Patronus

TABLE OF

CONTENTS

ON STONE OR SAND

PREFACE

FOR the generation that grew up during the Cold War, the recent momentous changes in Eastern Europe and the former Soviet Union have brought a sense of relief. The threat of nuclear destruction, while nearly unimaginable, was nevertheless a real possibility for most inhabitants of this globe. Now such an event seems remote.

The conflict underlying the differences between East and West seems to have disappeared from center stage, and the reason for this, of course, is the entire collapse in the East of communism as a viable social and economic system. The extended and intense rivalry between the "capitalist" West and the "socialist" East seems to have ended in favor of the West. The hundreds of millions who lived under the totalitarian regime of communism appear to have recognized that the promised paradise of socialism could not be attained; that, in fact, it was capitalism as practiced in the West that had produced prosperity on an enviable scale.

Many looked to the West with a hope for change and improvement in their lives. What they now faced in the East was not merely a matter of solving their problems within the context of socialism; there would have to be an entire revamping of society in the direction of liberty, democracy, and free-market values. Marxist philosophy was not only dead but decaying on the corpse of a system that proved fruitless precisely because of its empty philosophy. Nothing remained but to revolutionize the revolution.

This profound historical event has led some to speculate that history per se has arrived at its denouement. Is the centuries-long struggle of men and nations for truth and justice at its conclusion? Has the rivalry between capitalism and socialism finally been resolved in favor of capitalism? Does the apparent triumph of capitalism mean we have arrived at history's end? May we declare victory just yet?

There are many reasons to dismiss this sort of thinking not only as premature but infantile—not the least of which is that Christians should know that history does not end short of the moment that lies hidden in the counsel of God. But of even greater relevance, the struggle for capitalism, far from having been concluded, is actually about to begin. Although socialism for the moment has experienced a setback, it is not defeated—far from it.

The death of socialism in the East should not lead us to believe that it has lost its appeal in the West or, for that matter, that the East might not witness its rejuvenation. The reason for this has less to do with the relative success or failure of each system in the area of economics, though that is not unimportant; it has to do with the ethical and religious assumptions upon which each system is founded. This is the point that most deserves to be stressed.

Many have failed to understand that capitalism and socialism stand for wholly incompatible ethical ideals. The ideal of each represents not only a technique, an organization, a way of life, but intangible spiritual values and attitudes that frame life and human activity within the concept of an ethical *good*. So one may not laud the superiority of a free market system if one supposes it is possible to derive benefits from that system when the ethical outlook of its people is basically hedonistic. No economy is ever ethically neutral.

The foundation of a true national economy is reflected in the ethical and intellectual quality of its citizens. Warren Brookes, in *The Economy in Mind*, has said that "a society that has no values will not produce much value; a nation whose virtues are declining should not be surprised at a declining economy." Western societies today are at war with God's ethical absolutes. As a result, many people are increasingly willing to surrender responsibility (and self-respect and integrity and honesty) to organized political power. This ethical reshaping has caused socialism to appear attractive to large numbers of citizens who, though they suppose they live in capitalist societies, don't understand that recent events in the Soviet bloc are a warning of what might happen here.

In chapters five through seven of the Sermon on the Mount in the Gospel of Matthew, Jesus sets the authority of his word in matters of faith and conduct—*I say to you*—over against the traditions of men: *You have heard it said*. He declares an antithetical opposition to those traditions. Jesus also says that his word and God's word are the same. So when he contrasts the traditions of men with his own instructions, Jesus is doing so on the authority of God's word—which he identifies as *his* word. To hear and obey Jesus is the same as to hear and obey God, and vice versa.

At the very end of this portion of Scripture, at Matthew 7.24-27, in one of his well-known parables, Jesus summarizes the ethical issue of every life, in so far as it applies to each person's work in the building of entire cultures and civilizations. There he says that the difference between the wise builder and the foolish builder is the difference between one who hears his word and lives by it, and one who hears his word and refuses to live by it. The obedient person, then, builds his cultural and civilizing efforts on solid STONE, so they are firmly grounded and immovable, able to stand the winds of adversity. But the disobedient person builds all his work on SAND, and has no base beneath to anchor his efforts when the storm of God's judgment rises.

To get a mere glimpse of how far our culture has wandered from the foundation commended by Christ, note the statement made in "The Structure of Theories and the Analysis of Data," an essay on the hard science of math written by the philosopher and mathematician, Patrick Suppes, in which he deliberately contravenes Christ: "There is somewhere a beautiful quotation from deFinetti in which as part of defending the Bayesian use of far-from-certain prior information in making decisions, he says that it is better to build on sand than on a void. I believe we can rephrase this remark and say something that is as important for philosophy. When it comes to matters of knowledge, real houses are always built on sand

and never on rock."

Without recognition of the authority of the word of God over all of life, the struggle between capitalism and socialism will remain unresolved. As long as people refuse to submit in faith and obedience to the undivided authority of Jesus and God, the totalitarian temptation will continue to bedevil their efforts to erect a sound economic and social order. There are only two alternatives for mankind: a civilization built either *On Stone or Sand*. Only on stone is genuine capitalism possible; on sand, the tendency invariably will be toward some form of socialism. If mankind chooses the latter, as seems to be increasingly the case in the West, then we can be certain that mankind will get, as in the East, first tyranny, and then total collapse.

INTRODUCTION

SOCIALISM is "the watchword and the catchword of our day. The socialist idea dominates the modern spirit. The masses approve of it. It expresses the thoughts and feelings of all; it has set its seal upon our time."[1]

Ludwig von Mises offered this astute observation in 1922, at the beginning of a decade remembered as The Roaring Twenties, an era, we were once taught to believe, that epitomized unfettered, laissez-faire capitalism. Today we know that such descriptions are no longer accurate. Already in the twenties both capitalism and limited government were under assault from the forces of "progressivism." Mises's observation best sums up the prevailing social and moral attitudes of the day.

Socialism was in ascendence because of a radical moral and religious transformation that had been underway long before. Nearly two centuries earlier, the ethical ground was being prepared to receive an implanting of the socialist idea. Starting in the Renaissance (1400-1600), but not reaching maturity until the Enlightenment of the eighteenth century, a new secular religion of *humanity* began to replace the dominant faith and moral value-system of Christianity.

The leading minds of the culture declared the irrelevance of God to the affairs of life, and looked to science and reason as the way to fashion a better society. In time, the masses, as socialism termed them, would support this new course that sovereign man (as he now saw himself) had charted on his

1 Ludwig von Mises, *Socialism: An Economic and Sociological Analysis*, trans J. Kahane (Indianapolis: Liberty Classics, 1981), p 15.

own. The socialist idea, which will be discussed in detail later, overtook the modern spirit when belief in the "religion of man" became widespread. If by the early 1920s a residue of capitalism was still present, it represented a mere atavism, a throwback; the world of man's experience would take only a while longer to catch up with his beliefs. A little more time and a telling crisis were needed to ingrain the socialist idea into the consciousness of modern man.

Johnson has characterized the prevailing outlook at the turn of the century, an outlook embedded in the 1920s, as one of conspicuous moral relativism. He traces this to a scientific relativism that preceded it. Because of Darwin and Einstein, the world was seen to be in flux. Nothing, any more, seemed definite or certain; all was subject to change; there were no absolutes. Scientific relativity became a convenient tool for intellectuals to use to revamp the ethical foundations of society. Western civilization, without its foundation of Christian faith and law, emerged in the nineteenth century afflicted with cultural pessimism. A new basis was needed for the conduct of men and societies.

It was discovered in the ethical ideals, first, of the theory of evolution, and second, the theory of relativity: the death of absolutes in the world of nature confirmed the death of absolutes in the realm of morality. "At the beginning of the 1920's the belief began to circulate...that there were no longer any absolutes...relativity became confused with relativism."[2] But it was not only those in the cultural vanguard for whom moral relativism became fashionable. It was, as Mises noted, the spirit of the times. In the West, moral relativism reached the man in the street and it was no accident that both moral relativism and socialism attacked him at the same time.

The moral relativism at the center of the new religion of

2 Paul Johnson, *Modern Times: The World from the Twenties to the Eighties* (New York: Harper, 1983), p 4.

humanity was far from a simple belief in total chaos, or a kind of skepticism that found meaning in the denial of civilization as such. Rather, it was a conspiracy by modern men to replace the grip of God's absolutes with those of man's, and to reconstruct the entirety of society on that basis. Doubtless, "Among the advanced races [the Christian West], the decline and ultimately, the collapse of the religious impulse [of Christianity] would leave a huge vacuum. The history of modern times is in great part the history of how that vacuum had been filled."[3]

From a "transvaluation of values" would arise a new civilization whose course would be charted by the self-defined *needs* of man. This new civilization would be unhindered by any constraints other than those that men saw fit to make themselves. We should not be surprised if, in Johnson's words, this new civilization "would produce a new kind of Messiah, uninhabited by any religious sanctions whatever, and with an unappeasable appetite for controlling mankind."[4]

There is no question that socialism rises from that new religious impulse and seeks to fill the vacuum left by Christianity. It is precisely that form in which the new kind of Messiah now made its appearance.

When socialism first began to take hold of the thinking of nineteenth-century man, it was foisted on him as the inevitable conclusion of a truly scientific and rational society. It was said that socialism's emergence in history stemmed from underlying social and economic forces that necessarily moved society more and more in one direction. The old bourgeois society might hold out a little longer, but it was decaying and would soon collapse. Such claims, however, were by no means the result of unbiased observations by disinterested social theorists. Over and over, the conclusions

3 Johnson, p 48.
4 *Ibid.*

they reached were tinged with yearnings for a better world. Socialism was as much a wish as it was a scientific conclusion.

The prophets of socialism proclaimed it carried the hope of redemption; not only would socialism inevitably come in the future, but unless it did, civilization had no chance of survival. More than anything, the desire for socialism prejudiced the conclusions of social analysis. A religious conviction lay beneath socialism's veneer of scientific respectability: a heartfelt urge to jettison all cultural roots in Christianity and rebuild civilization on a new, man-centered moral foundation.

In the 1920s, as I have said, socialism was just under the surface, beginning to show through in places, perhaps, but awaiting a crisis to usher it in. Actually, the first crisis had already taken place: the Great War of 1914 to 1918. This was the culminating event in the deterioration of the ethical foundations of the Old World. It thoroughly convulsed the last vestiges of a civilization that had all but lost its connections to the Christian past from which it arose. At the same time, the belief in capitalism and liberal-democratic institutions in general was shaken to the core. For the first time, there was doubt about their inviolability, not to mention their practical superiority. Perhaps it is more correct to say that the war was the product, rather than the cause, of the loss of faith in that civilization. Nevertheless, it was an excuse to bury Christian civilization—or what was left of it—and to erect on its grave a version of the Brave New World.

One of the unanticipated yet widely welcomed effects of the war was the exaltation of the state to a central, all-encompassing role. "The effect of the Great War was enormously to increase the size, and therefore the destructive capacity and propensity to oppress, of the state." It "greedily swallowed up the independence of the private sector."[5] This increase in state power was not temporary; the war created

5 Johnson, pp 14-16.

a permanent regard for government power that continues to this day. In fact, "the war corporation of 1917 began one of the great continuities of modern American history, sometimes underground, sometimes on the surface, which culminated in the vast welfare state...brought into being in the late 1960s."[6] Once a few have possession of the sort of power that enables them to control the destiny of millions, you can well imagine there will be little inclination to give it up. The war, then, made it possible for those with power to practice messianism in a way that their nineteenth-century forebears scarcely dared to imagine. The god-state had arrived.

The Great Depression kicked the door to statism wide open. In Rothbard's words, "The chief impact of the Great Depression on American thought was universal acceptance of the view that 'laissez-faire capitalism' was to blame. The common opinion—among economists and lay public alike—holds that 'Unreconstructed Capitalism' prevailed during the 1920's, and that the tragic depression shows that old-fashioned *laissez-faire* can no longer work. It had always brought instability and depression during the nineteenth century; but now it was getting worse and becoming absolutely intolerable. The government must step in..."[7]

After the crash of the stock market in 1929, there was a clamoring claim that capitalism did not produce wealth and prosperity for everybody, but bred greedy tycoons who hoarded the wealth of the nation in their pockets; the depression allowed envy, before concealed, to emerge into the light of day. A "righteous government" must check this avarice in the name of the people. As a result, new vistas of governmental power opened up. The New Deal provided America with its first real experience of big government, and the growth of The New Deal has continued to the present day.

6 Johnson, p 17.

7 Murray N. Rothbard, *America's Great Depression* (New York: Richardson & Snyder, 1983), p 2.

When Hayek published, twenty-two years after Mises' appraisal, his now famous critique of modern civilization's death wish, *The Road to Serfdom*, his similar declaration echoed with even greater resonance. "Scarcely anybody doubts that we must continue to move toward socialism," he said, "and most people are merely trying to deflect this movement in the interest of a particular class or group."[8]

As matters presently stand, the vast majority of people in the once predominantly Christian West believe that socialism and welfarism, to some extent at least, contain the correct formula for prosperity, humanity, and justice. Sometimes we hear that the broader segments of society are not actually in favor of the socialization of society; that they are being manipulated by a well-positioned and politically vociferous minority—the media, for example, or special interest lobbyists, or self-serving politicians. This depiction is not wholly accurate. The broader segments of society, I believe, are morally adrift. And because of their unmoored state they are able to be manipulated.

In the course of politics, conservative programs do appear from time to time, calling for an end to the Leviathan state, or at least demanding that it be scaled back, but are rarely taken seriously; they are viewed as romantic fantasies of the past. The conservative programs that do succeed are attacked by the humanist establishment. Certainly, too, the burden of wealth required to maintain and increase the size of the welfare state is felt; and no doubt this is why conservatives sometimes bring the populace to pause, to reconsider the direction in which we are headed. But the burden that most people feel is economic, not moral. Most of them dearly want some form of government welfare; it's just that they don't want to have to pay for it. They have learned to think this is something to which they are entitled. To eliminate the

8 Friederich A. Hayek, *The Road To Serfdom* (Chicago: Univ of Chicago Press, 1944), pp 4 & 5.

welfare state would be to take away their "rights."

In his brilliant yet little recognized work, *Fire in the Minds of Men*, James Billington has brilliantly traced the origins and unfolding of what he terms the modern "revolutionary faith." It began, he claims, with a moral transformation at the heart of the Christian world, and was the work of intellectuals and a self-appointed cultural elite. Neither poor factory hands nor oppressed peasants initially rebelled against Christian and capitalist civilization. Accordingly, "...the characteristic 19th-century European revolutionary:[was] a thinker lifted up by ideas, not a worker or a peasant bent down by toil."[9]

It is a myth to believe that capitalism unintentionally but unavoidably gave birth to a "proletariat" which, because its existence itself was perceived as an injustice, saw as its chief responsibility the need to crush an oppressive social and economic order and to substitute a system more equitable. The image of capitalism as a form of social relationships that concentrated wealth in the hands of a few, to the impoverishment of the masses, originated with uprooted and alienated intellectuals who wanted to persuade themselves and convince others that unlimited powers ought to be entrusted to them, so they could redesign and rebuild society. They imagined themselves to be the messiahs already mentioned. With their unimpeachable expertise and knowledge of society, they saw it as their responsibility to save civilization from certain doom.

Socialism, which revolution was expected to usher in, was a "mental and spiritual revolt—born of a new vision rather than old grievances."[10] Today's intellectuals hold the same view. It is an illusion to think we can turn back the clock, they say. They have an emotional contempt for capitalism, less

9 James H. Billington, *Fire in the Minds of Men: Origins of the Revolutionary Faith* (New York: Basic Books, 1980), p 3.
10 Billington, p 232.

thought out than their nineteenth-century predecessors, but still there. Their hostility has nothing to do with a proper understanding of capitalism or, for that matter, socialism.

To argue against the material productivity of capitalism is difficult; it is obvious how well it outperforms any socialist society of today. But for most people the economic argument is not what counts; what matters is the appeal of socialism's moral and humanitarian qualities. The most important cultural and spiritual needs, and the aspirations of humanity, cannot be met by capitalism, they say. Capitalist society fosters impersonal relationships, dehumanizes man, and reduces him to the status of a mere thing, to be used at somebody else's whim. Socialism alone seems to hold out a promise of total enhancement of the entire man. It promises him inner fulfillment and the opportunity to realize his own best potential. This characterization of socialism descended from the genius of Karl Marx and remains imbedded in the consciousness of the shapers of today's culture, no matter how much they may or may not be committed to Marx's revolutionary program.

But the attraction of socialism is not limited to today's educated cultural leaders. By now it's on everybody's agenda. The average individual may not be drawn to it by an enraptured vision of a new social and moral order, but everybody seems to have grasped the political advantage of economic envy. Large numbers of people believe that others have benefitted from the world at their expense, and somebody better see to it that they get their fair share. They have been quick to learn that the "somebody" capable of carrying out their demands—because it has such a plenitude of power to coerce—is the state.

And since the form of our government is a democracy, the people's greatest interest seems to be in electing those officials who will promise to get *their* money back for them. The wealth that exists is perceived as the wealth of society, to be distributed to every member equally. The primary purpose of government, most people believe, ought to be the enhancement of what anybody takes to be his personal well-being;

and, as Hayek noted, most people merely try to deflect government in their direction.

The conflict between capitalism and socialism ultimately draws us back to the conflict between the Christian ethic and an anti-Christian ethic. The choice of the ethic is a choice of the heart and is expressed in faith, by a bondage of the will Luther best expressed. Or as Wilhelm Roepke says, "In the last resort, the distinction between socialists and non-socialists is one which divides men who hold basically different views of life and its true meaning and of the nature of man and society."[11] Roepke is partly correct when he says "...the ultimate source of our civilization's disease is the spiritual and religious crisis which has overtaken all of us... Above all, man is *Homo religiousus*, and yet we have, for the past century, made the desperate attempt to get along without God...we have set up the cult of man..."[12]

We must understand, however, that socialism does not merely deny God; it sets up another god: man himself. The God socialism wishes to rid the world of is the Christian God. Socialism is a religious substitute for Christianity, no more nor less—an absolute that accepts no compromise. It means to transfer total authority on all matters over to man alone.

What about capitalism, it may be asked? Isn't it as man-centered as socialism? Isn't it the product of the same religious impulse? Why does it create more problems than it solves? Why is strong government needed to rein in its excesses? Questions of this kind will no doubt arise.

The historical truth is that capitalism, in spite of the many faults attributed to it, never appeared as a system driven by the wish to evict God from the world. At the center of capitalist practices, no confrontation generally existed between God's commandments and the desire of man for moral

11 Wilhelm Roepke, *A Humane Economy: The Social Framework of the Free Market*, trans Elizabeth Henderson (South Bend: Gateway, 1960), p 4.
12 Roepke, p 8.

autonomy. That is, capitalism did not bear in itself this moral conflict as a necessary premise. If, under capitalism, men acted contrary to God's righteous decrees—and, unquestionably, many did—that does not indicate a moral flaw in capitalism itself.

Capitalism came under siege by the secular left *as a result of the decline of the Christian ethic*, which places man's will and actions in all matters under the authority of God. Capitalism is not only compatible with this arrangement; it cannot exist apart from it. While socialism is savagely hostile toward Christianity, because Christianity proclaims the supremacy of God's will over man's, capitalism aligns with Christianity's religious and moral outlook. Capitalism is not man-centered; it must be God-centered, if it is to work, and problems arise only when capitalism loses its ethical moorings.

Capitalism has not received favorable press in modern times. Hardly anyone believes that capitalism is morally superior to socialism. They've been taught the opposite. This is what generates socialism's appeal. In the West, socialism has helped contribute to a moral schizophrenia on economic issues. Many see that capitalism works better economically than socialism, yet socialism is perceived as necessary, in order to correct capitalism's "inherent" moral deficiencies.

Such notions are due, partly, to an ignorance of capitalist economics. Christians should know that capitalism—or whatever name one wishes to call it—originated in a culture where a biblical lifestyle prevailed, and it can function properly only as long as that lifestyle is intact.

Capitalism emerged historically on an ethical foundation. Men were imbued with a sense of responsibility toward God, the necessity of toil, respect for a just civic order, and moral self-control. No contradiction was seen to exist between prosperity earned by productivity and the obligations of godly behavior. In the Christian view, capitalism, productivity, and gain are some of those obligations. And one cannot say that anybody consciously invented capitalism. Those who practiced it hadn't the least idea they were devising a system that would be called "capitalist" by humanists and socialists for purposes of denigration.[13]

Although modern humanists have almost unanimously adopted the socialist creed, there are a few exceptions. Some are stalwart defenders of capitalism and brilliant adversaries of socialism. Their attraction is often their ability to communicate insights and scathing analyses in simple form, without the obtuseness associated with contemporary economics. These apologists of latter-day capitalism, through their masterful and lucid publications, have a growing influence among the educated and laymen alike. Besides Mises and Hayek, writers like Murray Rothbard, Henry Hazlitt, and others may be consulted.

Christians who have not succumbed to anticapitalist propaganda should be grateful that significant numbers of ideas have emerged in print. These can be used as source material in the struggle against socialism and humanist culture. However, since the critique of socialism comes substantially from a humanist viewpoint, further questions arise. In particular, how should Christians morally assess their defense of capitalism? What, for them, is the moral basis of capitalism? Should they present it as rooted in and dependent upon Christianity? Can capitalism exist on any other than a Christian foundation and still be capitalism?

The views and tenets of these contemporary proponents of capitalism have aroused, in a broad sense, a lively "reawaking of public interest in the intellectual tradition of *classical liberalism...*"—the tradition, in other words, of John Locke, Edmund Burke, Adam Smith, David Hume, Immanuel Kant, and others, who have been described as "the theorists of

13 Mises, in *Socialism*, pp 105 & 106 states: "the terms 'Capitalism' and 'Capitalist Production' are political catchwords. They were invented by socialists, not to extend knowledge, but to carp, criticize, to condemn. Today, they have only to be uttered to conjure up a picture of the relentless exploitation of wage-slaves by the pitiless rich. They are scarcely ever used save to imply a disease in the body-politic."

liberalism's Golden Age in the eighteenth century." This tradition is alleged to cherish "the dignity of the human individual and the moral primacy of his freedom, the virtues of free markets and the necessity for limited government under the rule of law."[14] The modern-day defenders of capitalism in this tradition, then, are often called "neoclassical liberals."

It is certainly true that today's neoclassical liberal thinkers have produced much-needed, often neglected material to weigh in against the collectivist mania of most intellectuals. They also have provided the basis for a reevaluation of what is now accepted dogma. Two outstanding examples are Ludwig von Mises and Friederich Hayek, whom we shall examine later. Both have warned us of the consequences of our modern society's drift toward a concentration of power in government; and both see Western civilization today as seriously threatened. What our forefathers struggled to achieve, and taught the generations after them to cherish: the way of liberty, independence, and self-determination—what everybody in our time takes for granted—today stands threatened by socialism. Hayek and Mises, among others, know full well that socialism means tyranny, not justice and humanitarianism. What they do not clearly understand is that socialism's real enemy is Christianity.

Humanists who defend capitalism are aware that Western civilization owes a great deal to Christianity: that the power of Scriptures ordered society. Once man's barbaric and predatory instincts were tamed, it became possible to create the conditions that allowed civilization and culture to flourish; most of the success in this can be credited to Christianity. But even the most enlightened humanists, it seems, want to minimize the extent of Christianity's influence.

In their eyes Christianity is often seen as a hindrance to the progress of culture and civilization—a fomenter of controversies and schisms, a denouncer of science and invention,

14 John Gray, *Hayek on Liberty* (Oxford: Basil Blackwell, 1984), pp 1 & 2.

an instigator of superstition, a cause of narrow-mindedness, factions, and power struggles. Worst of all, Christianity—or at least the Church—seems too intolerant morally and intellectually; it prevents free thought and the flow of ideas so necessary to the cause of truth. The list could go on.

In contrast, humanists look fondly at the time when man rediscovered Western culture's true roots, as they might put it. During the Renaissance and after, the ideals of ancient Greece and Rome fired men's imaginations with a new, autonomous, "rational" enterprise; there was the goal of transforming the backward medieval world through sovereign science, liberated from any authority but its own.

And then, of course, came the mighty Enlightenment. In place of the prejudices and superstitions that characterized the Middle Ages, the Enlightenment, supposedly following unbiased reason, substituted the modern ideals of liberty, free markets, limited government, and the rule of law. According to the neoclassical liberals, this humanist revival laid the foundations for modern capitalism.

This standard interpretation of the rise of capitalist civilization presumes that it was built upon the philosophy of human behavior developed by a few great minds around the end of the seventeenth and through the eighteenth century. Beginning with Locke, the political philosopher, and continuing past Hume, the moralist, to Adam Smith, the greatest economic thinker of all time, the neoclassicists locate the ideas that they believe created capitalism. And certainly the thinking of these men played a major role in that. Soon after them, though, capitalism was seriously opposed, and we must ask why.

From whence a watershed in the nineteenth century? At that time a growing anticapitalist attitude took hold, and continued into the twentieth century. Is it because today's opponents of capitalism simply misunderstand the doctrines of that older liberalism? But weren't those doctrines the product of untainted reason and science? Why shouldn't the logic that convinced those others continue to persuade rational minds today? Don't all humanists agree that we can arrive at the truth by open-mindedly following the voice of reason? Can the humanist proponents of capitalism convince today's socialists that capitalism is in accord with reason and science, while socialism is not?

As long as we fail to see that capitalism fell into disfavor as the result of an ethical change at a deeper level, we will fail to see what motivates the modern socialist. We must realize that he reasons from the standpoint of the thing that controls him. There has been a change of religion at the center of Western civilization; a great deal of the reasoning found in the old liberalism was influenced by the Christian ethic. With our religious unmooring there has come a change in the way we reason. And so it will be impossible to confront those in the grip of socialism unless we understand the religious and ethical assumptions that undergird it. Because the West lacks this understanding, it has been unable to offer clear advice to the Soviet bloc countries that wish to escape the tyranny of socialism at this century's end.

The old liberalism contained much that was antithetical to a Christian point of view. There was a mixture of Christian and non-Christian thinking in its notions. Present-day humanism is the consequence of self-consciously eliminating the Christian element and developing an entirely non-Christian perspective. If, then, there is any real difference between the earlier humanism and the humanism of today, it is that today's is far more consistent in its anti-Christian vision. When socialists look back at their intellectual and spiritual predecessors, they are appalled at the extent to which Christianity influenced them. They now realize that humanist principles are utterly incompatible with Christianity, and that if those early thinkers had been more conscious of their principles, then they, too, would have despised capitalism.

What is the common non-Christian element present in both the old liberalism and in modern socialist thinking? It is the ethical doctrine of utilitarianism. Utilitarianism states that what is morally right is whatever is useful in gaining the greatest happiness for the greatest number. It grounds all human activity on principles that rise solely from human experience, and conforms entirely to a self-defined "need." Moral obligation is only what the individual perceives to be in his own best interest, as circumstances allow. There are no antecedent and transcendent moral principles to guide conduct from the start, no absolute laws of good and evil, right and wrong, just and unjust. Man is his own judge of what is good, and is free to live by the laws he himself lays down.

Happiness, or moral good, is whatever produces pleasure, and moral evil is whatever produces pain. This principle holds for individuals acting together for social ends as well. "[T]he principle of utility approves or disapproves of actions according as they tend to augment or diminish the happiness of the individuals under consideration." But it is also true, according to utilitarianism, that "an action...is [deemed] morally praiseworthy according to the extent to which it seems to conform to the interests of society."[15]

What distinguishes the classical liberal school of thought from its modern socialist offspring is that the old school set greater store by the first half of this formula, the happiness of the individual, and the modern socialists look primarily to the second, the happiness of society. Of course on the premise of utilitarianism, the one leads inevitably to the other; the happiness of the individual is inseparable from the happiness of all, or, more precisely, the happiness of "the greatest number." The ethical perspective was bound to shift under the influence of utilitarianism, and everybody came to accept as an article of faith the premise that "no action can be moral except by reference to the needs or good of society."[16]

We must not forget, however, that the old liberalism did not present an untainted utilitarianism. Mixed in were principles that still reflected Christian values. When present-day socialists rebel against the old liberalism, it is because they

15 Elie Halevy, *The Growth of Philosophic Radicalism*, trans Mary Morris (London: Faber & Faber, 1972), pp 28 & 12.
16 Rousas John Rushdoony, *Christianity and the State* (Vallecito, CA: Ross House, 1986), p 30.

object not to utilitarianism, but to the influence of Christianity. Modern socialists want to rid society completely of every trace of Christianity, and to extend the application of utilitarianism without any encumbrances whatsoever.

The neoclassical liberals want socialists to return to the ethical roots of old liberalism. But before socialists will admit a common ground, they insist that the old liberalism be purged of all Christian influence. Neoclassical liberals are unwilling to do this; if they do, they will have to admit that socialism reaches the only consistent conclusion; humanist capitalists have no place to turn.

Are Christians at present willing to recognize that capitalism is a product of their religious heritage, that it flowered when Christianity had gained predominance over the culture? Many are not. One hears the same condemnations of capitalism that one hears of socialist humanism. It is said to be a system of selfishness and materialism; it atomizes and dehumanizes society by placing too much emphasis on individual behavior. It fosters tyrannical economic powers that only oppress the poor and the weak. Socialism, at least in some form, it is said, best expresses the Christian position, since it seems in accord with the biblical injunction to exercise compassion and justice. Socialism means order and fairness, concern for the poor and downtrodden. Socialism will save mankind from the rape of the environment and the pollution of nature. Socialism puts people ahead of profits.

Christian anticapitalists, like their humanist kin, ignore the "demonstrated failure of state-directed economic policies."[17] The morality of an economic system, they would say, is vastly more important than its efficiency. They assume that a choice between morality and efficiency is inescapable, and of course they will choose morality. Christian opponents of capitalism often do not fear the increase of state power and

17 See Ken S. Ewert, "Moral Criticisms of the Market," *The Freeman*, March 1989, Vol 39, No 3.

tyranny to which socialism leads. They are untroubled by the morality of those whose main ambition is to control the lives of others and dictate what they do. They are in favor of the modern Baal-state.

One book in particular by a contemporary Christian author, Bob Goudzwaard, represents an anticapitalist point of view.[18] If any work of recent Christian scholarship by the educated elite reflects an attitude of cultural pessimism about modern Western society, none does so more consistently than Goodzwaard's. The thesis of his book is that Western society in general, and capitalism in particular, is the result of a secular faith in progress, and capitalism is in no sense the outgrowth of Christianity. Not only this, but capitalism's cultural fruits are in direct conflict with Christianity, it argues. The author goes to great pains to dissociate capitalism from Christianity and to say that the two stand for opposite ideals. I will return to Goudzwaard's work later.

It is necessary to understand the past and present frame of mind on these issues, so that as we move ahead we will be reminded of all that is at stake. In the section that follows, I will explain the elements of the Christian ethic, and by doing so hope to lay the groundwork for an understanding of it. If portions of this section seem theological, this is purposeful, precisely because of the general ignorance among many Christians about what the true Christian ethic actually is.

In Part II, I will examine the ethical implications of the Christian outlook in relation to economic activity and the establishment of culture in general; and finally, in Part III, I will discuss the humanist alternative, and the sort of society it intends to impose on our present-day world.

18 Bob Goudzwaard, *Capitalism and Progress: A Diagnosis of Western Society*, trans Josina Van Nuis Zylstra (Toronto: Wedge, 1979).

PART I

CHRISTIANITY

Those who are possessed of a definite body of doctrine and of deeply rooted convictions will be in a much better position to deal with the shifts and surprises of daily affairs than those who are merely taking short views, and indulging their natural impulses as they are evoked by what they read from day to day.

Winston Churchill

ONE

THE FOUNDATION OF THE CHRISTIAN ETHIC

IN ORDER to understand the relationship of the Christian ethic to economic and social behavior in general, to the nature of capitalistic behavior in particular, and to understand as well its contrast to socialism, it is necessary first to clarify the principles that define the Christian ethic itself. This is incumbent upon any commentator because that ethic is scarcely audible in the corridors of human affairs at present, and among Christians its imperatives are not upheld with conviction. In matters of economic, political, and social application, Christians seem to be indifferent to the reigning secular ideals, and as a result are unwitting accomplices to the humanist agenda. From ignorance or willful choice, they have forsaken the principles that define who they are and what they stand for, and have adopted the ethics of humanism instead.

The first essential, then, is to keep clear in one's mind what the Christian ethic is, and what it is that causes it to be, indeed, *Christian*.

If the Christian ethic once held moral reign over Western culture, it is not necessarily because the church has been responsible to God, as He ordains. In the past, the church often attempted to assimilate the ideals of secularists into its body of beliefs and practices. When this happened, the clear and distinct message of the Gospel was compromised, and the ethical demands of Christian life were undermined. The church at times appeared to be motivated more by ambition for earthly distinction, and its leaders more skilled in the art of maneuvering for power than in shepherding the flock. When the church assumed it could pick and choose among humanist philosophies and values, keeping some and rejecting others, it wasn't long before the church assimilated these values, and became helpless to speak with any relevance to the cultural issues of its day.

Something like this has happened in our own time. The church of the modern era has retreated before the advance of humanism and has allowed itself, and its uncompromising message, to become infected with humanist values. In general nowadays one sees the same secular and man-centered trends in the church as in secular society as a whole. The practice of religion has been overtaken by subjectivity and emotional escape, with the emphasis falling on its ability to excite and entertain, rather than to edify and instruct.

In the process, the Christian message has come to be defined almost exclusively in terms of each member's personal experience. A preoccupation with *me*-ism has become as much accepted in the church as in the world, with the tragic result that secular standards prevail in the church, and man-centered criteria have come to regulate Christian practice. When one considers that Christians tend not to think about social, political, and economic issues in the light of Christian principles, the conclusion one reaches is that many Christians, consciously or not, are undisturbed by the trend toward socialism taking place, even as they watch Soviet-bloc empires crumble. There are even intellectuals in the church who applaud this trend, claiming that socialism actually represents the ethical outlook of Christianity.

A useful truism goes, There is no need for precise definition where there are no real things to define. In order to give a definition, or at least a description, of the Christian ethic, then, an understanding of what is meant by *Christian* is first in order. This involves in turn some form of doctrine—though to the majority of those who like to think of themselves as Christian, the word *doctrine* is repugnant. And so the present state of the church is one of widespread doctrinal ignorance.

This is no mere happenstance; it has come about by deliberate choice. In its preoccupation with religious experience, the church has come to assume that doctrine does not matter, and has brought ignorance down on itself; it has come to believe that a living, vital faith is somehow eroded by intellectual assent to precision in doctrines and definitions. It thinks of intellect as a burden to genuine faith, and an obstacle to wholehearted participation in religious life. One popular and prevalent attitude assumes that doctrinal knowledge is not only unnecessary for, but even detrimental to, a "meaningful faith-experience."

This hostility to doctrine (which simply means teaching) is part of an unbiblical religious subjectivism that has overtaken the contemporary church—one whose point of departure sets the "needs" of human experience over against the objective authority of God's revealed Word. What we *want* claims our allegiance more than what God *teaches*; and linked to this me-centered outlook is an escapist view of life in general, a desire to retreat from the world and forfeit our concerns for the broader issues of culture and civilization. The Christian community has turned in upon itself and seems barely motivated anymore by the greater goal of advancing the kingdom of God. This insularity has brought about the eclipse of the Christian ethic, tragically, from its once-dominant position as the ethical ideal of all of Western civilization. The systematic denial of doctrine is precisely why Christians have ceased to be the salt of the earth, and why the Christian ethic no longer seasons our culture.

We shouldn't let the present anti-doctrinal outlook deceive us about the actual state of affairs, however, because whether we want to admit it or not, a doctrinal position is something no Christian is without. In fact, every person, Christian or otherwise, holds to some set of beliefs about the meaning of life, the purpose of man in the world, the origin of things, and all the rest. We give expression to a system of belief, whether consciously or unconsciously, by the ideals we live for, the goals we pursue, the causes we support (or, perhaps, do not support), the values we place on things and on people, and especially the ends we wish to achieve.

If Christians reject doctrine, that doesn't mean they don't have a doctrine they adhere to; the question is whether the doctrine they adhere to is the truth. Whether that doctrine appears in a written and codified form, or is shared in a more or less non-verbal fashion, every Christian is governed by a set of principles he or she takes to be the truth. This is equally true of every non-Christian. It is an ineradicable part of our religious nature to *believe* in something, to hold as true something about the nature of being and all that exists in the world. And whatever we hold to be true will determine how we think about questions of good and evil, right and wrong, justice and injustice; it will influence the ethical position we adopt for ourselves and the society around us.

If Christians suspect that doctrine is dispensable, it's due to one of two things: they have refused to take the time and effort to understand the doctrinal system at the heart of the Christian message; or they have become influenced by one of the many unbiblical systems of belief in the world, and are unaware of it. Or perhaps it's a combination of both. The benign indulgence of Christians in the humanist culture *as a whole* reveals a schizophrenic moral consciousness in the Christian community; for having assimilated the humanist ethic into its consciousness, the Christian community responds, when the consequences of that ethic are applied to the culture, with shocked disbelief.

They seem unaware that humanism presents a unified moral vision at war with Christianity and means to acquire dominion over society. Christians, in turning in upon themselves, have lost their sense of separateness from the world; so when the world imposes a social agenda whose ethics are opposed to theirs, most Christians (if they think about it at all) are merely puzzled by what seems a loss of normality in society's otherwise civilized behavior.

Some time ago the church apparently began to think it could live at peace with unbelieving society; it could practice a dual lifestyle: be Christian in church, but in society be as the Romans. It believed life could be divided into categories, one portion of which belonged to matters of salvation, or spiritual concerns, the other to life, which could be withdrawn from God's revelation. Today we are reaping the fruits of this dichotomy, and are beginning to experience God's judgment on our failure to submit to His authority over all areas of life. In politics especially, an idolatry of the state is the policy more and more people support. Those elected to office intend to implement socialist programs and secular values. Righteous men hide while unrighteous men triumph, and the church seems undisturbed by this state of affairs.

The church even attempts to sanctify aspects of the culture—by using rock music, for example, with "Christian" words attached. These efforts only further divide the ranks and testify to the appeal of secularism in the church along generational lines—our kids like it. The message of life entrusted to the church has changed in recent years; human needs and expectations have replaced God and His precepts. Meanwhile, the threat of a total humanization of our culture makes it more and more difficult for the church to live inside its self-absorption.

Whether we wish to admit it or not, Christians, for all their antidoctrinal self-satisfaction, are governed by beliefs that color the way they understand the message they proclaim, the faith they practice, and the importance they attach to the Christian ethic. Their ethical position always follows their doctrine. Is that doctrine grounded in God's word, or are there elements of non-Christian ideals mixed in? A Christian ethic can be a Christian ethic only when it is a biblical ethic. An ethic is not Christian because it conforms to something called Christian experience, or perhaps *feels* Christian. It does not in any sense rise out of human experience; it is based entirely on "every word that proceeds out of the mouth of God" (Mt 4:4). Those who live according to the Christian ethic are those who submit themselves in obedience to the will of God.

That is the foundation of the Christian ethic. Christians must understand the fundamental content of biblical truth in order to apply it to every area of life; biblical truth is a single Truth that encompasses life's totality. Although we often speak of doctrine*s*, in the plural, there is really only one doctrine. All Christian truth forms a unity, and if it doesn't, unbiblical motives have insinuated themselves into it.

Today's Christian community has little concept of a unified understanding of biblical truth. Rather, there is a diversity of doctrinal *opinion*, and this suggests a serious problem at the heart of modern Christendom. No basic agreement exists among professing Christians over the nature of the ethic that should guide their conduct and interests, and few of them express to what extent, if any, they wish to see that ethic achieve supremacy over the culture. There is even a diversity of opinion concerning the content of the Christian ethic itself, or whether there is anything uniquely Christian in an ethical perspective—doesn't it owe at least part of its content to the collective insights and sentiments of mankind in general, some wonder.

For many Christians, the Bible is, of course, a great source of ethical wisdom, even perhaps the most important source. But traditions other than Christianity have produced great thinkers with much ethical insight, the argument goes, and surely we can learn from them as well. The Bible is mainly a book about salvation, they feel, and accept its uniqueness in that respect—but meanwhile look at what we can learn about life from pagans, both ancient and modern! Many Christians are willing, then, to cede territory to humanism for culture and society, and to confine the Christian ethic to the life of the church, or worse, to the personal lives of individuals. If the Christian ethic is a biblical ethic, however, we can be certain it is the ethic that God requires.

Is there any realm into which God doesn't quite fit? Would God fail to provide for our entire life, including our cultural and societal life, and not also require submission to His

Lordship in those areas? Isn't God's word sufficient for every good? The Christian ethic must stand alone or it cannot stand at all; it must include every area of life, or include nothing. Christians must come to understand that God is a jealous God who will not share His glory or authority with any rival. We must find our life in God, or else find it in ourselves, but we can't have it both ways.

And it won't do to pretend that we can speak of Christianity as a religion that means the same thing to all people. We may not gloss over fundamental differences between, for example, Catholics and Protestants, or between Calvinists and Arminians, and assume that all will happily agree on some indiscriminate and ecumenical notion of what it means to be a Christian. This is a popular trend nowadays. To insist on doctrinal accuracy, or even to believe that one doctrinal viewpoint reflects the truth more faithfully than another is thought to be divisive, a cause of unnecessary disputes. The idea is, we can all join together on the things we do have in common. If there are differences, let's not get worked up about them; love and brotherhood are more important than the truth. Let's put aside petty differences, since the matters of doctrine are merely matters of opinion anyway; knowledge puffs up, but love edifies, etcetera.

This attitude has led to the present etiolation of the church, in which the gospel and its ethical demands no longer speak with precision. A distinct Christian voice can hardly be heard above the din of the humanist clamor, and the church more than anything needs to realize that truth matters, is worth standing for, and must be *lived* in order to honor the Lord. The church should have no agenda other than the one given by her sovereign Head, and the church is called upon to achieve *His* purposes, not her own.

For my part, there is one doctrinal viewpoint that more faithfully and accurately reflects what is truly Christian than any other; this is the *Reformed* doctrine. In saying this, I offer no apology. I'm not claiming that unless a person is Reformed he's not a Christian; I'm asserting that the truth of Christianity is presented more justly, with greater faithfulness to biblical content, and more fully, in the Reformed system of doctrine than in any other. Nor am I saying that only certain churches, or denominations, are in possession of doctrinal truth, and that unless one is a member of those churches one cannot be Reformed in his understanding and confession. What I mainly have in mind are the doctrinal formulations contained in the Reformed Creeds and Confessions of *history*. My explanation of the Christian ethic is based on these documents' superior understanding and summation of the entire content of Scripture.[1]

What, then, sets the Reformed view apart from every other Christian point of view? It has to do with its uncompromising stand on Scripture as God's only Word to man concerning everything he has need of for faith and life, and its scrupulous articulation of the elemental content of that Word. The first premise of Reformed doctrine is the recognition that God's authority over man's life is supreme, and that God has declared that authority in Scripture alone, so that the authority of God is the authority of Scripture, and vice versa. Scripture, then, does not speak to man as the collective wisdom of sagacious and religious men, but as the word of God Himself. Its message isn't one of mere good advice, but demands unquestioning acceptance and obedience.

Man owes God obedience because he is God's creature. When God created man, He intended him to live in accord with His sovereign authority and understand that the knowledge of God and of His will was his highest good. Man did not have to search to find that will; in the garden God communicated it directly to him, and continued to do so throughout the course of history. God meant for man to be dependent on His word alone. When in sin and disobedience

1 My naming of the superiority of Reformed doctrine should not be taken to mean that Reformed churches are the best churches. In fact, these days Reformed churches and Reformed doctrine have only the word in common. To a great extent, Reformed churches have ceased to represent in substance the Reformed confessional point of view.

to that word man separated himself from God, he cut himself off from the truth, and so from life.

He was cast out of God's presence and initially barred from reentry into communion with God. But in mercy and compassion, God restored man in righteousness and truth, and granted him knowledge of the way of life. This knowledge came to man again in God's word, as the revelation without which man could not know truth and life. That word, which can be found in Scripture and nowhere else, demands that man's whole being be brought under it in submission.

As the Westminster Confession of Faith puts it: "The whole counsel of God, concerning all things necessary for His own glory, man's salvation, faith and life, is either expressly set down in scripture, or by good and necessary consequence may be deduced from scripture: unto which nothing at any time is to be added, whether by new revelations of the Spirit, or traditions of men."[2] We must pay particular attention to the phrase "traditions of men," for it touches profoundly on our understanding of the Christian ethic. Christians are not to name anything as good or evil for self or society, but only what Scripture names. Justice, fairness, equity, truth, righteousness and the rest, must be what Scripture says they are, and not what any person, for whatever reasons, supposes them to be. Which implies that Christians ought never to think that the "good of society" or any other such maxim can govern the ends of ethical conduct. Christians are obliged to take God's purpose alone as the goal of their conduct. They should not suppose they hear God's voice in reference to any such goals apart from Scripture.

2 This Confession may be obtained separately, or found in the books of church order or hymnals of Reformed churches, such as the *Trinity Hymnal* of the Orthodox Presbyterian Church; the numbering of the document is by chapter and paragraph, each sentence or relative clause bearing footnotes that refer to proof texts in the Bible; this extract is from I, 6, from the William Blackwood edition reprinted in Edinburgh in 1963.

Reformed teaching recognizes the revelation of God in nature; but God doesn't speak through nature with either express commands or clear propositions. Nature in itself cannot tell us how to live or what it is that is right for us to do. This is true whether we think of nature as our environment, or as a conscience within us. God's word to us comes as a special revelation from Him, and Scripture is the record of that revelation. This further implies that nothing can verify Scripture as God's word but Scripture itself; or as the Westminster Confession states: "The authority of the holy scripture, for which it ought to be believed and obeyed, dependeth not upon the testimony of any man or Church, but wholly upon God (who is truth itself), the author thereof; and therefore it is to be received, because it is the Word of God" (I,4). More exactly, "our full persuasion and assurance of the infallible truth, and divine authority thereof, is from the inward work of the Holy Spirit, bearing witness by and with the word in our hearts" (I, 5). Our full acceptance of Scripture, then, is the work of God's Spirit, received in faith, and does not rest upon scientific proofs, not even on the science of *history*. Science, for the Christian, cannot be a principle of authority independent from the Word of God.

It is from Scripture that we learn of our purpose in the world and the place our cultural efforts are to occupy. Scripture alone must define the value we place on the results of those efforts; that is, whether they're good or evil, beneficial or not. Every ethical judgment, for the Christian, should be based on Scripture and nothing else. History, the record of mankind's cultural efforts over time, is, by itself, incapable of telling us whether developments over the years have been good or evil, profitable or the source of misery. If we wish to evaluate capitalism or socialism, then, our basis of evaluation must be Scripture. To use supposedly empirical observations of mankind's material welfare, and nothing more, is to ignore the ethical dimension. Scripture must be our ethical perspective at the outset.

Until science has collected and evaluated all the data, it cannot presume to be neutral to Scriptural authority, and it is doubtful that it will be then. Because of the "darkening of the understanding," as the apostle Paul states in Romans, no person is capable of evaluating the propriety of his actions by reason alone. If we don't begin with Scripture, we won't end with Scripture, and as far as our accomplishments are concerned, we must go *outside* history, as it were, to find the basis on which to judge past deeds *in* history. The eternal must illuminate the temporal.

With man's life and culture resting on the foundation of Scripture, then, Reformed doctrine proceeds to define the content of the outlook on life and on the world that Scripture demands. It comprehensively explains the "religious motifs" that pit the Christian point of view against pagan and secular views of the meaning of life, besides the origin and purpose of all that exists, including mankind. All Christians recognize the primary motifs of Scripture—Creation, Fall, and Redemption—but Reformed doctrine has given a more biblically faithful account of their essentials and of the place they should occupy in the Christian world view and ethic.

Creation

To begin at the beginning, all believers need to grasp the importance of the concept of creation, and how it informs our understanding of both God and man.

Our starting point must be God, for Scripture teaches that He is the Creator; all that exists is His handiwork, His accomplishment, and until He called everything into being, there was nothing whatever—no primordial matter that had been eternally in existence, no material chaos: a void. He made everything out of nothing, and the first lesson we learn from this is that God is not a quiescent or an inert God. He is a God who works, who glorifies Himself through industrious attainments, which issue entirely from His purposes. He has made all things for a specific reason, and by deliberate design. He exercises His power, and manifests His being, in productive labors; He builds with a goal in mind. Closely related to this is that God has a direct and positive interest in the work He performs; He cares for all He has made. After creating all things, He did not withdraw His concern from any particular aspect of creation, but in His providence continued (and continues) to oversee every specific detail. God created all things for the purpose of glorifying Himself, so we can be certain that the world and all it contains does indeed, by its very existence, glorify God.

There is an important corollary in the relationship of God to His creation. Though all that exists was formed by Him and depends on Him for its existence, there is an absolute distinction between God and His creation. The technical theological term for this distinction is *transcendence*. God transcends, or exists beyond and apart from all that He has made (so nothing in creation can be identified with God or worshipped and served as if it were Him), yet all things are dependent on Him and Him alone for their existence and meaning. We shouldn't think of this connection in a mechanical fashion, as a necessary dependence that binds God to all of creation, but should see it as a gratuitous dependence, based on the good pleasure and sovereignty of God Himself. He causes all things to depend on Him, but He is not bound by anything He has made.

God's transcendence should not blind us to the other side of His relationship to all He created, however: His *immanence*. God's immanence is His intimate presence within, and watchful care over, all He has made. God does not absent Himself from the affairs of this world, but takes direct responsibility to see His purposes carried out everywhere and always. God's immanence in the world, then, is an omnipresence; He sees all and knows all that happens; nothing escapes Him. But more than being present merely to observe, God is present to make sure that the least detail of His purposes for the creation are accomplished. The significance of this immanence to man is far-reaching, for every single Christian is compelled to say that his life is carried on in an environment that God both created and directly controls.

This means that "God is man's ultimate environment and this environment is completely interpretative of man who is to know himself."[3] The Christian's entire experience in Creation, in all he endeavors to achieve and intends to realize, including his interaction with nature and the building of culture and civilization, has been "predestined" by the greater purposes of God. Our life is not the product of evolutionary chance, but a result of God's design. God's transcendence and immanence form, therefore, essential presuppositions of the Christian ethic.

In contrast to this view is every non-Christian concept of God and His relationship to the universe. While the non-Christian speaks with many voices, there are usually one of two perspectives the non-Christian takes—which shouldn't necessarily be seen, however, as antithetical. Both complement one another, for both represent rebellious attempts to reinterpret God; both derive from the sinful need to redefine the true nature of God's transcendence and immanence. The motive behind this is not a desire for a true knowledge of God, but a hope that by reinterpretation of Him, man will be seen as the absolute authority over life, with the ability to define his relationship to the world, or to know good from evil on his own terms.

On one hand, God's transcendence is redefined in a *deistic* manner; that is, God is viewed as not only separate from the world, but without connection to it in any way. Non-Christians wish to loosen the connection of the dependence of all things on God; they wish to set life free from His jurisdiction. They begin by saying the world is an eternally existing, self-operating "machine," and does not need God to explain it and its processes; and while it may be true that this machine

3 Cornelius Van Til, *The Defense of the Faith* (Philadelphia: Presbyterian and Reformed, 1972), p 43.

shows stress and strain, or malfunctions in its natural operations, this is simply due to the nature of the machine itself. It is the normal state of affairs for sickness, disease, disaster, and death to be present in the world; nature is wise in its own way, these redefiners assert, and has its own means for correcting the aberrations that occur; it has brought forth man himself, and endowed him with "reason," a capacity that provides him with nearly limitless ability to penetrate nature's mysteries and master them. So the world does not need God; it has man. These non-Christians can only accept a god so transcendent that he's absent.

On the other hand, some non-Christians like to retain a god who is immanent. They, however, reinterpret God's immanence in an *pantheistic* manner, identifying God with the universe itself. This is the opposite of deism, but the reasoning, which means to set man up as his own god, is the same. Once God and nature are made identical, the next maneuver is to say that God requires a means by which to communicate Himself, and the instrument best suited to that is man, since man is a self-conscious being, the highest form of existence in nature. So man, as the consciousness of God, is freed to be the voice of God Himself.

Without man, no god could exist; the existence of God necessitates the existence of man, in this view. Not only has man freed himself from dependence on God, he has made God dependent on him. The implications are clear; man is the most significant being in existence: his will is God's will, and God's will is his; what he does is what God does, and what God does is what he does. In short, man is God, and God is man. The ethical effect is that no being stands outside history to judge man's endeavors; all evaluations, wholly immanent, are determined by man himself, and no standards of conduct exist but the ones he sets up.

Both of these non-Christian perspectives are formulated to replace the biblical God with a god of man's own devising: man himself. The God of Scripture is not man's ultimate environment, but nature, altogether impersonal and self-existing, is, and the consequence is apparent: "[I]f the most ultimate environment that surrounds man is impersonal it is in the last analysis the task of the consciousness of man to determine the nature of that impersonal environment."[4] Since man must decide for himself who he is and what his purpose is in the world, he naturally begins with the assumption that he is not God's creature, and that the world is devoid of intrinsic purpose. If some purpose can be discovered, it must be found by man and lie within his design. Every effort at building civilization and culture will be stamped with this assumption; everybody will proceed on the basis of whatever seems compatible to those independent from God.

From the Christian viewpoint, creation also has something important to say about man: man was not simply created by God, but created to be *like* God, though on a finite scale. God created man in His own Image, Scripture teaches, and this alone constitutes the biblical and Christian definition of man. The significance of this, above all, relates to the purpose behind life and culture. "The creation of man according to the image of God...had as its nearest purpose that man should fill, subdue, and have dominion over the earth."[5] The creation of man in God's image bore in it the original mandate to build culture and civilization. "All this teaches very plainly that man was not created for idleness but for work. He...had to go straight into the wide world in order to subdue it to the power of his word and will... He was given an assignment which would cost him centuries of effort to accomplish."[6] Like God who works, man too was destined to work, and to seek out productive accomplishments. Man's purpose in this was not merely for his own benefit, not even primarily for that: "Man had to cultivate the earth so that it

4 Cornelius Van Til, *Christian Theistic Ethics: In Defense of the Faith* (unpublished class syllabus, 1974), Vol. III, p 10.

5 Herman Bavinck, *Our Reasonable Faith* (Grand Rapids: Baker, 1977), p 215.

6 Bavinck, pp 215 & 216.

would more and more become a revelation of God's attributes."[7] Man's principal task is never complete if he fails to realize the glory of God in it, and in the next chapter I will take this up.

The Fall

The second central motif of Scripture is the Fall; or the fall of man into sin, which is also necessary for an understanding of the Christian ethic. Reformed doctrine affirms, as virtually every other Christian viewpoint does not, that the fall of man into sin, as well as the resultant curse upon the earth, was known in the eternal counsel of God, and was predetermined by His purpose. Yet God may not be held responsible for man's disobedience and fall; man alone is culpable for his disobedience to God's express command not to eat of the tree of the knowledge of good and evil.

If man suffers the consequences of his disobedience in the present, he must take the blame; it is not the fault of God that life has become difficult and precarious for generations of men. Once more, the Westminster Confession best summarizes this: "God from all eternity did, by the most wise and holy counsel of his own will, freely and unchangeably ordain whatsoever comes to pass: yet so, as thereby neither is God the author of sin, nor is violence offered to the will of the creatures..." (III, 1).

The entry of sin into the world of God's creation did not surprise Him, nor did it force Him to alter His original intentions for His creation in general. What is more, the Confession, explicating Scripture, states that sin did not enter the world at the moment of creation itself, since the creation was originally free of sin, and perfect. Sin entered after the creation of man, with the historical (space-time) disobedience of Adam in the literal (space-time) Garden of Eden. "Our first parents, being seduced by the subtlety and temptation of

7 Bavinck, pp 215 & 216.

Satan, sinned in eating the forbidden fruit. This their sin God was pleased, according to His wise and holy counsel, to permit, having purposed to order it to His own glory. By this sin they fell from their original righteousness and communion with God, and so became dead in sin, and wholly defiled in all the faculties and parts of soul and body. They being the root of all mankind, the guilt of this sin was imputed, and the same death in sin and corrupted nature conveyed to all their posterity descending from them by ordinary generation. From this original corruption, whereby we are utterly indisposed, disabled, and made opposite to all good, and wholly inclined to all evil, do proceed all actual transgressions" (VI, 1-4).

From this biblical interpretation of the fall, a number of corollaries follow that need to be kept in mind in order to further define the Christian ethic. First, the present condition of the world, the relative misery of human life everywhere, the fact of physical as well as spiritual death, all exist as consequences of the fall. When, for example, we consider such disturbing facts of life as poverty, vice, crime, oppression, or war, we need to understand that the real cause of these is sin and its results; they are part of God's curse on the world for man's rebellion. Each of us has inherited a corrupt nature; we are *born in sin* (Psalm 51). The natural predilection of all of us, then, is to do evil. All our inclinations, in every aspect of life, tend in that direction.

But we should never think we act this way against our wills. In the biblical view, none of us may offer such excuses for our behavior, or seek to remove the blame for the acts we ourselves commit. We may not blame the environment, the circumstances of our birth, or society in general for the maladies that overtake us. The biblical view is that all human misery is the result of each person's daily disobedience towards God; and that all we do in this life "that does not spring from obedience to God is sin."[8] It follows that sin and the curse are what God says they are, and may not be explained away by what we suppose them to be.

When God created man and supplied him with a purpose in creation, He also stipulated how man was to conduct himself in accomplishing that purpose. At the outset, God planted His law in the heart of man in order to instruct him how to discern and to perform all that was good. To confirm His law, God set before man the form of a test, to see if he would obey Him and live, or disobey and die. In God's counsel, the tree was used to see whether man would accept His authority over life. The "tree of the knowledge of good and evil" was not forbidden because of anything inherent in the fruit itself, but because it symbolized that everything in man's existence must be subordinate to the will of God. By testing man with something that could be consumed as food, God was instructing him that all that pertained to his "material good" must serve "spiritual ends," the "lower" realms of life existing for "higher" purposes, or good.

We see, then, an interesting paradox: starvation would result from eating the fruit, whereas nourishment and prosperity was promised if man refrained from eating it. There never was, and never will be, an automatic mechanism to insure the production of wealth and well-being in God's world: material prosperity was originally fused with man's religious and moral response to his Creator. No one will ever attain and enjoy wealth or happiness in an ethical void. Man set Satan's word next to God's, weighed them in the balance, and made his choice: Satan. So now man must accept, whether he wishes to or not, the dominion of Satan over his life—a harsh slavery indeed.

The meaning of the fall for us is that it is God to whom we must give an account. Every ideal of justice, right or wrong, good or evil, must refer first to God's righteous requirements

8 Van Til, *Christian Theistic Ethics,* p 25. *Cf* Romans 14.23b.

before they apply to our "needs." Since the fall, however, man does not have the capacity to know what is truly for his own good. When the question is asked, "Wherein consisteth the sinfulness of that estate whereinto man fell?" the Westminster Larger Catechism (Question 25) replies: "The sinfulness of that estate whereinto man fell, consisteth in...the corruption of his nature, whereby he is utterly indisposed, disabled, and made opposite unto all that is spiritually good, and wholly inclined to all evil, and that continually." The condition of man, then, after the fall, is "a natural tendency to hate God and neighbor."[9]

Every act and accomplishment, all industry, science, labor, art, civic involvement, hermeneutics, and the rest, all have been affected by the vile transformation that occurred in man and now expresses itself primarily as hatred. Hatred now qualifies and colors every human relationship. You need only look at the record of history to note that every cultural endeavor, every attempt to create a civilization, every undertaking of man is always and everywhere stained by violence, warfare, plunder, or oppression. Our natural tendency is to hate, and like our master, Satan, we would rather destroy than build. If any truly civilized accomplishments have been achieved, they are due to God's restraining grace over our behavior.

What is the exact nature of sin? Whatever best describes Scripture's view of it will have implications, too, for the Christian ethic. In answer to Question 24 of the Westminster Larger Catechism, we read, "Sin is any want of conformity unto, or transgression of, any law of God, given as a rule to the reasonable creature." The law of God was, from the beginning of time, man's only measure of what may be called just, holy, and righteous. From the moment God called man

9 *The Heidelberg Catechism*, Question 5. The text of this translation was adopted by the Synod of the Christian Reformed Church in 1975 (Grand Rapids: Board of Publications of the Christian Reformed Church, 1975).

to exercise dominion, He expected him to do this in reference to His standard of ethical measure, His law. God's law, in fact, was to be the instrument itself for subduing the earth. The fall into sin didn't alter this. For man to be able to carry out, once more, his original purpose, he must be redeemed from sin and the curse. God's law cannot help him in this respect, for the law cannot save; it is not the instrument of redemption. But this doesn't diminish its intention to serve as the instrument of dominion for redeemed man. The measure of ethical conduct, in every sphere of human endeavor, continues to be God's infallible law.

The Westminster Confession (XIX, 2, 5) echoes that truth: "This law, after his fall, continued to be a perfect rule of righteousness... The moral law doth for ever bind all, as well justified persons as others, to the obedience thereof; and that not only in regard of the matter contained in it, but also in respect of the authority of God, the Creator, who gave it. *Neither doth Christ in the Gospel any way dissolve, but much strengthen this obligation.*" Can Christians cherish any desire but to see every righteous demand of God implemented in life, and not remain on a Christian foundation? There are many who seem to think so, but anything less is not in conformity to the Christian ethic. And if we do not have the Christian ethic to guide us, we will get the ethic of humanism, which means the rule of hate.

Non-Christians should be expected to deny not only their status as God's creatures, but the truth that they live at present in a fallen condition. The non-Christian assumes that the Bible's explanation for mankind's miseries, corruption, and death is a myth, sheer fantasy. As far as non-Christians are concerned, there never was a perfect world that fell into its present state. God did not create man, they say, so man certainly cannot derive his purposes in life from God. The non-Christian "takes existence, as it now is, for granted."[10]

10 Van Til, *The Defense of the Faith*, p 62.

To the unbeliever the present condition of life is entirely normal. But the problem of evil confronts him daily, and he is driven by a need to solve its enigma. He is quite certain that it is solvable, and that the solution lies within his wisdom. We can only expect that the non-Christian will, as history testifies, continue to deny that man is in any way responsible for evil in the first place.

From the unbeliever, then, "The most commonly presented solution is the one to which sin does not live in man nor come out of man but attaches itself to him from without." Or: "The evil lies in the circumstances, in the environment, in the society in which man is born and reared."[11] Man himself is good, the reasoning goes, but the world around him is bad; if anything, it entirely influences the way he behaves. To improve his lot, the solution is to change society. This is the assumption at the basis of the famous Marxist dictum: philosophers have only interpreted the world in various ways; the point however is to change it. This view has gained increasing approval, and not solely with Marxists. Or perhaps it would be better to say that outside Christ all men have become Marxists, more or less; revolution in general is the driving passion of the non-Christian. His efforts are expended on overthrowing, tearing down, but never building up, in his endless quest to solve his basic problem, evil. And in searching out a solution, he has become a law unto himself.

If by chance non-Christians admit that, at least in part, there is something amiss in man himself—some disturbance in his makeup that causes evil behavior—he attributes it to "the sensuous nature of man," or his psychology. Some natural infirmity in man's condition is responsible for the ills and vicissitudes that attend this life. Non-Christians aver that if we would only realize that man is descended from the

11 Bavinck, *Our Reasonable Faith*, p 225.

animal, and in his heart is really still an animal, how simple it would be for us to understand that "sin is nothing more than a vestigial influence and remnant of the earlier animal condition."[12] The evolutionary hypothesis was invented to make it easier to rid ourselves of responsibility and guilt.

This is the real reason the non-Christian seeks a different explanation for misery from the one found in Scripture; he means to free himself from any blame. If God possessed the original jurisdiction over all human conduct, then only He could set the terms of guilt or innocence. But if man were free of that authority, he would be at liberty to decide these matters for himself. Christians need to recognize that every present-day effort to explain man's origins and present condition, when in opposition to the Scriptural account, involves a fundamental difference of opinion over who is to be the final authority on ethical behavior—God or man.

As Van Til has pointed out, "The main point of dispute was that of authority. The Christian position maintains that man, as a creature of God, naturally would have to inquire of God what is right and wrong...the non-Christian position holds that man does not need Scripture as a final authority...the non-Christian does not believe that man ever needed to be absolutely obedient to God. Non-Christian ethics maintains that it is of the nature of the ethical life that man must, in the last analysis, decide for himself what is right and what is wrong."[13] This is the underlying assumption of the non-Christian, regardless of other differences that may come between him and a scriptural perspective on culture.

These two tendencies—to blame either the physical makeup of man, or something in the nature of man's environment—dominate the non-Christian explanation of the fall, in opposition to the Bible. Together, the two constitute the belief system of the ethic of humanism; they help foster the

12 Bavinck, p 226.
13 *Christian Theistic Ethics*, p 33.

notion that man is able to serve as his own authority on matters of ethical conduct. This notion is the fulfillment of the Satanic assertion, "You shall be as God, knowing good and evil" (Gen 3.5). All cultural endeavors, from science and economics to politics and education, are based on our religious inclinations to be our own god. Just as the non-Christian conceives of God as either deistically transcendent or pantheistically immanent, so he interprets himself and the nature of his experience to exclude anybody but him from having the final say on questions of good and evil.

Redemption

Of the motifs of creation, fall, and redemption in Scripture, redemption is the most pervasive. The express purpose of Scripture is to make known to us the single possible deliverance from our sin and misery. In redemption, the other motifs are taken up and find their proper interpretation, for with redemption, the fall receives its corrective, and we are restored to our proper place in creation: *to subdue and have dominion over the earth.*

To understand the implications of redemption to the Christian ethic, we must see its significance in relation to both God and man. It will also be necessary to compare the Christian and non-Christian viewpoint, because we shouldn't suppose the Christian ethic is a redemptive ethic, while the non-Christian ethic isn't; both are imbued with redemptive ideals. To distinguish between those ideals is an act of Christian discernment.

According to Scripture, the fall of man into sin and misery was the consequence of the "disobedience of our first parents, Adam and Eve, in Paradise."[14] Reformed doctrine refers to this as original sin, not simply because it was the first sin committed, but more especially because it was the origin of sin in the human race. All men have become sinners *in Adam.*

14 *Heidelberg Catechism*, Question 7. Cf WCF, VI, 4.

God imputes the guilt of Adam's sin to all his progeny; he was not just one man among many, but the "head" of the race. Mankind was represented in him; when he fell, we fell, and "this fall has so poisoned our nature that we are born sinners—corrupt from conception on."[15] As the Westminster Confession states it, we "became dead in sin, and wholly defiled in all the faculties and parts of soul and body" (VI, 2). The Reformed call this the doctrine of *total depravity*; in this state all men are "bound over to the wrath of God, and curse of the law, and so made subject to death, with all miseries spiritual, temporal, and eternal" (VI, 6). We cannot in the least deliver ourselves from this state.

How, then, shall we be saved? Where must we look to find redemption as Scripture conceives of it? "Are we," asks the Heidelberg Catechism (Question 8), "so corrupt that we are totally unable to do any good and inclined toward all evil?" The answer provides the Scriptural viewpoint on redemption: "Yes, unless we are born again by the Spirit of God." The source of redemption is none other than God Himself.

It may seem a simple truism to say, as far as Christians are concerned, that God is the source of our redemption; it goes without saying that this should be the unanimous declaration of every Christian. On the other hand, the non-Christian sees himself as his own savior. He may wish to disguise his intentions, or pretend to himself and others that he, too, trusts in a superior being of sorts, but Christians should have no doubt about who the non-Christian actually believes in and serves. There would be little reason to dispute either point, if it weren't that even for many Christians God is not always so exclusively the source of redemption.

Every concept of redemption must be *total*, and whoever is man's redeemer will not only deliver and restore him, but assume the status of Lord and Master. To whom is accorded the responsibility to save goes the right of exclusive authority;

15 *Ibid.*

or, as Rushdoony notes, "Because salvation is a total concept, a savior has dominion and authority over every realm of life. If his lordship is not total, his salvation is not effectual. Therefore, anyone who claims to be a savior must of necessity assert an overlordship over every realm of life and thought."[16] So when Christians claim that the source of redemption is God, they ought to mean, at the same time, that God alone has total authority over every area of their lives; the scope of His redemption must be entire. This was inherent in the confession Moses taught Israel: "Hear, O Israel, The Lord our God is one Lord" (Deut 6.4). Note that it is not the Lord our God is one *God*, as if there were some philosophical issue at stake concerning the number of gods that may, or may not, exist. It is rather a matter of whose God is the *Lord*, or who has absolute authority over man—indeed, over all creation. This confession was to teach Israel that next to the true and the living God they must set up no rival gods, no other lords. There was only one Savior.

In redemption we see more clearly than elsewhere the absolute difference between the Christian and non-Christian ethics. Neither ethic is, or can be, expressive of a view of life and conduct that is not rooted in a redemptive ideal. Both represent distinctly redemptive programs for the whole of life and society, because the Savior at the center demands nothing less than total sovereignty over all he redeems. Both visions are equally totalitarian in nature, and because redemption is a total concept, it becomes, at the same time, an exclusionary one. So both the Christian and non-Christian ethics emerge from redemptive ideals that are everywhere, and at all times, opposites to each another. Often the church has neglected or doubted this, to its own peril.

Today, in fact, the Christian ethic has all but surrendered to humanism in virtually every area outside the church. The unbeliever unequivocally states that he is his own savior and,

16 Rushdoony, *Christianity and the State*, p 27.

therefore, his own lord and master. The difference between this view and the Christian's is the difference between grace and works, and salvation as a gift from God or as the accomplishment of man. In the end, however, there can be only one Lord; either the true God or an idol.

I will discuss the non-Christian ideal of redemption more fully in the next chapter, but for now let me simply state that in our contemporary society, perhaps more than at any other time in the history of the West, Christians believe that it is possible for the Christian ethic and the non-Christian ethic to exist side by side, in a kind of live-and-let-live environment. Which means that many have refused to reckon with the scope of the redemptive ideal that underlies both the Christian and the non-Christian ethic. One or the other must triumph, and unless the church wants to become even more impotent—defenseless in today's secularization of culture—it must come to terms with the redemptive ideal. That ideal must inform its ethics and its opposition to every other ideal. The resistance may be mighty, but the challenge is not insuperable.

Finally, I want to offer a few comments that touch on the matter of a Christian philosophy of history. As with everything else, history too must be based on a doctrinal foundation that upholds the Christian ethic. Even more, a Christian ethic is incomplete without a comprehensive outlook on the rise and development of human culture. History is the human record of that process. Yet the record of history cannot simply present the deeds of men in chronological order and neglect to say anything about the meaning and purpose of their outcome. It is imperative for Christians to understand that history is ultimately the product of the purpose of God, and that the progress of civilization does not issue from the will of man.

A Christian philosophy of history asserts that God's providence is behind every human accomplishment. Everything that has transpired in history, whether good or bad, has been predetermined by God's plan; it is a product of His will. He did not leave His creation to its own devices, and our willful pursuits do not thwart the goal that He intends to realize. Thus in the Heidelberg Catechism (Question 27), we read, "Providence is the almighty and ever present power of God by which he upholds, as with his hand, heaven and earth and all creatures, and so rules them that leaf and blade, rain and drought, fruitful and lean years, food and drink, health and sickness, prosperity and poverty—all things, in fact, come to us not by chance but from his fatherly hand." History would not be possible, not at all, nor could we achieve anything on our own behalf, unless God had ordained whatsoever comes to pass.

The Christian view affirms that predestination, not chance, regulates even the hairs that fall from our heads (Matthew 10.30). The essential point, once again, is that in order to make sense of history, and to fathom, as it were, the evils that it records, as well as the rich expressions of culture it has defined, we must consult God's word to learn what it is that He intends to accomplish. And the way in which He expects us, from generation to generation, to act in the course of history's developments, which are His accomplishments. Apart from His truth, history is sound and fury, signifying nothing. Every deed, whether it is good or whether it is evil, must be set in the light of Scripture, the eternal illuminating the temporal.

Because the Christian views history as the purposes of God accomplished, he is not so disturbed when times of evil and regression overtake the cultural marketplace; these, too, have a place in God's plan. On the other hand, Christians should not adopt a fatalistic attitude toward everything that occurs in the course of history; their chief concern shouldn't be with the product of history per se, but the purpose that transcends every historical circumstance—the advancement of the will of God on earth. This should undergird our philosophy of history, and our confidence in its realization should not rest on the deeds of history, but on the transhistorical promises of God. These promises imbue the Christian with a guiding ideal of history, and give him a sense of purpose in the building of culture and civilization. Unlike the non-Christian, the Christian does not lose faith when history fails to achieve its ideals, but knows that his labor is not in vain in the Lord.

For this reason, the Christian doesn't cower in a corner to escape his role as an actor in the drama of history, but works in the expectation that God will ultimately cause his goals to be secured. In the final analysis: "For the orthodox Christian, the dynamics of history are in God the Creator, and man accepts those dynamics and rejoices in the blessings thereof when man accepts Christ as Savior and then follows the leadings of the sanctifying Holy Spirit."[17]

Christians should see as their highest calling the need to develop culture and civilization in conformity to the righteous requirements of God. The life of the Christian should be consciously directed by this purpose, or his actions will cease to be wholly Christian. So for the Christian: "To accept this biblical philosophy means to accept the responsibility of the creation mandate. Man must exercise dominion in the name of God, and in knowledge, righteousness, and holiness."[18] Anything less is unworthy of a Christianity that would call itself Biblical.

17 Rousas John Rushdoony, *The Biblical Philosophy of History* (Phillipsburg: Presbyterian and Reformed, 1979), p 8.
18 *Biblical Philosophy of History*, p 16.

TWO

THE TWO ETHICS OPPOSED

THE Christian ethic is shaped in every essential by nothing more nor less than the sovereign word of God. The central content of His word—creation, fall, redemption—furnishes the foundation for that ethic. The ethic is not Christian because it was invented by Christians or wise thinkers, or was approved by the Church, or was found to conform somehow to something that *felt* Christian. It is the principle of behavior given to man by divine revelation. Christians are to receive it with unquestioning faith and obedience. It demands a life of responsibility and dedication to the purpose and will of God—a life through which, the apostle Paul says, "the world has been crucified to me, and I to the world" (Gal 6.14).

In more celebrated terms, it is a way of life in strict conformity to the things of the spirit and not the flesh. If anything, these two terms—spirit and flesh—denote the real difference between the Christian ethic and every other ethic that exists. Two antithetical principles cannot coexist, and Paul asserts the impossibility of their mutual existence: "Those who live according to the sinful nature have their minds set on what that nature desires; but those who live in accordance with the Spirit have their minds set on what the Spirit desires" (Romans 8.5). Peter adds that the "sinful desires are at war with life and the soul" (1 Peter 2.11).

To realize God's glory is the entire purpose of all of life. This is the goal of the Christian ethic, and it is achieved only by conforming to divine revelation. Man was created in God's image in order to reflect a total response of the creature back to our Creator. As the image of God, man "is that entirely and completely, in soul and body, in all faculties and powers, in all conditions and relationships."[1] It is not simply that when we are involved in worship we reveal characteristics of God's image, but the entire unfolding of civilization exhibits our nature as the image of God. To engage in any pursuit as an image of God means to act in the greatest God-glorifying manner possible. Yet at the same time, we act out of a concern for our own highest good.

Originally, man wished to do what God commanded because he realized it was for his own good. Man would work the best possible work—the greatest self-aggrandizing act he was capable of—by attempting to carry out self-consciously what God had ordained as his purpose in life; the two would work together. In Eden, man was no doubt moved to carry this ideal into practice, and did, as long as he remained obedient to God. But when he rebelled against God's explicit commandment, he sought to put an end to the purposes of God. At the instigation of Satan, man saw his own good and the glorification of God as separate ends, and set up an alternate ideal—the glorification of himself. Or as the apostle Paul has said, "They exchanged the truth of God for a lie, and worshipped and served *created things* rather than the Creator" (Rom 1.25).

Instead of understanding that his highest good depends upon seeking to glorify God, man now thinks of this seeking as an obstacle to his own good, to his *happiness*. In the

1 Herman Bavinck, *Gereformeerde Dogmatiek*, vierde onveranderde Druk (Uitgave van J. H. Kok te Dampen, 1928), Vol II, p 516. "En hij is dat geheel en al, in ziel en lichaam, in alle vermogens en krachten, in alle toestanden en verhoudingen."

beginning, when man acted in accord with God's will, he did what he understood to be righteous. Before sin entered the world, there was no conflict in man between seeking to please God (doing what was righteous) and seeking to increase his own happiness. God has purposed that man's well-being should be conditioned in every respect by his faithful response to God's commands. Prosperity and righteousness were mutually compatible goals. When man sinned, however, by disobeying God's rule not to eat of the tree of the knowledge of good and evil, he assumed that doing what God required was not necessarily essential to his well-being; his happiness and God's law were seen to be at cross-purposes. Man presumed that to achieve God's glory amounted to a sacrifice of his good. And man's good became paramount.

It is the nature of sin to blind people to the notion that good can be achieved only by obedience to God's word. At the heart of the non-Christian ethic, which lies at the base of all humanist cultural endeavor, is the belief that man's welfare in this life must result from obedience to man's will, not the will of God. Because of the fall, then, man cannot seek to glorify God *as a matter of will*.

Christians generally concur that "man not only became blind through sin, but he became totally unwilling to do the good."[2] If man now hopes to achieve anything good for himself, the good must be a free gift. He must be redeemed from error and willful rebellion by having his conscience cleansed from vanity and self-idolatry, and his heart renewed. Through the power of sovereign grace he can again take up for himself the fruitful task of glorifying and serving God. Without this restoration—and it depends upon God to give it—man may never expect to achieve any real happiness.

It must be a primary concern of the Christian ethic to call men to faith and repentance because, above all else, it is sin

2 Van Til, *Christian Theistic Ethics*, p 78.

that is our primary problem. Whatever difficulties attend the development of civilization and the unfolding of culture, they derive from sin. In this respect, whatever we may mean by a "disclosure of society,"[3] the disclosure can't accomplish anything if we fail to make clear the basic problem at the root of man's cultural obligations: sin and rebellion.

The entire content of the Christian ethic is derived from biblical revelation alone, not from the auto-suggestion of human wisdom. We do not serve God simply because we want to, nor may we serve Him in any way we please; indeed, no service is rendered if it is not rendered according to God's revealed will. Every issue of life must seek its resolution in the authority of God's word. All Christian endeavor consists of the adoption of God's purpose as the chief end of man. That ideal is pervasive and lays claim to everything in the creation; it has a programmatic work to accomplish that defines and delineates every cultural task. Its purpose is the building of God's kingdom on earth.

The Kingdom of God

Students of theology quickly note that the phrase *the kingdom of God* (or *heaven*) appears in Scripture almost exclusively in the gospels. Not that the concept is absent elsewhere; but as an expression, the precise wording is limited primarily to the first four books of the New Testament. The authors of the gospels were concerned with bearing witness to Jesus' central teachings about the kingdom of God. The preeminent reason Jesus came into the world was to make known to sinners, through the good news of salvation, the coming of God's kingdom on earth. The establishment of this kingdom was conveyed as the fulfillment of God's purposes for the world, and His intention from the outset. All that pertains to the forgiveness of sins and the obtaining of eternal life can be summed up as entrance into the kingdom of God.

3 Goudzwaard, *Capitalism and Progress*, p 186*ff*.

The first words Jesus spoke when he entered the short period of his public ministry were "The kingdom of God is near. Repent and believe the good news!" (Mark 1.15).

The Christian ethic must be as applicable to human life and as extensive in scope as the redemption this basic message proclaims. That redemption, as we shall see, left out nothing that referred to the creation mandate and all that it implied for human life on earth. Jesus' own ministry surely enlightens us as to how comprehensively God views the matter, and how extensively, therefore, we ourselves ought to consider the scope of the gospel.

When Jesus announced the coming of God's kingdom, he meant nothing less than the kingly self-assertion of God Himself. In more specific terms, "Everything in the announcement of the kingdom is concentrated on the divine...on his [God's] self-justification and self-assertion against anything that opposes his kingship."[4] This thought isn't sufficiently appreciated in the present even by Christians. The kingdom of God, as Scripture speaks of it, does not base its concern in the realm of human needs; its purpose is to declare God's sovereignty over all His creation. Scripture views the world, and the life of man in it, as existing for God's purposes, not man's. When Jesus proclaims the kingdom of God, he means therefore "the reassertion and maintenance of God's rights on the earth in their full sense."[5]

These rights are regarded as having been usurped by man's self-declared independence from God—his disobedience to the original command. It involved a supreme effort by man to exclude himself from obedience to God's authority. The coming of the kingdom of God, according to Jesus, is a rectification of this state of affairs. It means no less than total reclamation of the original relationship between

4 Herman Ridderbos, *The Coming of the Kingdom*, trans H. de Jongste (Philadelphia: Presbyterian and Reformed, 1973), pp 19-20.
5 Ridderbos, pp 20-21.

God and man. At the place in Scripture where Jesus instructs his disciples how to pray, he tells them that they must pray, first, that God's kingdom may come, and that His will may be done on earth as it is in heaven; that is, perfectly (Mt 6.10).

The two thoughts are inseparable for Jesus—the implication being that they ought also be united in the minds of seekers of the kingdom. The plea of Jesus' disciples should be for rule at every moment by God's Word and Spirit, and so should reject their own wills (see Heidelberg Catechism, Q & A 123 & 124). One must conform one's conduct to that for which he prays, so if we pray for God's will to be done on earth, shouldn't we be committed to that end? This is not an injunction limited solely to the personal lives of Christians; for as the Heidelberg Catechism puts it—"Help us and *all* men to reject our own wills..." Whatever else the kingdom of God means in Jesus' teaching—and whatever other benefits accompany it—the supremacy of God's authority over earthly life is its chief consideration. And because the kingdom centers so surely on God's glory and will, it becomes the supreme object of human pursuit. As one author interprets the matter, "The Kingdom means the subjection of all temporal affairs, of all ethical activities, of all spiritual experiences to a transcendent life-purpose in God."[6] The priorities of the kingdom are inherent in its nature.

While it may be true that, from the standpoint of the history of redemption and biblical revelation as a whole, Jesus, in his earthly ministry, "never speaks of the kingdom of God as previously existing"—that, "to him the kingdom is throughout something new, now first to be realized"[7]—nevertheless, he is well aware that the kingdom had been God's purpose for the whole world from the outset. In

6 Richard B. Gaffin, ed, *Redemptive History and Biblical Interpretation: The Shorter Writings of Geerhardus Vos* (Phillipsburg, NJ: Presbyterian and Reformed, 1980), p 15.

7 Geerhardus Vos, *The Kingdom of God and the Church* (Nutley, NJ: Presbyterian and Reformed, 1972), p 15.

Matthew 13.35 we read that Jesus' use of parables had a special revelatory purpose that bore in particular upon the kingdom. Quoting from Psalm 78.2 Jesus declares, "I will open my mouth in parables, I will utter things hidden *since the creation of the world.*" That is, he makes known the way of the kingdom of God as it was intended to be, from the moment of God's creation. What Jesus intimates has been lost to the kingdom, he now sets about, through his designed purpose, to bring to fulfillment. With this in mind, it would be helpful to examine more carefully the original mandate as it is found in the first chapters of Genesis.

Those who wish to allegorize this portion of Scripture, or deny historical truth in order to appeal to modern science, invariably distort the truth of Jesus' message as well. If a real Adam never lived, Jesus' role in the creation becomes enigmatic; at best, the disclosure of a purely subjective gospel—one designed to get people into heaven, or make them feel good, but with no actual connection to daily life. Many Christians believe that the great commission has nothing to do with the cultural mandate. For them Jesus provides, at most, an escape from our present afflictions; he does not have a program for achieving victory through them. A reconsideration of the original kingdom is imperative in order to regain the essence of the Christian ethic for our time.

When God created man He did not, as it were, simply toss him out into the world and leave him on his own to figure out who he was or what meaning his life should have. Man was never for a moment left to his own devices, or the merit of his wit, to conjure for himself out of a cold and unforgiving environment some purpose by which to justify existence. On the contrary, when God created man, He had for him a programmatic ideal—a constructive plan of action, a purpose for him from the beginning—and He expected him to express his approval by bringing that plan to realization. God's entire purpose for man, set before him at creation, was nothing less than building God's kingdom on earth. This was no part-time endeavor; every moment of every day should find man engaged at the task. Idleness was not an option.

Constructive, productive work defined the nature of man's life in God's world. The biblical account calls this *having dominion*.

The original purpose of man is found in Genesis 1.26-28, but this text in itself can't do entire justice to the biblical explanation of man's purpose, or the manner in which he should carry it out. In Genesis 2.15, after the creation of Adam and Eve, God enjoined them to "Be fruitful...fill the earth and subdue it." From the start, their lives, and their children's, and their children's children's, were to be dedicated to the productive dominion and replenishment of the earth. They were to have prosperity by a proper and systematic use of the earth and its resources. Here we might add: *all* the earth was to be brought under their sway. Unquestionable benefits would accrue from this. The task would not be completed at once; it was long-term and progressive.

The idea of progress in the work of man in dominion must be kept in mind, for I will return to this theme in Part II. In the meantime, however, let me say that progress is a thoroughly *Christian* ideal of life and culture; and history is the record of the progress of God's kingdom on earth.

Man was made in God's image, and this truth is significant to man's life in this world. Because God works with a purpose, man, too, since he is like God, works with a purpose. We could put this in a slightly different way by saying that man was created like God, but on a finite scale, and so, like God, he was intended to be a *creator*. To be precise, he was meant to carry out his work as a *re*-creator of everything God himself had once for all created; without doubt, "to create" means, "to interpret," and man could not be expected to be the original interpreter of the world any more than he could be expected to formulate his life's purpose.

At best, man could only reinterpret what God had already interpreted. As Van Til says, "Christian theism says that there are two levels of interpreters, God who interprets absolutely and man who must be the reinterpreter of God's interpretation. Christian theism says that human thought is therefore analogical of God's thought."[8] Once man sinned, he refused to see that the ideal of his life was to reinterpret what God had originally interpreted. Only then did he set before himself the goal of being the original interpreter of his own life. At the outset God expected man to build culture in accordance with *His* plan; but man now assumes that his job is to build civilization according to a plan he devises for himself. This can only be a delusion; God will bring his purposes to pass in spite of what men do.

It is at this point that the correlative statement in Genesis 2.15 comes to bear. In that passage we read, "The Lord God took the man and put him in the Garden of Eden to work it and take care of it." To some this verse appears to stand in opposition to the original mandate mentioned in 1.28. The latter proclaims the *whole earth* as the territory of man's activity; the former seems to limit man's work to the Garden of Eden. Bible interpreters almost always fail to understand the relationship in which Genesis 2.15 stands to the mandate given in 1.28. Many even think that 2.15 contains the real purpose of man at the beginning, and would confine that purpose to what is also alleged to be man's dwelling place, Eden. The Garden belongs to man, and his purpose was to "tend and care for it." If this means anything, it indicates that man's original work was meant to be agricultural.[9] The assumption often read into this is that men led pastoral lives

8 Van Til, *Defense of the Faith*, p 47.

9 See G. Ch. Aalders, *Genesis: Bible Student's Commentary*, trans William Heynen (Grand Rapids: Zondervan, 1981), p 93. Here we are dealing with what we might well call the beginning of 'agriculture.' Aalders does grasp, however, a more significant meaning to the Garden: that "the need for 'caring for' the Garden...implies that there were hostile forces against which man was to be on guard." Even at that early moment Satan was on the prowl—the task of attending to the Garden indeed takes on an added dimension.

that limited the nature of their activity. Because of sin, it is said, man now despoils the surroundings that would make this idyllic lifestyle possible. Man would seem to prefer the cluttered and congested life of the city, with its large-scale industry and commercial preoccupations.

Sin, apparently, ignited a feverish desire to mass together in compact locations to engage in manufacturing and other material pursuits. Man should have spread out and busied himself with rural occupations. Many back-to-nature movements have found romantic justification by pointing to the myth of man's original bucolic existence.

To suppose we should understand from this passage that man was destined for the simple country life of agriculture, against which he rebelled, is a notion that does not fit with Genesis 2.15. In fact, nothing is specifically said about agriculture in this verse, nor should one assume its implication in the words, "to work and take care of it." A proper understanding of this text requires it to be joined with 1.28; the two form concomitant parts of the same enterprise. As I've pointed out, man was given dominion over the whole earth; his work was to reinterpret, to recreate, what God originally created and interpreted. To discharge his responsibility faithfully, man would have to consult the Creator's original in order to discover the blueprint for making his copy. In Genesis 2.15 we learn how man was to have made that discovery: by working the Garden. In the Garden he would find the pattern for exercising dominion. Man was never left to his own imagination in the matter.

At the same time, man would learn in the Garden, in a most explicit manner, that his kingdom task had to be subordinated to God's absolute authority over his life. This was epitomized in the prohibition regarding the tree of the knowledge of good and evil. It stood as a reminder for man that success depended upon holding fast to the law of the Lord. It was meant to teach him that though he was commanded to rule over all of God's earth, his authority was a delegated authority, and he was really a viceroy. He served at the pleasure of the Great King. In reference to his service, the tree taught man that his whole life, and all the fruits of it, were to be consecrated to the Lord. The whole of his life was to be centered in God; it came from God and it must be lived to the glory of God.

We misunderstand the importance of the Garden if we think of it, in the first place, as a dwelling place solely for human beings. The Garden is properly the dwelling place of God, who grants man the privilege of dwelling there in union and communion with Him.[10] This dwelling together is a condescension on God's part, on the condition of man's obedience. All of man's life was summed up in this relationship. The "material" was meant to serve spiritual ends. The end of that relationship resulted in death.

To appreciate this truth we need only consult Ezekiel 28.13 & 16. There we read specifically that the city of Tyre was called the "garden of God." We can compare this passage to others that offer a redemptive equivalent: Exodus 15.13 & 17, Psalms 43.3 & 78.54, and Isaiah 2.2. The idea of God possessing a dwelling place within creation itself is not common knowledge to Christians nowadays. But God always meant to dwell in a place that would be compatible with the habitation of man; this essential truth of the kingdom is inseparable from a comprehension of that kingdom. God did not intend to be an absentee landlord, but planned to cohabit the earth with man, in what, theologically speaking, has been termed "covenant fellowship." He charged man with the responsibility of building His kingdom, but the arrangement was to be a joint enterprise, with God as senior partner, taking man, the junior partner, into His counsels, and piece by piece revealing to him all that was to be accomplished.

As man finished one job, he would be entrusted with greater responsibility, until in God's providence everything

10 Geerhardus Vos, *Biblical Theology* (Grand Rapids: Eerdmans, 1948), p 37: "The garden is 'the garden of God,' not in the first instance an abode for man as such, but specifically a place of reception of man into fellowship with God in God's own dwelling place."

was brought to completion. God in fellowship with man is the only basis for His kingdom. The implications for culture and civilization, for science, technology, commerce, art, and industry are thus far-reaching. From the pattern in the Garden man could have transformed the unformed world into an image of that paradise. How different the world has become on account of sin! Instead of extending paradise, we have become afflicted with "thorns and thistles." Yet God remains concerned about the fulfillment of His kingdom on earth.

Scripture testifies to this truth when it records the long process by which God, in spite of the curse, is moving forward to reestablish His dwelling place among men; everything relevant to redemption is couched in those terms. For example, in Leviticus 26.9-12 we read, "I will look on you with favor and make you fruitful and increase your numbers, and I will keep my covenant with you. You will still be eating last year's harvest when you will have to move it out to make room for the new. *I will put my dwelling place* among you, and I will not abhor you. I will walk among you and be your God, and you will be my people." In the long history of redemption, the tabernacle and temple give partial fulfillment to that promise.

But with further study we learn that it will be in the coming of Jesus Christ that God will ultimately reveal exactly how He will dwell among us—in the form of man himself! "The Word became flesh and lived [lit: *tabernacled*] among us"(John 1.14). In Jesus we see what that original covenant, fulfilled in Himself—the true covenant Son—should have been. "I tell you the truth, the Son can do nothing by himself; he can do only what he sees his Father doing, because whatever the Father does the Son also does. For the Father loves the Son and shows him all he does" (John 5.19 & 20).

In the Second Adam, or Christ, the partnership between God and man is reestablished. The Garden was the original link between God and man; the Son is now that link, serving as vindicator and mediator between God and man. So the basis of the Christian ethic is a personal communion with the living God, and it involves submission to the Father's will: doing what the Father does.

Although the original covenant was forfeited, and man was expelled from the Garden, God did not abandon the world, or retract His original mandate. He established it on a firmer foundation, settled upon His Son. Those who serve the Son serve the kingdom of God. Because of sin, however, the progress of God's kingdom is seriously challenged by an alternate kingdom: the kingdom of man.

The Kingdom of Man

The conditions and circumstances that encompassed Israel and, in particular, the cultures of the nations surrounding her, and gave rise to the era of the prophets foretelling judgment and salvation to come, have been described by E. J. Young:

> It was an age of particularism, of various religions and cults, of various peoples. In such conditions salvation was not to be found, and *the old spirit of Babel again asserted itself*. As never before in the history of the world the idea of conquest gained ground, and one nation sought to subdue other nations and to make them a part of itself. Thus, the Assyrian king appeared upon the horizon, and his appearance signalized the striving for *a new order of things*. A reaching for *universalism* such as the world had never before known now began to appear, and a reaction against the old order took place. Again, the spirit of Babel was present, and again man began to exalt himself as he has tried to do at Babel. There would be no tower to reach into the heavens, but there would be *a world empire*. Mankind would not be concentrated in one spot; he would cover the earth but would belong to one kingdom, *the kingdom of man*. Man was to rule and to extend his sway, and man's kingdom was to cover the world so that *man alone would be exalted* through such universalism.[11]

Young is primarily referring to the world power of Assyria, but also has in mind the kingdom of Babylon that followed. Both were centralized state regimes, ambitious for military

11 Edward J. Young, *The Book of Isaiah* (Grand Rapids: Eerdmans, 1970), p.5. All emphases mine.

conquests and world dominion. At the same time, Young wants to illustrate the influence that these earthly powers had upon the impressionable minds of God's people, Israel. The emergence of these kingdoms was for Israel a spectacle she feared and envied. The extent to which Israel was at a corrupt distance from the Lord can be seen in the way Israel esteemed these principalities as secure and prosperous, or cringed at their power. Israel was seduced away from the Lord by the prospect of a similar kingdom of man.

The prophets teach that this lust for a worldwide empire, which would signify the supreme exaltation of man, is really the consequence of sin. It is in this inevitable direction that the rebelliousness of man gravitates, and the prophets announce that God will render sweeping and permanent judgment against such sin. "The Lord Almighty has a day in store for all the proud and lofty...the arrogance of man will be brought low and the pride of man humbled; the Lord alone will be exalted in that day, and the idols will totally disappear" (Isa 2.12, 17 & 18). At the same time, this judgment works to bring salvation to all who put their trust in God alone. "In the last days the mountain of the Lord's temple will be established as chief among the mountains, it will be raised above the hills, and all nations will stream to it" (Isa 2.2). This exaltation of God displaces the attempted alternate: the exaltation of man.

What should concern us at this point, however, is the necessity to understand the nature of sin in all of life. We cannot hope to understand the motive that is the guiding ideal of the non-Christian ethic, in whatever form it expresses itself, apart from insight into the genuine dimensions of sinfulness; and we must lay bare the drive in us that underlies all our endeavors and colors our achievements in every area, whether scientific, political, or economic.

The covenant structure overarching the whole of humankind has a paramount bearing on the way in which sin, because of the fall, reaches fruition in life. Not only did Adam himself stand in original covenant communion with God, but through him that privilege extended to all humankind. At the same time, man was created in a covenant interrelationship with his fellow man. The connection had more than a merely psychological quality (a feeling of *oneness* or *harmony*), or biological blood relationship; it was a spiritual unity. One may say that as there was a union and communion with God, so there was, in a derivative sense, a union and communion with the members of the human race, through our common head, Adam. This unity was focussed in him. Whether he responded to God in obedience or disobedience, his response would include the entire human race. There was originally, then, a societal dimension to sin or righteousness. Man was to be a "kingdom" creature; his life's purpose was united with organized activity; he sought societal expression for that experience. This was as God intended.

When man sinned, the structure of his existence, though seriously distorted, was not abrogated. So sin comes to assume all the features of a *kingdom*. We are compelled to admit that "if we could penetrate through to the essence of appearances, and trace out the root of sins in the hearts of people, we should very probably come to the conclusion that in sin, too, there is oneness, idea, plan, pattern—in a word, that in sin too there is system."[12]

In every way in which man was destined to act as a covenant keeper, he now acts as a covenant breaker (Rom 1.31). Mankind can never be a mere collection of individuals, and so sin can never be the mere deed of an isolated person. It is the nature of sin always to seek some organized social structure. The implement most ordinarily seized to give sinfulness a systematic expression is the *state*. As Rushdoony notes, "During most of history, the state has been man's central institution and therefore the central manifestation *in corporate form* of man's original sin."[13]

The state is the instrument most readily available to the

12 Bavinck, *Our Reasonable Faith*, p 248.
13 Rushdoony, *Christianity and the State*, p 35.

kingdom dynamic of sin. Genesis 1.28 affirms man's purpose to rule; the state has endless potential for the sinful form of that mandate. It is not, of course, scriptural to say that the state as such is the product of sin. It is to be an instrument in the service of God's kingdom. In order to be effective, it was granted vast powers; it was to use these to check the rise of sin wherever it threatened social order. But the state can become a tool in the hands of the organized power of sin, and be used to serve man-centered ends. The direction it takes will depend upon the ethic that controls the center of society.

The Westminster Larger Catechism defines sin, we saw, as "any want of conformity unto, or transgression of, any law of God, given as a rule to the reasonable creature." This definition, while correct as far as it goes, does not explain the kingdom dynamic of sin. It clarifies the juridical aspect of sin, revealing it as a transgression, or violation, of law. However, sin possesses a positive quality that must be taken into account, too. This quality is the motivating power behind sin's tendency to strive for systematic expression; it is, in essence, nothing less than the desire to be "as God." Every actual manifestation of the work of sin in man's life is an expression of that central, dominant motivation. Man was created to be under the law; sin is the ambition to be above the law, in the sense that man wants to be like God, who *gives* the law.

This is an attempt on the part of the creature to act as his own judge of good or evil; to lay down the law for himself, as it were, beyond which no appeal is permitted. "By transgressing the command of God and eating from the tree he [man] would in this sense make himself like God, for he would set himself *outside and above the law* and, just like God, would himself judge and make up what was good and what was evil."[14] In order, of course, to become god, it is necessary

14 *Gereformeede Dogmatiek*, Vol III, p 6. "Door het gebod Gods te overtreden en van der boom te eten, zou hij in dien zin zich Gode gelijk maken, dat hij zich buiten en boven de wetstelde en, evenals God, zelf beoordeelen en uitmaken zou, wat goed en wat kwaad was."

to declare independence from the true God. The desire, then, to be *as God* implies hatred of the true God, a hatred that basically expresses itself in opposition to His law.

The divine origin of that law prevents man from gaining the sovereignty he covets; it is the strength of man's opposition to the law that gives sin its kingdom quality. Therefore, "in principle and essence it [sin] is nothing less than enmity against God, and in the world it aims at nothing less than sovereign dominion. And every sin, also the smallest, being as it is a transgression of Divine law, serves this final objective in connection with the whole system."[15] The kingdom of man reveals the systematic form that sin inclines to take.

Professor Young, whose comment opens this section, without hesitation identified the kingdom of man with "the old spirit of Babel." The tendency of sin to seek a systematic, societal form, as in the Tower of Babel, was asserting itself again in Assyria and Babylon, in their struggle to achieve world empires—empires that would permit man alone to be exalted. The chief policy of these governments was to bring all of humankind under one regime. Assyria and Babylon did not act out of a new set of political ambitions in the history of man; they simply tried to revive the program that first appeared among the men building the Tower of Babel. The ideal of the kingdom of man is never dormant.

There is a common failure to understand what the Tower of Babel really means in biblical revelation. Many have seen its construction as a misplaced but well-intentioned effort by ancient man to find his way back to God after the fall. If anything, it represents the attempt of man to insure his independence once and for all from God—to make certain that God never again has authority over his life. It should be instructive, then, to consider the principle at work at Babel, for it is the same principle found wherever and whenever men seek to raise the state to absolute power over all of life.

15 Bavinck, p 249.

At Babel, the systematic inclination of sin becomes fully manifest.

The relevant passage in Scripture is Genesis 11.4: "Then they said, 'Come, let us build ourselves a city, with a tower that reaches to the heavens, so that we may make a name for ourselves and not be scattered over the face of the whole earth.'" The building of this tower served two purposes: to make a name for man, and to foster unity, or a one-world empire. The tower was meant to enhance the glory of man by organizing and centralizing culture. To achieve this, however, meant defying the living God, who said specifically that man was to exercise dominion over the whole earth under His authority.

That would have required a broad dispersion of man over the surface of the earth; it would have resulted in diverse enterprises. Every culture would work to build God's kingdom and glorify Him. Naturally, then, such a dispersion was a threat to the kingdom of man. If it weren't halted, it would prevent man from serving the advancement of his own sinful purposes.

For man to be glorified (or "make a name for himself") he had to coerce all of society toward this one goal. It was not that man didn't intend to make himself lord over the earth as a whole; it is only that he meant to achieve it by means of a locus that would "bind the whole of mankind together in a world which should find its strength in might, and in the glorification of man [as] all its purpose and endeavor."[16] In other words, through military conquest man would achieve glory for himself, and by force preserve his fame. If there was to be a purpose to any cultural task, it was that it would be cultivated as long as it promoted a unified society under a single state. The tower was a perfect example of this; standing tall over the city, it symbolized man's achievements. It would provide a constant inspiration and overawe any conscience

16 Bavinck, p 50.

not willing to submit to it. The tower would make visible to man life's purposes; it would stand as testimony to his impulse to set some god over his life to give that life purpose. The motive behind building the kingdom of man is religious. The tower "that reaches up to the heavens" is not a tower to God, but a symbol for a substitute god.

It is altogether correct that in the Tower of Babel "for the first time in history the idea arises of concentrating and organizing against God and His kingdom the whole of mankind in all its strength and wisdom, and in all its arts, and science, and culture."[17] In other words, *the Babel principle* is man's self-conscious effort to build his own kingdom in opposition to the kingdom (or will) of God. The incident at Babel should make clear that the non-Christian ethic is the antithesis to the Christian ethic. The former intends to replace the latter as the central and organic code of humankind. To work for the kingdom of God, then, is to summon opposition from the kingdom of man. If one of the goals of the kingdom of man is the exaltation of the state, its people must be regimented and controlled. The "good of society" must define every human act. The logical conclusion of the Babel principle is a totalitarian society.

Socialism rises from that principle, with this exception: contemporary developments in socialism indicate further maturation in modern man of the principle at work, and, therefore, greater historical progression in the accomplishment of its goals—all the more reason for Christians to become aware of the principles undergirding their own ethic, and the contrast it provides to the ambitions and energies working on behalf of the kingdom of man. In this regard, there is consolation in the truth that "greater is He Who is in you, than he who is in the world" (1 John 4.4).

That two kingdoms exist in the world side by side, locked in mortal combat, has been a distinctive theme in the history

17 *Ibid*.

of Christian thought; perhaps it finds no grander depiction than in the writings of St. Augustine. In *The City of God* he intended to show how two antithetical principles—two opposite kingdoms—actively operate in history and strive to overmaster human civilization. Each has a distinctive outlook that shades and stipulates every desire and deed of every human being. The most significant difference between men lies in what divides them into two opposing religious camps.

Or "...although there are many great peoples throughout the world, living under different customs in religion and morality and distinguished by a complex variety of languages, arms, and dress, it is still true that there have come into being only *two main divisions*, as we may call them, in human society: and we are justified in following the lead of our Scriptures and calling them *two cities*. There is, in fact, one city of men who choose to live by the standard of the flesh, another of those who choose to live by the standard of the spirit."[18]

Augustine said about the motive at work in each of these two cities, "in one city love of God has been given first place, in the other, love of self."[19] His description of the cities corresponds exactly to the perspective at the foundation of the Christian and non-Christian ethic. Love is a religious function of the heart, for "where a man's heart is, there is his treasure as well" (Mt 6.21).

The principle of Babel is the first dramatic expression in the Scriptures of "a dream of a unified order in which man totally controls and unifies every aspect of life under his own dominion."[20] It represents the aspiration to replace God with man as the final source of truth (and justice, and good and evil) and thus exclude God from the culture man intends to build. No doubt, it would be very easy for us, now, to dismiss

18 *St. Augustine's City of God*, trans Henry Bettenson (New York: Penguin, 1984), Bk XIV, p 547.
19 *City of God*, p 573.
20 Rushdoony, *Christianity and the State*, p 11.

the story of the Tower of Babel simply as myth, a product of the ignorance and superstition of primitive men. In our contemporary world, we think with a smile, Babel would be simply a device, useless. We are far too sophisticated to believe in the efficacy of a mere tower.

It is the spiritual principle of Babel that should concern us, not the peculiar form it happened to take. If as modern men we do not seek to build a unified culture by means of a literal, physical, material tower, nevertheless the idea behind it continues into our time. In fact, it has become more a part of the life of modern culture than of any other period in recent history. And while a crude symbol no longer supplies strength to a spiritual principle, the need for symbols abounds. Modern, sophisticated man has merely discovered a more effective means by which to throw off the yoke of God's dominion, take on the yoke of the kingdom of man, and rally the nations to its cause: Nature.

Nature is the most recent symbol for belief in man's independence from God. Nature has been called upon to assist in man's real ambition: to become his own god. By insisting that reality is the product of self-generation, no explanation for which can be found outside the physical cosmos, and that all of it is ordered and governed by laws inherent in it (which have nothing to do with a transcendent law-giver), man has found a way to transfer sovereignty from God to nature.

Introduce the theory of evolution and the case is closed; no further explanation is needed for man's existence. Natural law, the highest governing principle of nature, is not seen as the product of a personal God, who in wisdom fashioned the world and man's life to serve His purposes; it is seen as the outcome of impersonal, random forces somehow part of matter *as such*. If human life is to have any purpose, man thinks, it must come from whatever purpose I see fit to give it.

One of the instruments man has used is the realm of science; reason is the only authority he deigns to submit to. It is necessary to stress that in the history of ideas, the concept of nature that first took hold during the Renaissance became more and more secularized, as men began to seek an explanation for natural phenomena on a basis other than the cosmologies of Aristotle and Scholasticism. Without entering into detailed discussion of the reasons that prompted man to alter his theory of knowledge, it should be sufficient simply to say that the idea of nature which emerged at that time generally followed two different stages of philosophical interpretation.

First, under a still pervasive Christian influence, and up to the advent of the philosophy of Kant, the concept of nature continued to be viewed in an objective manner. That is, both the structure and laws of nature were assumed to exist outside of and beyond the mind of man, and so they formed an order of things to which man was compelled to assent. Nature was seen as an authority, demanding the submission of the human mind to its seemingly external imperative. This outlook can be partly explained by examining the field of epistemology, or the theory of preconditions, standards, and modes of knowledge: reason was seen to be a mere instrument, a tool of empirical investigation fitted for the job of sifting and evaluating the data of experience, so that man could understand causation in nature, and thereby control it, in order to bend nature's benefits to his own ends.

The accumulation of knowledge included, naturally, a utilitarian motive. As a founder of this new outlook, Francis Bacon (1561-1626) proclaimed, in *Novum Organum*, "...the real and legitimate goal of the sciences, is the endowment of human life with new inventions and riches." One can easily see from this how science was destined to guide a cultural program that rested at the heart of man's autonomous nature. The Promethean spirit of scientism, however, had not reached maturity; that would require some time. But matters pointed in this direction.

Ambiguity can already be read in Bacon's thinking on this matter; while he proudly declares that "the empire of man over things is founded on the arts and sciences *alone*,"—on the other hand—"nature is only to be commanded by obeying her."[21] At this first stage in the *idea* of nature, man did not yet feel free to create nature as he wished, or in his own image; he still felt bound to respect an order of things not wholly of his making. The Christian influence, which regarded nature's laws to be God's laws—to be the product of His creative will—continued to prevent man from assuming complete autonomy. Still, the deistic doctrine behind this new outlook on nature opened such a chasm between God and nature that the idea of nature began to dim. It was regarded, more and more, as imbued with immanent powers not attributable to the providence of God. Yet it seems God was needed to explain at least the origin and functioning of nature. If nature had an order and a purpose, from whence did these arise?

The second phase in the new concept of nature, beginning with the philosophical revolution of Immanuel Kant (1724-1804), turned from an objective to a subjective viewpoint. From that turn, nature ceased to be seen as an orderly system of experience having even partial legitimacy, apart from the mind of man. Instead, especially in post-Kantian idealism, nature came to be viewed, both formally and materially, as the product of man's reason.

Nature had always meant order, design, or purpose. At first it appeared as a given to man, more or less ready-made, that structured and predetermined his actions and the way his life developed, either individually or socially. But beginning with Kant's "Copernican Revolution" in epistemology—his reversal of the relationship between the subject and the object, making the object depend upon the constructive powers of the subject—man had the means by which to explain the principles of nature as the result of his own reason. Until, with Kant's help, man discovered that nature's order actually lay in his own mind, he didn't realize there

21 Francis Bacon, *Advancement of Learning & Novum Organum* (New York: Colonial Press, 1899), pp 339 & 366.

was a means at hand to sever him and his cultural efforts from God's revelation. Creation by a personal God was no longer necessary, even formally, to explain "order" or "purpose;" nature received its order and purpose from man's mind.

With the publication of *The Origin of Species*, the theory of evolution put the capstone on the construction of the idea of nature that had begun in the Renaissance, and laid to rest, once and for all, the belief that the world received its origin and purpose from God. The order of things we call nature cannot be attributed to anything but total random occurrence, science now said, leaving open the notion that man exists in an environment which he alone can imbue with meaning. The theory of evolution was formulated to serve the interests of the kingdom of man. It has enabled men to say that no real purpose to life existed until man himself, from the sanctum of his evolved rationality, oozed upward and proclaimed that purpose. For as North points out: "What is most offensive to modern science is the idea of cosmological purpose prior to the evolutionary advent of man."[22]

Evolution is the child genius of the spirit of Babel, and derives its strength from devotion to that conglomerating spirit. Those who assume they can buy evolution's "scientific" insights without the religious ideal that goes with them are on precarious footing, mere sand. They have already surrendered to the ethical vision of Babel.

22 Gary North, *The Dominion Covenant: Genesis* (Tyler, TX: Institute for Christian Economics, 1982), p 16.

THREE

CENTRAL COMPONENTS OF THE CHRISTIAN ETHIC

ON THE surface, non-Christians appear to stand for many different, even contrary, ethical systems. It may seem, then, that no single ethic has a permanent upper hand in our culture. History teaches us that non-Christians have never been able to agree upon a common purpose for civilization. There is a struggle between one set of principles and another, with the winner often gaining only pyrrhic or temporary victory. Soon a new set of values replaces the one that has been our standard, only to be replaced by yet another. One may even ask whether such a thing as a non-Christian ethic exists. It does. In spite of appearances to the contrary, a single religious ideal lies at the base of every non-Christian principle. It is the idolization of man.

For those within the framework of the Christian ethic, this idolization represents man's desire to be free from God's sovereign authority over life. Man will never think of himself as truly free from God if any portion of the world of his experience—his culture or civilization—remains without liberation; man wants everything under *his* sovereign authority. Whether he always realizes it or not, he sees every aspect of his experience in the light of this ambition, which is a religious ambition. Most especially, he wants to usurp

God's exclusive prerogative to declare what is, and what is not, good. This is of primary importance in understanding the ethical issue at stake between the Christian view of life and all of the world, and the view that emerges from the non-Christian ethic.

At creation, God made a declaration concerning all that He created (including the life and purpose of man): That it was good. For Christians this means that God alone has the right to decide the fundamental questions about everything that exists, including its purpose in the life of man. It also means by implication that God has reserved exclusive right to decide when that which was originally good became perverted, or evil.

Because of sin, man claims the right to judge this matter for himself. And man unquestionably assumes that everything concerning his life in this world must have as its final justification whatever "good" it provides on his behalf. As we shall see, every question of value and purpose is judged from the view of the good of society; or, in technical jargon, "social utility." Beginning with the Babel principle and its mate—man's declaration of independence from God—there arises the need, the absolute necessity, to reconstruct society; to organize it so every individual realizes that his actions, ambitions, and accomplishments are achievable only when they further "the good of society."

This is true whether the underlying principle is democracy, or another, more centralized manifestation of the same principle. The tendency of the Babel principle is always toward some form of totalitarianism that is agreed upon by everyone. It naturally arises, then, that whenever men decide on their own initiative what is good for them and society, they find that the only power able to insure that their desires will be realized is the state. Government is pliable; it can be made to serve whatever purposes its citizens wish, as long as it implements what they would call their utilitarian plans. The chief concern, however, is for government to be man's servant, not God's, and for it to conform to man's dictates alone. In the end, the logic of Babel pushes every society into totalitarian civil government. The idolization of man leads to idolizing the state, and the state must keep this idolatry under its control.

It was my contention at the beginning that capitalism (or whatever term one wishes to use for it) is not, and never was, a set of social relationships or economic activities that grew out of a Babel-inspired, man-glorifying culture. Yet capitalism is greatly maligned at the present. The very word evokes derision. North says, "the strongest philosophical and theological argument in favor of the free market is that it thwarts the attempt of power-seeking men to imitate God by centralizing the economic planning system through the civil government, thereby directing the lives of other citizens in terms of the goals of some elite central planning board."[1] North does not defend capitalism because of its utility, a common argument of humanists. That is, the Christian's argument for capitalism does not rise from its proven ability to increase vastly the goods in society and so augment the comfort of man, even though this may be true.

The argument for capitalism's material benefits should not be the Christian's chief consideration; rather its value to thwart the sinful desire to establish the kingdom of man in society. By the same token, capitalism allows the kingdom of God to increase, by preventing certain men from usurping the place of God over others. Indeed, capitalism is a witness to the progress of that kingdom on earth; it is a system of behavior that comports with God's sovereign authority over culture. Capitalism is possible only through the biblical recognition that a person's behavior is overseen by the Lord and made fruitful by His blessing. Its direction is not governed by the belief that everybody must work for the "good of society." Man labors to please his Lord.

Power-seeking men who want a society controlled by the state cannot tolerate anyone outside their jurisdiction, nor

1 *The Dominion Covenant*, p 10.

anyone prospering without their approval. This is the nub of the issue between socialism and capitalism. To argue over which one materially benefits a greater number of people, although significant, is of far less importance than the question: Which religion does each system serve? Capitalism—genuine capitalism, not the various state-sponsored hybrids that continue to use the name but in practice reject it—is a form of social behavior in which individuals recognize God alone to be sovereign over everyone's affairs; socialism, on the other hand, knows no sovereign but man acting through the state.

Presently there are conservative humanists who, in an inconsistency of belief, admit that a society under state control eliminates capitalism, and the prosperity accompanying it, and they are concerned about the implications of this for future civilizations. They have shown that capitalism could never function justly, according to some blueprint designed by a group of planners for an idealistic goal called the "good of society." In a truly capitalistic society the thousands of people who act, either individually or in association, in the market place, exchanging their goods and services, would never think of coercing their fellow entrepreneurs with laws meant to benefit an idolized "good of society."

In a Christian society, rather, each would know that he may engage only in those acts that honor and serve God. At the same time, each would know that the aggregate benefits to society of his actions lie beyond one's capabilities to grasp fully, ever; those possible benefits could never serve as a basis by which to act. Results must be left in God's hands. Each person is always reminded that his plans are contingent upon God's sovereign plan.

"What is your life? You are a mist that appears for a little while and then vanishes. Instead, you ought to say, 'If it is the Lord's will, we will live and do this or that'!" (James 4.14 & 15; Cf Ps 39.5b6a; 144.4). When the conservative humanist, then, sets out to defend capitalistic behavior on a utilitarian basis, he is not aware that he is taking an ethical perspective which is antithetical to free, decentralized economic activity.

Utilitarianism, because it is the invented ethic of sinful man, always insists that some immanent principle of behavior governs each action. Utilitarianism comes to view the good of society as the highest principle of behavior. Once detached from the Christian ethic, this becomes the inescapable viewpoint that is always assumed.

At present, however, even among Christians, the Christian ethic is not acknowledged. There is a profound difference of opinion among professing Christians about the Christian ethic and the exclusive authority it demands of us and our culture. Many believe that the Christian ethic should not guide any cultural task. More than that, many are persuaded that this would be catastrophic; that the Christian ethic, if anything, would stifle cultural development. At best, they are content to see the Christian ethic *share* in the guidance of modern culture. To them, the non-Christian ethic does not present an entirely contrary view of the world—it is not acknowledged, in other words, to be rooted in the Babel principle, whose purpose is to build the kingdom of man.

The church today offers a compromised gospel because it fails to see that a religious war is being waged beneath the exterior forms of society. The spirit at work in the world has penetrated the church itself. Not surprisingly, the church listens attentively to the subtle, tempting voice of non-Christian theorists who claim that society should be seen as an aggregation of diverse beliefs; that all viewpoints must be tolerated equally; that none must prevail over the rest.

This sounds so reasonable to many Christians that they accept the possibility of coexisting with other value systems that do not recognize Jehovah as sovereign over all. They willingly acquiesce to what is termed *pluralism*, which alleges that all value systems in society must respect each other's outlook on some supposedly neutral basis. This basis is never defined. Society, they say, can expect to achieve only a similitude of civil justice that exists independently of any particular religion—any religion, that is, but humanism. This perspective eliminates the Christian ethic from having any say in the public square about the goals of culture. This is understandable; the Christian ethic is absolute and uncompromising, because God is absolute and demands unilateral authority over every activity.

Christians fail to be obedient to God when they do not strive to make *all* men obedient. Today, the church practices a largely personal piety, withdrawn inside its walls to hear the simple message of Jesus. But no message of Jesus is true that does not proclaim Him Lord of the universe, and no piety honors Him that does not work for the increase of His Lordship in all that we do under the sun. When the church fails to make this message clear, when it equivocates on this point, it does not advance the kingdom of God; it tacitly promotes the kingdom of man.

It is disturbing to hear Christians maintain that they have no right to impose their values on society, as if the Christian ethic were something Christians manufactured on their own. One should rather insist that Christians impose nothing that God Himself does not impose. A genuine, biblically-grounded Christianity wants what God wants: total authority over every facet of experience. When Christians withdraw into cloisters to practice their religion of self-satisfaction, they should not feign astonishment when they see humanism directing civilization. Its influence, of course, will drive society steadily in a totalitarian direction.

It is no exaggeration to say that it has been only within the framework of Reformed doctrine that the Christian ethic has remained consistent with the Bible. The Heidelberg Catechism, in Question 91, asks, "What do we do that is good?" This is the most basic question that any system of ethics seeks to answer: what of man can be called good? How may we know that that which a person does is truly good? Is it on the basis of results achieved by his acts, which add to his happiness or the happiness of others? Is an act good in itself, or must it achieve some result that is defined as *good*? In other words, are good ends achieved only by good means; or may good be gained by any means? These and similar questions always come under consideration when we reflect upon the ethical viewpoint that governs life; and this is true when

Christians endeavor to understand the Scriptures.

Before we can answer these questions, however, we must define the meaning of good. And we must define it according to Scripture. We may not first consult our experience to decide what it is; we must take it on authority, like it or not. The Heidelberg Catechism, in broaching the question of good, provides in its answer the best summary of the scriptural viewpoint: "Only that which arises out of true *faith*, conforms to God's *law*, and is done for his *glory*; and not that which is based on what we think is right or on established human tradition." This stands in stark contrast to every assumption of the non-Christian ethic. In the Christian ethic, good is what conforms to God's word; in the non-Christian ethic, good arises solely out of man's inclinations and desires.

These, then, are the indispensable components of the Christian ethic: faith must be the *motive*, God's law the *standard*, and God's glory the *goal* of every Christian worthy of the name. Nothing has a place in the Christian experience that does not conform to each of these ethical stipulations. None of these elements may be missing when we speak of a Christian's ethical obligations. In the Christian world-view it is not simply a matter of desiring to exalt the claims of Christ over culture; the exact way in which Christ intends to be exalted is equally important. If we wish to see all of culture and civilization submit to Christ's dominion, we should understand that our efforts will fail if we exclude any of these scriptural teachings.

Faith as Motive

The motive of faith is not merely a matter of one's inner disposition. Nor is the Christian ethic a product of human experience, as I've said, or even of Christian experience; it is all that conforms in word and deed to God's authoritative Word. Although I speak of faith as the *motive* of the Christian ethic, what is paramount is the object to which faith is directed—the deepest incentive for all we do. The foundation of this is Hebrews 11.6: "And without faith it is impossible to please God, because anyone who comes to him must believe that he exists and that he rewards those who earnestly seek him." To this we should add the latter half of Romans 14.23: "Everything that does not come from faith is sin."

Faith is the dynamic of the Christian ethic; it should influence our understanding of the relationship between that ethic and society, economics, and politics. It seems obvious to say that within the Christian ethic God is the object to which faith is directed. Unfortunately, in our day, many think they believe this, but few practice it. We may pay marvelous lip service to the God of Scripture—He is Lord and Father—but we seldom trust Him unequivocally.

Today, as throughout the history of God's people, many rival gods are present to draw our allegiance away from the one and true God. What the Hebrews text says has nothing to do with resolving a philosophical problem about whether it is reasonable to believe that God exists. Its purpose is rather to command us to exercise unquestioned belief and trust in the only God who does exist, and who reveals His intimate concern for our lives, thereby teaching us that it is on Him alone that we may depend for our welfare, now and forever. The text also implies that we can depend upon nothing, or no one, else.

Faith has to do, above all else, with the one we take to be the ultimate source of our life and livelihood, the one to whom we give allegiance, and in whom we place undivided confidence and trust for the good of our selves—and, we should add, for society. Faith is that on which we place our reliance for our eventual success in every cultural enterprise. The essence of faith answers the question, Who holds in his power the course of events and has the ability to cause everything that happens to achieve a purpose, so that we don't feel history hurling onward without rhyme or reason?

The text from Hebrews further implies the one to whom we should submit on every question of right and wrong, good and evil, justice and injustice. For wherever we discover the source of our well-being, there we venerate its provider as our highest authority. And whoever in turn stands in our lives as that authority becomes the object of our greatest affection, service, and devotion. The one on whom we place our confidence is the one we will attempt to please in every sense; and trust, and obey, and look to for direction and motivation. In short, that one will be our god. Hebrews invites us to understand that it is on the God of Scripture—who has revealed Himself in Jesus Christ—and on this God alone that we may rely, and that to place our trust elsewhere is vain. From the last half of Romans 14.23 we learn that anything less is sin.

In our day, the god on which more and more people have come to rest their hope is the state. Multitudes look to it for every need. From the standpoint of the Christian ethic, this is idolatry. The reason the God of Scripture alone can be relied upon to benefit our lives has to do with the character of His relationship to the material cosmos. The realm of nature does not exist apart from Him, as an independent entity over which He has no control. When God promises that He will reward those who seek Him, we should understand that His word applies to every circumstance. His power is not limited to the salvation of individual souls, but is effective for the life of man, his cultural labors included. However it may appear to us, God is capable of causing nature, with its seemingly inviolable laws, to serve in the interest of those whose service is dedicated entirely to Him. Nothing in man's experience—not poverty, disease, oppression, or any evil—can prevent God from delivering His promise to those who put their faith in Him.

We should not, of course, view faith merely as a means for achieving material blessing. The promise is not automatic; often the wicked prosper; reward for Christians in this life may seem never to arrive. But the faith of a righteous man does not expire on that account. Instead, it ascends still higher, to the perception that God's reward reaches beyond the grave—to the belief that God will bring life out of death. There is simply no obstacle to God's purposes. So our labor in the Lord is never in vain.

Calvin best conveyed the attitude of faith we should have: "Faith...having grasped the love of God, has promises of the present life and of that to come, and firm assurance of all good things, but of such sort as can be perceived from the Word. For faith does not certainly promise itself either length of years or honors or riches in this life, since the Lord willed that none of these things be appointed for us. But it is content with this certainty: that, however many things fail us that have to do with the maintenance of this life, God will never fail."[2] Faith is the motive of the Christian ethic, not because it brings about an exclusive, material well-being, but because it entails the singular conviction that our entire lives rest in the care of the only God capable of rewarding those who entrust themselves to Him without reserve; faith looks to His blessing alone.

But as we examine faith more closely, as the motive of the Christian ethic, we should understand that economic welfare is no more withdrawn from reward than any area of life. And in fact we see that God rewards obedience economically, as well as other ways. Once again, many Reformed statements make trust in God's promise of reward particularly applicable at this point. In answer to Question 125, "What is meant by the fourth request in the Lord's Prayer, 'Give us this day our daily bread?'" the Heidelberg Catechism supplies an incisive biblical explanation: "Do take care of all our physical needs so that we come to know that you are the only source of everything good, and that neither our work and worry nor your gifts can do us any good without your blessing."

Faith is not mere fideism, a self-absorption in the experience of belief itself. Faith is not concerned only for the soul, but for the whole of life, and means walking in dependence on God, to realize His purposes. It is not a withdrawal from life; it is the fountainhead of all we do. Our economic well-being is covenantally conditioned on perfect trust in

2 *Institutes of the Christian Religion*, John T. McNeill, ed, trans Ford Lewis Battles (Philadelphia: Westminster Press, 1975), Bk III, Ch II, p 574.

God, who promises to "reward those who seek Him." Believers cannot rationalize their economic behavior apart from faith in this promise from God. For, quite simply, the blessings of prosperity are blessings to the whole of man; his heart should find complete satisfaction in whatever enrichment he experiences. The economic benefit, both to himself and others, is of little effect without the understanding that it stems from the blessings of God.

Faith in God's promise gives long-term meaning and stability to life, and therefore long-term stability to any economic endeavor. These are the only conditions under which wealth can be achieved and enjoyed. It is this outlook alone that turns men into producers of permanent results. Taken together, God Himself is man's reward, for He alone can give true satisfaction to every heart. Calvin strongly concludes the matter: "godly men must hold to this path...let them neither desire nor hope for, nor contemplate, any other way of prospering than by the Lord's blessing."[3]

Are we permitted, then, to accept the pervasive modern belief that man's welfare lies in the state? That is the ethic of socialism. Socialism invites us to put all our hopes for our well-being in the state. We begin to look to the state, not to God, for our prosperity in life, and as a consequence more and more people are turning to politics as the solution to all their problems, particularly economic ones. Many Christians, too, are lured into the false belief that the state alone has the means by which to bring about positive benefits and sanctions in our lives. But Hebrews 11.16 is unequivocal: no other source exists for our welfare than the God of Scripture.

Our economic and social selves must be included in a comprehensive framework of dependence on Him for every good we expect to receive in this life.

To put our faith in God's promise for one area of life, and deny its relevancy for another, is to adopt divided loyalties,

3 *Institutes*, pp 698-699.

which the Christian may not do. A Christian may not look to God to save his soul, and to the state to save his body. Christians are bound to frame the issue of prosperity exclusively in covenantal terms. All of our cultural efforts, including economics, rest on the foundation of God's kingdom alone, or they serve to advance the kingdom of man; we trust in God or trust in ourselves. And frankly, we haven't grasped the importance of this principle of reward until we understand that it covers *everything*—all that God has ordained for us to do.

Is our reward from God, or is it a product of our individual might? God formulated this issue, gave the answer, and warned against the common humanist response in Deuteronomy: "Otherwise, you may say in your heart, 'My power and the strength of my hand made me this wealth.' But you shall remember the Lord your God, for it is He who is giving you power to make wealth, that he may confirm His covenant which He swore to your fathers, as it is this day" (8.17 & 18).

Which principle of reward governs the outlook of capitalism? Which socialism? Under the view of the Christian ethic, the concept of reward must relate to and determine the entire dominion task of man. Man was never left to himself to carry out this original obligation, as mentioned earlier, but was always dependent upon God to guarantee the outcome of his labors. This has not changed. Calvin has captured the essence of the scriptural outlook on all of life. It is an outlook that badly needs to be restored to the Christian community in our day.

God's Law as Standard

Next to complete trust in God's reward as the motive for our labor, the Christian ethic upholds the law of God as the only standard by which to pursue that reward. Socialism is not only a turning away from dependence on God, it is a refusal to accept God's law as the standard of justice and righteousness. In the question raised by the Heidelberg Catechism—What is the good we do?—we learn that only that which rises from true faith, from an undivided trust in God, is good. But we also learn this: only behavior that "conforms to God's law" can be called good. This sets the biblical ideal of good in contrast to what we think is right or permissible according to human tradition.

So the Christian ethic insists that nothing that man does is good if it does not self-consciously rest on the revealed will of God. It doesn't matter if it seems good to us; if our behavior in life doesn't conform without question to God's law, it is no good; in fact, it's evil. This is as true for our life within society as it is for our personal conduct. If we expect God alone to provide for our well-being, we must listen to Him alone in all matters of conduct relating to life. Since He is the source of life itself, He is the supreme authority over all of life.

Here I ask you to recall the content of Chapter One, of salvation as a total concept, so that whoever becomes man's redeemer also becomes his lord. Anyone actually concerned about the advancement of God's kingdom here and now on earth, should recognize that his duty is to work for the increase of His Lordship over every dimension of life. We must establish God's law as the basis of every act; and at the present, we can be certain that the carrying out of this responsibility will meet with the stoutest resistance.

When we take time to consult Scripture, we discover these two components of the Christian ethic to be inextricably bound into one. That is, God's blessing—His life-giving and life-building reward—is contingent upon righteous obedience on the part of man. And it is God's law alone that teaches us which behavior is fit to be called righteous and which unrighteous. The blessing of prosperity was never promised as a matter of course, but was meant to accompany righteous deeds. The fruitfulness of man's life in every respect depends upon perfect obedience to God.

Certainly, we must take into account the fall, and man's loss of ability to satisfy the obligations of perfect righteousness; and, too, the complete restoration made possible through Christ, who fulfills righteousness on man's behalf and assumes the punishment for man's refusal to walk in obedience to God. Christ makes it possible for us to be obedient again to the standard of the law; he causes the law of God to become active in our lives, and transforms us from creatures of rebellion into doers of righteous deeds. This alone makes us fit to be the builders of culture, as servants of God's kingdom. It gives us the confidence to work for productive ends in all we're given to do in this world.

Tragically, many Christians embrace an ideal of justice that leaves out God's law. Like the heathen they live among, they see God's law as an obstacle to justice. They believe it is possible to achieve a prosperous society without reference to the righteous behavior determined by God. The best possible justice in the world, they suspect, is a pluralistic accommodation to the values of humanism. And not surprisingly, they accept a form of socialism as the goal toward which public policy should be directed. Like secularists in general, they have come to think of capitalism as the epitome of injustice and greed, and therefore the enemy of civilization. But the real enemy is a deep-seated lawlessness. A widespread antinomianism (which means "against the law") lies behind most of society's institutions now, and with it comes the desire to dominate the lives of others.

The Christian ethic upholds the centrality of God's law in the entire experience of life. When Christians deviate from it their offense is more grievous than the non-Christian's. Christians today have largely adopted the relative-values outlook of the secular world; Christian values are viewed as relative to Christians only, and so they ought not to be imposed on society. Society is the product of many values, this view insists, and Christians should not expect theirs to receive any special favor. This attitude has come about mainly because Christians have made their personal feelings, rather than God's word, their touchstone of faith. They have retreated from the obligation to promote God's kingdom on earth, which can be accomplished only as God's will is consciously brought to bear on the lives of all. Self-absorption with religious experience per se causes indifference in Christians to divine law. This law demands that we take an interest in things that do not in the first place pertain to ourselves, but to God and our neighbor—interests out of keeping with our present age of narcissism.

By the same token, we shouldn't suppose that antinomianism among Christians has the same perversity as with non-Christians; their outlook derives from a profound hatred of God, and so, too, of His law. The premise of the entire culture of the non-Christian is this hatred, although various value systems of the non-Christian speak with eloquence about the rule of law; societies have sought to establish principles of justice using the law as a final court of appeal. But non-Christians oppose any principle that even remotely includes God's law. Human-worship, or the religion of humanism, excludes any principle of law whose source is not in man himself. Humanists cannot accept a transcendent source of law, and as a result the notion of what is lawful changes with every alteration in what men define as good or evil, just or unjust, within changing circumstances. The only constant is whatever people choose as useful for promoting their self-defined happiness. Law is simply a means to that end; its value is relative.

Where God's law does receive a modicum of respect and reverence, there often remains an insufficient grasp of its sovereignty over all of life, public as well as private—when it should apply to everything that God has given us to do under the sun. This is why Ecclesiastes addresses its "gospel" to the world of meaninglessness and vanity in these terms: "Fear God [motive] and keep his commandments [standard], for this is the *whole duty* of man. For God will bring every deed into judgment..." (12.13 & 14). Far from offering an escapist concession in the face of a tormenting and intractable world, this injunction provides the only hope available to us in our cultural endeavors. It states that the law of God is to be the spiritual criterion by which every material activity is measured and performed.

People in our age express disillusionment at civilization and what it has come to mean. They despair over the fractured and impersonal nature of our modern materialistic lifestyle, and the threat of industrialized societies to the health of people and the environment. See how shallow and empty we've become, with our idolizing of youth, our pursuit of pleasure—living, it seems, only for the next thrill. Or, in revolt against modernity, seeking consolation in the drug and rock-music culture, in which mindlessness has possibly reached its apogee. Many see the problem as dehumanization, a transforming of "meaningful relationships" into mere mechanical interactions, with human beings treated like pawns rather than persons. Yet at the same time, those who voice these concerns are quick to locate the blame anywhere but in our rebellion against God.

They point the accusing finger at one factor or another in our culture: they blame government for dereliction of duty, society for callous indifference, and especially like to lay the blame on education, for its failure to inculcate proper values—science is, after all, infallible, as they see it; men of reason rarely make mistakes.

But the worst offender is capitalism! Nothing has been more responsible for the ills of modern man than this hated economic and social system. Anybody with rational sense *knows* that capitalism is the chief cause of our miseries, responsible for greed and selfishness, aggressiveness and war. On it rests the blame for every psychic and social disturbance we define. It fosters a form of relationship that can be measured only in terms of cash. It has taught us to see all men as laborers or owners of "things," and nothing more. We have lost a sense of the past and tradition, which gave our lives a basis and a continuity, because of capitalism's single-minded pursuit of technological advancement—*progress*. Capitalism can continue to be justified only by its ability to keep men constantly interested in satisfying merely sensual cravings. Notions of this sort have been the *obiter dicta* of socialist zealots for so long that people believe them; they promote the image of socialism as the good guy needed to rescue mankind, and to restore justice and meaningful human relationships based on compassion and "caring."

Many reasons have been given to explain why we suffer

from meaninglessness in our lives, or social injustice, poverty, crime, disease, and the rest; but not one of them ever gives the reason as rebellion against God. The standard of God's righteousness, His law, which ought to rule over our lives, is universally assailed as central to the problem. Naturally! It stands in the way of our religious ambition to be our own law-givers and arbiters of good and evil. Rebellion against God's law does not remove the need for law to govern life. Man is unalterably a creature of law; it's in his makeup, indelibly part of his nature to live in accordance with law.

From the outset, the law was implanted in our being to limit our behavior: God's law, the only rule of righteousness, was thoroughly meshed with human personality. Man was created to act in accord with that law as a regulative principle, and was destined from the beginning to be God's obedient servant. By acting out of obedience, man indeed would have become master over God's creation; he would have succeeded in his kingdom work. Van Til has observed, "As a creature of God man had to live in accordance with the law of God, that is, in accordance with the ordinances that God had placed in his creation. This law was for the most part not verbally transmitted to man but was created in his being. Man would act in accord with his own true nature only if he would obey the law of God and, vice versa, if he would live in accord with his own nature, he would obey the law of God."[4]

It was the very essence of human nature to live according to that law. No definition of man can exclude this and be a true definition. When man rebelled, he denied that truth. It is this revolt that is the chief cause of his dehumanization. A flat denial of God's law as a principle part of our being turns our experience into vanity, sheer meaninglessness; but the restoration of this truth leads to true liberation and provides the foundation on which to rebuild culture and civilization.

Since man is a creature of law, the bearing of his life and

4 *The Defense of the Faith*, p 15.

society will be directed by whatever ideal of law gains control. If he will not have God's law as the standard of his conduct, then he must find a substitute law, and the source of that law will be, as I have said, his god. The essence of modern humanism is a transference of law from God to the state. "Modern humanism, the religion of the state, locates law in the state and thus makes the state, or the people as they find expression in the state, the god of the system."[5] This transference of the source of law from God also involves a transference of sovereignty from God to the state. The laws of the state acquire divine status; no appeal to a higher source of justice exists beyond the state. In the final analysis "any change of law is an explicit or implicit change of religion."[6]

In the Westminster Confession of Faith we read, "God gave to Adam a law, as a covenant of works, and perpetual obedience... This law, after his fall, continued to be a perfect rule of righteousness... The moral law doth for ever bind all, as well justified persons as others... Neither doth Christ, in the Gospel, any way dissolve, but much strengthen this obligation" (19:I, II & V). Or as Calvin remarks, "There is no doubt that the perfect teaching of righteousness that the Lord claims for the law has a perpetual validity."[7] And then elaborates further, "the law has been divinely handed down to us to teach us perfect righteousness; there no other righteousness is taught than that which conforms to the requirements of God's will..."[8] The Christian ethic holds nothing to be right, just, or good in any sense, if it does not have reference to the standard of God's law.

The centrality of this law in the Christian ethic should not

5 Rousas John Rushdoony, *The Institutes of Biblical Law* (Nutley, NJ: Presbyterian and Reformed, 1973), p 5.

6 *Ibid.* Either God or the state stands at the center of man's religion, and his worship and his expectation of reward attaches to one or the other.

7 *Institutes*, Bk II, Ch VIII, p 371.

8 *Institutes*, p 372.

be viewed as a sort of "categorical imperative," which we are dutifully obliged to obey whether it is to our benefit or not. Rather, God's law well serves His covenant framework. Obedience to God's will contains the promise of fruitfulness and blessing: disobedience, the threat of curse and punishment. Observance of the law is the instrument of covenant reward; contempt for the law insures evil and misery. God conditioned all of man's life on obedience to His will. What we in the present-day culture need to discover, if we wish to avoid a continual descent into chaos and calamity, is the proper place of the law of God in our lives and our work.

This is the real issue of our time.

Finally (and sadly) we must admit that the increase of lawlessness in our day is due above all to the growth of a deeply rooted antinomianism in the church itself. It is the Christian community that most deserves blame for having aided and abetted every non-Christian ethic, by denying the importance of God's law over every area of life. There is no doubt that Rushdoony is correct to assert that "pietistic antinomianism has been atheism's greatest ally."[9] The church in the modern world, by a radical shift in its doctrinal position, has encouraged society's attitude toward God's law. The church now teaches a new form of piety, one that insists that grace or faith stand in opposition to the righteousness of God's law. This teaching rises from the belief that the message of Jesus and the Apostles in the New Testament formed a dispensational discontinuity with the teachings of the Old Testament. The prevailing teaching says that since the Old Testament era has been superseded by the New Testament era, God's revelation in the former has ceased to have any validity for the life of God's people, much less for society as a whole. Christ's death and resurrection ushered in a new age, we hear, in which the experience of grace is entirely disconnected from the law of God. This altered

9 *Christianity and The State*, p 52.

doctrinal outlook, the opposite of what we find in The Westminster Confession and in Calvin, eventually spilled into the realm of culture as a whole, and rebellious men needed no encouragement to jettison God's law. But it certainly didn't displease them to discover that the modern church was entirely in agreement with them.

Modern man wants nothing more than to be free of the law of God, for His law is the means of His authority over man. Man wants to be free to locate law elsewhere, and more and more has settled it on the state. Society may continue to believe in something called the rule of law as the highest norm of right and justice, but since the idea of law has been uprooted from its transcendent source, the ideal of the rule of law now represents law created by man. Increasingly, this ideal has become a tool to those strong enough to wrest political control in the public domain. Their whim becomes the law; their "vision" for society, justice.

Capitalism is incapable of functioning in a social and moral environment in which lawlessness holds sway over the consciousness. Those who speak of capitalism as still being present in the world are not aware that they apply the term to a residue that perhaps is partly visible but that in substance has all but vanished—if it actually existed in the first place. Even those who are termed capitalists subscribe to the ideal of the socialist vision, hoping by this to protect themselves against the vicissitudes of a competitive environment. Justice has come to mean whatever benefits *me* at somebody else's expense. By means of law—man's law—men have come to approve of actions that are the antithesis of law and justice.

Their hopes to create order out of chaos are offered at the altar of the state. Under God's law, men can govern themselves; but under man's law, all men must bow to the state.

God's Glory as the Goal

The third and final component of the Christian ethic has to do with the end of man's endeavors, or the goal toward which all work aspires. What should be the ultimate purpose of man's life and labors? For those who hold to the Christian ethic, Paul's injunction from First Corinthians supplies the answer: "So whether you eat or drink or *whatever you do*, do it all for the *glory of God*" (10.31). This is the bottom line. God's glory always and everywhere is the real reason we do anything in life. Within the Christian ethic, God's glory is the answer to why all things were created, and to the destination toward which all things are ultimately headed.

That creation was meant to exalt and manifest God's glory was not something man could have discovered for himself, but had to be determined by God on His own behalf; and was declared to be the underlying purpose of all He has made. God's purpose was to glorify Himself in all that He created, but expressly in the commission He gave to man: to exercise dominion over the earth. This meant that all of man's accomplishments were to be done to achieve glory on God's behalf. God set this goal for man. It was not anything man would have planned to do out of merely utilitarian motives.

The mere existence of every aspect of the creation does indeed glorify God. The fall has not altered matters in this respect. The Christian ethic maintains that even with the fall God purposed to achieve glory on His behalf. The fall should not be viewed as an event that has rendered null and void the God-glorifying purposes and destiny of all of creation. In fact, we must assert that the fall reveals the predestined means by which God achieved glory for Himself. God's original intent was that the glory to be accorded to Him should be the chief desire of all His creatures—specifically man—and that man should freely and self-consciously offer Him this glory.

Man, created in God's image and likeness, was given the capacity, on a finite level, to *want* to do all he did for the glory of God. God implanted this desire in man and expected it to increase in strength as man more and more fulfilled his responsibility to build the kingdom of God. The fall, to be sure, has redirected the course of man's intentions and desires; instead of wanting to glorify God, man thinks only of achieving glory for himself. Through redeeming grace he can again be set on the proper path; he is expected to have as his highest ideal the glory of God, as Paul reminds us. Further, Christians are expected to bring the whole world to that end as well. This is the greatest thing any man can do with his life.

For many Christians, this raises the question of whether, by seeking to do all for God's glory, they might place an obstacle in the way to achieving any good for themselves. It has become so ingrained in our thought that God's glory and our own good are opposites that we tend to see them as opposed to each other. Is it possible to achieve both simultaneously, or is one possible only at the expense of the other?

As far as the Christian ethic is concerned, doing everything for God's glory is the greatest good anyone can perform on his own behalf. This has to do with the covenantal condition God has built into our lives, which ties our well-being to the advancement of God's glory. In this respect, doing everything for the glory of God should not be seen as an abstraction separate from the rest of the Christian ethic: our lives do not glorify God if what we do is not motivated by faith in Him alone; nor is God glorified if His law is impugned in our conscience and excluded from its place of authority. And whoever does not glorify God will not partake of life.

FOUR

IMPLICATIONS OF THE CHRISTIAN ETHIC

IN ORDER to cover the main contours of the Christian ethic, we must follow the implications of its outlook for both individual and society. And then resolve this question: which of the two, capitalism or socialism, accords more with Christianity? Unless we are able to articulate the perspective we should hold on life, as Scripture has conceived of it and Christians ought to proclaim it, the Christian ethic can have no relevance to, or influence on, our present culture.

It should be with sorrow that every Christian admits that it does, indeed, have little if any relevant influence. Much of the blame for this must be placed on the leaders of the Christian church over the last century, but it would be unwise merely to state that and stop there. The fault also lies in each of us, as members of that church, for none is as discerning of the Christian ethic as we are called to be, not one. All the more reason, then, to pursue a definition and description of the outlook we are to hold toward life and culture, over against the antithesis, a non-Christian ethic. We can never appreciate the ethical antithesis that distinguishes capitalism from socialism until we have done this.

Although I have not yet focused on the peculiar features inherent in each system, socialism and capitalism, I have alluded to the principles and ideals behind their differing points of view. A more complete discussion of these will come. First we must see the implications of the Christian ethic for the individual and, second, for society. I must add that this is not an attempt to be exhaustive. I will provide only an overview of the perspective that derives from a Christian understanding of experience in both realms: individual and societal. Until we hold this overview in mind, our understanding of the problem is incomplete.

Concerning the Individual

The appositeness of the Christian ethic to the individual, as individual, cannot be overlooked in any discussion of humankind's behavior as a whole. I don't say this because I assume that mere individuals compose—like so many loose bricks—the basic building blocks of society. Nor do I contend that the individual is the highest reality, and that his or her self-interest (enlightened or otherwise) should serve as the basis for moral considerations. Nor that society derives from a confluence of individual wills which have discovered that there are certain advantages, or safety, in numbers. The individual is not an onotological absolute, with society merely the offshoot of many individuals' voluntary association. To see the actions of individuals as actions of isolated entities that have formed social bonds for self-serving reasons is to be out of touch with the Christian ethic. That is a nominalist perspective foreign to Christian thought.

Yet the flowering of the value of the individual in mankind's ethical estimation, especially the estimation of Western man, has primarily been due to the influence of Christian thought throughout history. The spread of Christian teachings acted as a moral antidote to the poisonous low esteem that contaminated primitive and pagan man's regard for the sanctity of an ordinary individual's life. Everywhere in the ancient world the individual's uniqueness was subsumed into the holier cult of the community, be it the tribe, the clan, or the *volk.* History over and over records how the individual was subordinated to the omnipotence of a group—

especially as groups became manifest in the state. A person's life was cheap in comparison to the life of the community; one belonged body and soul to the divine *city*. You were expected to renounce your self in dedication to the interests of society; every person had to sacrifice everything for the sake of whatever was said to be beneficial to the state.

Christianity broke through this pagan ideal and taught that the individual has distinct value and meaning in the scheme of things, because each life must be seen, before anything else, as it stands in relationship to God, and so has worth according to Him. Individual achievements are thus a mainstay in contemporary Western moral estimation.

We shouldn't be surprised to find, however, many secular thinkers claiming that the rise of the ethical value of the individual came about as the result of ideals first promoted by ancient pagans, and especially the Greeks: "Greece made no greater contribution to human history than by establishing the supremacy of the private conscience."[1] And, too, secular thinkers would like us to believe that the recovery of those ancient ideals in the modern era, following their neglect in the "superstitious" Middle Ages, began with the revival of humanism in the Renaissance, and then reached a peak in the Enlightenment of the eighteenth century. The reestablishment of ancient Greek ethical values supposedly taught us to venerate individual human rights above everything else, including the state.

If these thinkers pay grudging lip service to any Christian influence, it has to do with the urgency that Christianity put upon the salvation of the individual soul. The philosophy of human worth as we understand it, however, and as it has pervaded the consciousness of the Western world, has its origins, they assume, in the Greek genius. We should not be deceived by this assumption. The truth is that when we

1 C. E. Robinson, *Hellas: A Short History of Ancient Greece* (Boston: Beacon Press, 1948), p 100.

examine statements from the Greek city-states, we find a different story. The ancient political communities—whether the smaller city-states of the Greek peninsula or those of the transnational Roman Imperium—took pains to submerge the lives of individuals in communal entities. The purpose was to make the state absolute in the life of every citizen.

No one better sums up the prevailing consensus in both the Greek and Roman worlds, perhaps, than Aristotle. In the *Politics* he reasons, "Every state is a community of some kind, and every community is established with a view to some good; for mankind always acts in order to obtain that which they think good. But, if all communities aim at some good, the state or political community, which is the *highest of all*, and which *embraces all the rest*, aims at good in a greater degree than any other, and at the highest good."[2] Aristotle's conclusion was, in general, the widely held opinion of the ancients. They assumed a hierarchy of *goods*, at the height of which was the state—the highest good. To do all one could to promote the interests of the state, therefore, was the greatest moral duty one could perform. Any lesser good that individuals might achieve on their own was to be subordinated to this supreme good. That, anyway, was the theory; in reality the pursuit of any good that didn't advance the state came to be viewed with hostile suspicion. No nonpolitical interests, no mere private goals, were allowed to interfere with the advancement and cause of the state.

To confirm this attitude in people's minds, Aristotle attempted to make the generally recognized assumption rationally inescapable, glossing it with a scientific aura of respectability that is always sought for in the value systems of the non-Christian. For Aristotle, the state was posited as the *whole*, from which everything else derived logically as its *part*. Conveniently, no single part could be explained or be

2 *The Basic Works of Aristotle*, Richard McKeon, ed (New York: Random House, 1941), "Politica," p 1127. The emphases are mine.

justified simply from the standpoint of *part* as such. It had no logical existence separate from the whole, which was, of course, the state. Aristotle argues, "As in other departments of science, so in politics, the compound should always be resolved into the simple elements or least parts of the whole. We must therefore look at the elements of which the state is composed..."[3]

Aspects other than the state are "simple elements" of the state, whether we consider these to be individuals or social groups, such as the family, for example. If it is not the state, then it is an element of the state. And as the whole is more valuable than the parts, according to the laws of logic, so too the state possesses greater value than the parts that make it up. "The state is by nature clearly prior to the family and to the individual, since the whole is of necessity prior to the part."[4] By prior Aristotle meant of greater importance. And by now it should be clear that, according to this philosophy, no matter what aims and aspirations, duties and responsibilities a man held dear, none could take preeminence over the powers and purposes of the state. To serve the state's interests was the citizen's highest moral obligation. The parts are interchangeable, the whole is permanent; the claims of the state take precedence over every other. No endeavor is justifiable if it fails to meet this ethical requirement.

Whatever value, then, was attached to the individual in ancient philosophy, it was important only to the extent to which the individual submitted himself to the state; duty to it was one's first duty. So it is more correct to say that, according to the ancient or classical view, if the individual had any value at all *as an individual*, it was exclusively for promoting the broader political entity, or state, to which that individual happened to belong.

In the history of the West, with the rise of Christianity, the

3 *Aristotle*, p 1127.
4 *Aristotle*, p 1129.

dreadful precariousness of the life of the individual was, to a considerable extent, granted more stability. The consequences to each person's life that this ancient ideal imposed, in reality, were removed; the individual achieved a status of respectability unimaginable in the ethical thinking of Aristotle. And the emergence of individuality has proven to be of inestimable benefit to the progress and development of civilization and culture—and, dare we say, to the increase of God's kingdom on earth? This benefit stands in antithesis to the deprecation it receives in non-Christian nations. In both the ancient world and in the modern non-Christian world, the state is everything, the individual is nothing.

Yet at the present in the West, where Christianity has made its greatest gains, beginning at least from the start of the last century, we can observe an ominous growth of statism and socialism—to an extent, indeed, that the ancient thinkers never dreamed of. More than with these men, the new vision for society contains an abundance of presumably scientific claims. Modern sociology reveals a series of rationalizations on the part of secular thinkers to justify a state-dominated society and culture. In the writings of sociologists you find virtually unanimous agreement that the individual must be viewed as a piece of a large and more valuable puzzle.

The individual's outlook on life, they say, simply reflects, in microcosm, the outlook of the social group into which he was born and reared. He is a conditioned reflex of previously existing customs and mores. His interests and ambitions are predetermined by what is "socially acceptable". Whatever values he stands for are the values society has given him, and the state exists to institutionalize those values; it implements the *will* of society—and society is absolute.

Rushdoony has suggested why ancient thinkers depicted the individual in this way; they had a profound distrust of man as man. On the other hand, they seemed infinitely trustful of philosophical man, or the man of *reason*.[5] This attitude is as pervasive in the present. At the very least we should be aware that the problem of man as an individual lies in the problem of man per se. The difference between the Christian view and every other view is crucial at this point; we can't appreciate the role of Christianity in enhancing the value of the individual without understanding the Christian definition of man.

It would be helpful to consider the development of the idea of man as it appears in the history of modern thought—because we have to understand our present outlook if we hope to make the Christian alternative clear. For assistance, I draw freely from interpretations found in an excellent book by Franklin Baumer, *Modern European Thought*.[6] For the most part my comments follow Baumer's exposition, and for a fuller understanding one would do well to consult this highly recommended work.

We begin at the seventeenth century. Because the onset of the seventeenth century was a time of great intellectual ferment and change, brought on by scientific discoveries, it upheld a view of man that was influenced by the shadow science cast over all of life. Specifically, it was because of man's role as a doer of science that "science inspired two new images, one of man *in* nature, another of man *over* nature.".[7] This definition then devolved into contraries: as an element of nature, man was viewed as a creature of passion, volatile and threatening, wretched and brutish. But as one who stood over nature, he was a creature of reason—conquering and subduing. So a dualism emerged in the definition of man.

Yet an optimism prevailed, by and large, maintaining that reason was more powerful, and that through reason man would learn to master and control his passions. This was

5 *Cf Christianity and the State*, p 14.

6 Franklin L. Baumer, *Modern European Thought: Continuity and Change in Ideas, 1600-1950* (New York: Macmillan, 1977).

7 Baumer, p 93.

made possible by knowledge and science. Science would teach man to bring the warring aspects of his animal nature into check, and would tame his passions and channel them into civilized pursuits, bringing order to his appetites and desires, and adding virtue, somehow, along the way. Wars would become a less common feature of life, making it possible for peaceful and prosperous societies to flourish.

This optimism continued in general through the eighteenth century, the era of the Enlightenment. But the dualistic definition of man also prevailed. Other dimensions began to be added, however, to this definition, complicating the purpose of man in the scheme of things, and suggesting a future crisis: most notably the notion that human nature was infinitely perfectible. This implied that human nature was malleable and could be manipulated for a variety of reasons. Meanwhile the centrality of man in the scheme of things—and with this the centrality of scientific man, man as *reason*—seemed unassailable. In fact, at this time, "the study of man...became the queen of the sciences"[8] displacing theology and, therefore, God.

Passions ceased to be regarded as the product of, or under the influence of, sin, and without further ado assumed a normal place in the life of humankind. These passions, though, still needed to be brought into submission to reason. At the same time, a machine-like image of man began to emerge (in conjunction with the view of nature, in general, as a machine), and this view threatened to deprive newly exalted man of his freedom and creativity. The concept of man being composed primarily of reason, though, was not dethroned. As far as science went, the general optimism continued to bolster an optimism about humanity, whose nature was seen to be fixed and unalterable. The value of man in the total order of things remained the central feature

8 Baumer, p 160.

of the Enlightenment: "Only the presence of man made the existence of other beings significant."[9] Gathering storm clouds, however, could be seen on the horizon.

With the advent of the nineteenth century, a gradual shift in emphasis occurred. Beginning with the previous century's acceptance of the perfectibility of human nature, particularly through education, the moral view of man changed; his nature was no longer seen as fixed but in constant mutation. And now reason, as the epitome of what man could be, was replaced by a growing preoccupation with the irrational and sub-rational. In particular, a Romantic reaction rose up, in an essentially negative turn: out of rebellion against reason as the epitome of man, and the fixity of human nature. This rebellion began in an anarchy stemming from science itself; instead of a geometrical model governing science, a new model—of history, of change, of development—came into vogue. History replaced reason as the queen of the sciences, and everything was seen as subtending to history, which stressed the relative, the momentary, the unique, the particular. This ended in historicism and ethical relativism; all was in flux, all undergoing change. *History*.

Under the influence of Romanticism a transformation in the general definition of man came about, for "universal among the romantics [was] a strong sense of the irrational, even of its primacy, in human life, and an emphasis on particularity or individuality, as opposed to generality."[10] From the ethical standpoint, this concern centered on mankind's creativity. Out of the subterranean flow of irrational impulses, humankind would discover and state its own values. No basis existed for right or wrong, good or evil. People were left in all circumstances to decide for themselves. Together with this redefined moral outlook, a new nature mysticism emerged. Nature was no longer a realm to be

9 Baumer, p 161.
10 Baumer, p 271.

conquered by reason, but a mystery to be approached in ecstatic contemplation. In conjunction with this nature mysticism, the Romantics "commonly saw man in the context of great cosmic forces that enveloped him in a whole or infinity greater than himself."[11] This had the effect of again submerging the individual in a larger whole.

The Romantics saw as the key to the meaning of man his *unconscious*. They searched the subconscious for something that would give unity (long since dissolved in the acid of rationalistic science) to the experience of mankind in general. And there they discovered a suppressed sense of "community feeling." Romanticism inspired an emphasis on the *volkgeist*, which found expression in the sentiments of nationalism and statism, and as art was subsumed under state interests, *kitsch* and *poshlust* arose. The state once more became the highest goal of human striving, the sole means by which to recover mankind's lost unity.

Romanticism offered the cult of state worship to a civilization longing for a cultural leader pointing toward utopia. Every interest was to coincide with the nation-state to such a degree that "romantic thought depicted the nation itself as an individual."[12] And from nationalism and statism a new *messianism* arose, which incorporated a belief in futuristic utopianism; "collective humanity became the new god."[13] "Society...was 'a new spook, a new supreme being,' taking the place of all the old spooks, or gods, in whom men no longer believed".[14] Men had little difficulty believing that "man's basic instincts were good and had only to be set free to deliver mankind from servitude and hate."[15] All it took, apparently, was the unleashing of the regenerative power of the state. A new confidence was placed in "collective man."

11 Baumer, p 283.
12 Baumer, p 290.
13 Baumer, p 316.
14 Baumer, p 324.
15 Baumer, p 293.

Collectivism, then, or socialism, was more and more seen as the savior of mankind, as a new lease of life was given in the nineteenth century to the spirit of Babel. Scattered efforts were made to recover the place lost by the individual, but nothing could stem the tide; the damage was done. The Christian foundations were too badly eroded for collectivist man to value the status of the individual anymore. Nothing was to impede the greatest happiness for the greatest number, and the moral assertion that rose from this view was an arrogant demand: the good of society must take precedence over "selfish" individual concerns. A cultural elite, as at the present, expostulated about the duties of social consciousness and the need for every person to develop his own.

The masses, as they were seen, increasingly succumbed to transient fashionableness, and became easily manipulated by public opinion. And then, at mid-century, as if reinforcing the pretensions of Romanticism, the theory of evolution arrived. Through its influence, "it was man's irrational nature that would be most talked about—his instincts, his aggressiveness, his kinship to the animal world."[16] The dignity of man, as the Christian world had for so long understood it, was jettisoned, and with it the very idea of civilization. Once God was removed from modern man's "belief system," it wasn't long before man was knocked off his pedestal as well, which was necessary in order to make the statist dream a reality.

We are living nowadays off the pottage of this Romantic revolution. Emerging ostensibly as a rebellion against the idolatry of reason in the Enlightenment, Romanticism should really be viewed as inventing the reason for its own existence—a self-conscious rebellion against Christian and Western civilization. It conveyed an attitude of cultural pessimism and hatred, and was antithetical to the purposes of God in creation; it wanted to build a world without Him.

16 Baumer, p 16.

Through Romanticism, the very idea of culture underwent a philosophical revaluation. Unfortunately, the corollary to this movement can be found in the Church itself, in pietism.

Pietism shares with Romanticism a refusal to have anything to do with the kingdom of God. Romanticism was a more sinister influence, because it seemed entirely rational in its irrationalism. It had all the decadence of a counterculture movement (and could, indeed, be seen as the first one) which was then offered as a culture all its own, as in our day. It intended to remake man into a being adaptable to its ideals, and uprooted the meaning of man from the Christian view, in order to remold him into the future Socialist.

At present, the very concept of man is problematic, but we should never doubt that this is exactly what the elite of our contemporary culture desire. Nowadays, there can be no definition of man that implies a permanence in his nature. No, human nature is viewed as a relative product of the surrounding moral and social environment. The one given that may be allowed is the "infinite plasticity" of the self—the implication being that we are mere effects of our cultural conditioning. "The qualities that characterize us are relative to a certain kind of society, education, and environment."[17]

In our day, every action in life is value-relative; nothing matters beyond the sensual satisfaction of the moment. This is the legacy of Romanticism. It has inspired the propaganda that an absolute state must exist in order to enforce in us tolerance for everyone else's self-defined and self-indulgent moral perspective. This is libertinism that comes at a price, because it promotes the chaos of a thousand conflicting opinions, undermining the possibility for social order and threatening human existence with a precarious lawlessness. The result is that, with increasing arbitrariness, the state imposes its order on society. In a situation of moral anarchy, upon what can a system of order be based?

17 Baumer, p 421.

Anarchism, by exalting the ultimacy of every man, and the independence and autonomy of every man, leaves no common ground between men except coercion. The result is a war of the gods, or would-be gods. In a world of autonomous men, the only contact between man and man is coercion, imperialism. Self-determination in the anarchic sense of autonomous man means that the only common or general will among man is the imposed will of one.[18]

If we do not have a generally agreed upon moral obligation, no social order is possible, and as Romanticism came to accept only that which was relative, particular, and momentary, so do we. We reject a universal ethical standard, except the facetious one which says, If it pleases you, or if it feels good, do it. The only order that exists, then, is the order the state imposes from the top down. So external coercion is often all that rebellious man ever comes to identify as society, while he reviles what alone can make genuine culture possible: the free and mutual interaction of individuals.

In the Christian world view there is an alternative to this descent into the abyss. Christians need to reassert a biblical anthropology as the truth about human nature. And a scriptural philosophy is basic to the Christian ethic, for it makes it possible to account for man both as an individual and as a member of society.

Every non-Christian interpretation of mankind has sought to explain man *immanently*, that is, without reference to anything or anyone outside his immediate physical experience; and every definition of this kind, apart from Christianity's, is behavioristic. Man is explained in terms of that which is observed, first of all, in the nature of his empirical actions—an explanation that stems from a need to deny the essence of man as image of God. To admit this is tantamount to understanding man in terms of his relation-

18 Rousas John Rushdoony, *Law and Society* (Vallecito, CA: Ross House, 1982), p 297.

ship and responsibilities to his Creator. Non-Christian thought prefers to look downward, to identify man with anything here below, and to exclude God altogether. But for a Christian it must be the *image of God,* along with man as a being directed and oriented toward God, that is the beginning definition. We have to start with Calvin's dictum: "It is certain that man never achieves a clear knowledge of himself unless he has first looked upon God's face, and then descends from contemplating him to scrutinize himself."[19]

But how is this possible? How does one look upon God's face? Only through the person of Jesus Christ, the Son of God, who himself became man. There the Christian begins to discern himself. Jesus is indispensable for a Christian anthropology, because in him is revealed not only the truth about God but, equally important, the truth about man.

Again it is Reformed thought that has grasped, more clearly than any other, the key to explaining this, as in these enlightening words from the Westminster Confession: "It pleased God, in His eternal purpose, to choose and ordain the Lord Jesus, His only begotten Son, to be the Mediator between God and man, the Prophet, Priest, and King..."[20] Here are the terms that reveal the truth about man: he is *prophet*, *priest*, and *king*.

Jesus assumes the responsibilities for these tasks through his incarnation; they fit and adorn him for his role as Savior and Mediator. We rightly understand these terms to indicate the offices and duties he exercises on our behalf, but we often fail to appreciate what they imply for a Christian philosophy of man. More than merely acting on our behalf, Jesus reveals, through these offices, what we are meant to be as images of God. And the offices signify what we can again become through the power of His redemption. A prophet, a priest, and a king—nothing comes closer to defining man as an

19 *Institutes*, Bk I, Ch 1, p 37.
20 *Westminster Confession of Faith*, VIII, 1.

image of God than these terms.

The offices give us insight into the biblical definition of man. A prophet is, in the first place, a person who interprets life in the light of God's word. A prophet's first responsibility is to clarify the truth, and to enjoin obedience to God's absolute will above every other. In the beginning, Adam was the first prophet, and would have passed the responsibility to all his offspring, instructing them in God's warning about the tree of good and evil. Each generation, in turn, would have been required to transmit this truth to the next, so that every man would proclaim God's authority in this matter.

Once sin entered the world, through Adam's rebellion against God, God set about, in redemption, a process of restoring this fundamental task to man. He would again cause man to be a prophet, who would proclaim the authority of the will of God as one's highest duty. Initially, however, only certain individuals were given the privilege of serving in the role of heralds of the way of life and death. But it was always God's intention, on one day, to anoint all of His people with the prophet's responsibility (Joel 2.28 & 29). In God's kingdom every person, to some extent or other, was to act in the capacity of a prophet. No individual is without that obligation; each must interpret his life, as well as the lives of others, as bound up with the keeping of God's will. There is no exception; there can be no compromise.

A priest is one who is granted intimate communion with God, and whose chief purpose is to offer himself, and all that he does, unreservedly to God as "a living sacrifice" (Rom 12.1), calling always on the name of the Lord. A priest consecrates the whole of each of his endeavors to God and, in doing so, confesses that it is God Who gives him life and breath and prospers his way and makes him fruitful. A priest looks to God's blessing alone as the source of every *good*. At the same time, a priest never neglects to remember that he is also a prophet, and so seeks in all that he does to conform faithfully to God's authority over all of life.

Once again, at first there were only a select few who could serve in the office of priest; but the writer of Hebrews brings us to understand that in Christ every individual believer enjoys the privilege of coming boldly into God's presence to sacrifice on his or her own behalf (10.19-22). In God's kingdom each person *individually* acquires the high calling of the priesthood. This great privilege established for the individual a new status before God; and once it was seen how the individual's value had become elevated in God's estimation, the Christian outlook historically tended to exalt the status of the individual in the presence of men as well.

When we say that man was created to be king, we mostly mean man's responsibility to rule and have dominion over God's creation. It was his job to subdue the creation to the glory of God. Each person is given special gifts and talents for that purpose. And again this office comes to the fore as a prominent feature of God's redemptive program in His kingdom. We learn that every individual believer will possess, first of all, the "gift of the Spirit;" as well as special "gifts" from the Spirit for the purpose of realizing the kingdom of God. Each person must cultivate his particular gifts in order to advance toward that goal.

If we wonder how these offices apply to the individual, we should think of each person as having the obligation to develop himself in terms of them; that is, the self-realization of the image of God in each person is what God intended for the individual as individual. To be sure, the idea of self-realization has become modish nowadays. Non-Christian psychologists and educators make much of the idea of personality enhancement through self-awareness and self-expression. The achievement of self-esteem, they say, cannot be replaced by any higher moral duty. Very often, this notion is accompanied by the idea of values-clarification, or values-positing, as the way of defining one's responsibilities.

The goal of self-realization in non-Christian thought has to do only with achievement in the kingdom of *man*. The Christian understanding of this obligation is directed toward God. We are expected to develop our potential for the purpose of becoming fit vessels for the working of God's will within His creation. At the same time, the realization of one's potential should be viewed as a legitimate personal goal.

In the beginning, there was no inherent contradiction between these two. The pursuit of personal ambition was no obstacle to serving God's purpose in this world. In fact, God meant for all of us to cultivate our special interests and abilities in order to contribute, each in his own way, toward the furtherance of His glory. What is more, God designed the world in such a way that it would become subordinate to man, gradually, over time. An historical progression was the path people walked in order to understand themselves, as well as the world in general. Individually speaking, this means that "man was created a character and yet he had to make himself even more of a character."[21]

Whatever God had placed within a person, as a talent to be developed, had to be applied with every ounce of energy in order to bring it to maturity. In this effort, one engaged his whole self: "As renewed in all the aspects of his being it is the glory of the Christian that he may seek to cultivate all his gifts without exception. He may cultivate his emotions as well as his intellect or his will. No one aspect of his being is more acceptable in the sight of God than are the others. The whole man is acceptable and the whole man may dedicate himself to God."[22] Through the realization of himself, man would realize the kingdom of God on earth. That is the way it was; that is the only way it ever will be.

So, then, which social and economic system do the implications of this ethical perspective comport with, capitalism or socialism? There is no doubt that capitalism represents the product, as well as the continued progress, of this ethical perspective. Capitalism is the only system mankind has known that places the premium it does on the opportunities and initiatives of individual endeavor. It allows full scope to every individual's particular abilities and interests. In fact,

21 Van Til, *Christian Theistic Ethics*, p 44.
22 Van Til, *An Introduction to Systematic Theology*, p 35.

capitalism does not make them possible; it is the outcome of their realization. It develops spontaneously as a system that generally encourages and rewards those who seek to realize their unique talents. These rewards need not be monetary, although that shouldn't be considered inappropriate. An individual's reward should be viewed in its totality, which is what it is in service of the kingdom of God.

Capitalism holds a high view of man, because it rises from the notion that man as image of God is capable of self-realization, and capitalism works only in a context in which this notion has ethical preeminence. It sets great store by man's entrepreneurial skills, which are every bit as much a talent to be developed, and exercised on behalf of God's kingdom, as any other. If any gift is stifled, then civilization on that point is retarded, and culture declines. More importantly, God's glory is not advanced as He intended.

Socialism, on the other hand, cannot tolerate anything that has to do with the free play and initiative of individuals. Socialism's goal is to coerce everyone to submit to the desires and ambitions of a few. In its moral high-mindedness, it speaks of the good of society as the only ethical good worth working for, as Aristotle did. It looks on anything less as contemptible selfishness. And it manages, by this moral deception, to create a state-dominated society for the political, social, and economic good of those in charge. It hates God's purpose for free expression among men. It insinuates that that purpose would amount to chaos and tyranny, when in fact it is socialism that always delivers such desserts.

I do not pretend that this view of the individual and of capitalism will lead to utopia. Utopia is what preoccupies the socialist mind. Nor do I deny that sin has profoundly affected all of life, including the aspirations and pursuits of us all. Capitalism does not promise that men will not cheat, lie, or steal from one another, and this is where God's commandments serve as a natural hedge. But capitalism, for its shortcomings, surely dissipates the power of sin as socialism does not. Socialism organizes it and gives it the sanction of the state as its enforcer. Anyone who doubts this has not grappled sufficiently with the Babel syndrome in the history of man. To conclude, whatever purposes God intended for man as an individual, He also had a plan for those purposes in terms of the social side of man's experience.

Concerning Society

No one can deny that God created man to give expression to his life in a communal or social context. In our daily lives we see social bonds of every kind, inescapably present. They were there from the moment we arrived by birth on the scene, and that structure of existing societal relationships is indeed the reason behind birth, the family, and the covenant.

These social bonds have the appearance of an ordered permanence that we are unable to attribute to anybody's personal or arbitrary design. They influence our behavior and inclinations in ways we seldom appreciate, since for many years they remain hidden from our explicit perception; we take them for granted. But they constitute the environment in which we grow up and mature, and then carry into our day-to-day affairs. And when we do pause to reflect self-consciously on the nature of our social experience, we soon find, both in history generally and in the history of ideas especially, a variety of theories, philosophies, and explanations that attempt to justify human experience on the basis of exactly this kind of inner, self-contemplation.

For centuries man has pondered the question of his social nature, and has always come to the conclusion that human experience ought to form in some sense a unity; men should cooperate in mutual interaction and reciprocity, since the unfolding of civilization and culture seems dependent on just such a joint venture. No other creature in God's world has, nor was meant to have, the developed social nature of man—the suppositions and hypotheses of naturalists and environmentalists notwithstanding.

This alone should cause us to wonder to what extent sin has destroyed not only the relationship between God and man but between man and man, man and woman, man and his neighbor, along with the devastating result it has had on our calling to exercise dominion. And yet... the restoration of a right relationship to God should bring restoration of a right relationship with our neighbor. The Christian ethic reveals a social as well as individual dimension, and only on its foundation can we lay the basis for societal interaction .

And now we must attenuate the assertion that God's word and will is for the development of individuals *as* individuals. This is true, but in order to avoid misunderstanding, we shouldn't suspect that individual self-realization is possible only in opposition to the purposes of God for mankind. We are not faced with this sort of unresolvable contradiction, but we should not be surprised to find it informing the history of most of non-Christian thought. Non-Christians tend to assume that individual self-realization always opposes the goals of society, so that one finally cancels the other out.

The notion thus prevails that because a tension exists between these poles of experience, the only solution is to allow one or the other to triumph. It is no exaggeration to say that in the history of social analysis we find a continual attempt to devise some scheme or theory whereby the perceived disparity between the individual and society is resolved, or at least ameliorated—when not done away with altogether. The justification for almost any theory rests on its prescriptive intent, not its descriptive content, and so we saw Aristotle attempt to resolve the problem: the individual as a mere *part* of which the state made up the whole. The interests of the state under this philosophy take precedence over individual needs, and the enhancement of the whole is held in higher esteem than any individual. Ancient man offered answers to the problem, and modern man continues to try to; in fact, it is only recently that the problem between individualism and socialism has become acute. More than ever, man seems driven by a need to find some solution to this social crisis.

It has been the natural tendency to fight out this supposed conflict, between the part and the whole, in the realm of politics. In modern times, beginning with the Renaissance, the state rose more and more as sole arbiter in the clash of interests between private well-being and social good; it gained ascendance as the institution best able to mediate the social concerns of every individual. This concept gained a virtual monopoly in the political theories of late-medieval thinkers. Marsilius of Padua, Dante, and Machiavelli argued, often in innovative ways, for the supremacy of the state over other societal forms. And I also believe, although it may cause some dispute, that the thinking of William of Occam contributed to this perspective. It might seem ironic that a school of thought such as nominalism, which stressed particulars over universals, individuality over generality, could, as a social theory, give in to this growing statist ideal, but it did.

This probably had to do with the psychological factors that reverberate through the nominalist outlook. Since individuals are unable to avail themselves of any genuine universal principles—because for nominalism they do not exist, in reality—they tend to feel isolated and morally helpless, and so find themselves seduced into accepting the strongest structure capable of creating social order out of the scramble of competing wills. By propagating "a new individualism," nominalism played into the hands of the emerging statist universalism. It didn't matter that the state was seen as the product of contractual agreements on the part of individuals, as adumbrated in Marsilius's thinking, and more generally accepted as theory later in the seventeenth and eighteenth centuries. When the world is divided in this way, power invariably gravitates toward the state.

Meanwhile, the sense of unity that was a part of medieval man's experience, and was made possible by a variety of feudal institutions to which everyone for the most part subscribed—this unity began to vanish with the emergence of state supremacy. The state absorbed into itself every communal form and made them seem outmoded. This period of the Renaissance experienced (and not for the first time in the history of mankind) the "atomization of society," the end result of which is "the isolation of the individual from the smaller groups of which he may be an active member, and his sudden facing of the terrifying countenance of the

State machine, with which he has no existential bond, but which dominates him nevertheless".[23]

It was the intention of Machiavelli, whether in theory or practice, to elevate "reasons of state" to an exclusionist principle. The result was that "Machiavellianism was also the most definitive expression of the trend toward weakening and abolishing the intermediate bodies between the individual citizen and the ruler of the State."[24] Molnar later dilates on this, helping us understand the frame of reference into which modern theory and practice plunged:

> The two models that helped the medieval theorists visualize society and the body politic were the human body and the macrocosm, that is, the total order of the universe... The feudal system itself was a political expression...the wisdom of which, among other things, consisted in setting up innumerable buffer zones between individual and State power, and between smaller power focuses. Already in medieval theory there was a trend, however, that, according to Gierke, stressed the 'concentration of right and power in the highest group, on the one hand, and in the individual man, on the other, at the cost of all intermediate groups. The Sovereignty of the State and the sovereignty of the Individual...[became] the two central axioms.'[25]

The dichotomy between these two axioms has become the central feature of our modern age. The struggle for supremacy of one over the other is the driving engine of modern social and political theory. Most theoretical efforts are bent to help resolve this supposed crisis, such as the present tendency to extend the application of state power, and so impose a presumed order on you and your neighbor. By the state's piping, we all are to dance the same dance. And Christians have abetted the trend, by failing to lay sufficient

23 Thomas Molnar, *The Decline of the Intellectual* (New Rochelle: Arlington House, 1958), p 87.
24 Molnar, pp 16 & 17.
25 Molnar, *ibid*. The portion of his quote that includes the reference to Otto Gierke may be found in Gierke's *Political Theories of the Middle Ages* (Boston: Beacon Press, 1958), p 87.

emphasis upon the structural foundation of God's creation. While in the medieval world there rightly existed a variety of buffer zones to limit the social nature of each person's experience, many of these mediating institutions were arbitrary constructs that represented artificial perspectives on God's creation.

In particular, think of the rise and spread of monastic institutions. These communities were based on a faulty understanding of the Christian's obligation to separate himself from the world. Over this same period, a growing struggle was waged between Church and State for control of the institutions in which men carried on their livelihoods. Great power and wealth were at stake. For a long while the church prevented the state from acquiring a monopoly, or absolute hegemony, over all of social life, but at what cost? The church often substituted its own monopolies.

It began to reflect an unbiblical hierarchicalism that tended to concentrate its power and wealth at the top. Any such top-down organization is bound to force a conformity upon the free exercise of other institutions. If anything, the medieval social experience represented an imperfect set of arrangements which, when they were called into question by late-medieval theorists, gave way to a social perspective in which power flowed toward the state alone. With the rise of the middle class, nearer our own age, the emphasis shifted back for a time; but lately it has shifted again in the direction of the state.

God's intent for mankind in his original creation-order was not to allow it to establish antithetical poles of individualism and universalism. This tendency can only be traced, in the final analysis, to the aggravation of sin. We might say that originally mankind would have sought to realize its potential within the framework of institutional structures; self-realization then would have included a concurrent understanding of communal forms. And man's personal development would have taken shape in harmony with distinct societal structures and expressions, such as the family, commerce, industry, technology, science, art, and so on.

With the entry of sin, we have to add *state* to this list. The Christian viewpoint allows a legitimate place for the state, and for the functions of politics and government. But statism is the perverse attempt on the part of some to usurp the rightful independence of others, including institutions and individuals, and therefore to exalt the state as absolute over all lives. Statism reflects the ingrained religious goal on the part of fallen man to usurp from God His sovereignty over life; and socialism is the moral justification of the idolatry of statism. The two go hand in hand; without the coercive power of the state, the social experience of man tends naturally towards pluriformity, or diversity.

Socialism arrives with ideological tools that are able to produce only uniformity. It comes armed with a subtle logic that tempts us into an addictive dependence on the state. "I'm owed it," people will say, and many in the church have fallen under the same spell. The spirit of Babel, and the syndrome it produces, eventually overcomes everybody's resistance.

The societal forms of creation, designed to structure man's experience, did not make their appearance all at once. God intended for them, like man's task of self-realization, to be gradually realized. As history moved on, the institutional experience of man should have increased in clarity of form and purpose. Each institution should have acquired a greater sense of its own space and function, but at the same time left room for others to develop. And as individuals worked to achieve their potential, they would have discovered that the possibility for that potential had to take place within prescribed societal relationships, in which others sought, too, to apply similar skills and talents. Each would learn as he worked with others that the increase of everyone's potential was becoming possible. And the institutional framework would assume, at the same time, a greater definition of meaning. Self-realization of the individual is attainable only within a wider, inter-individual, context. As we quicken in response to God, we should quicken to the needs of our neighbor, with the result that a rich and satisfying social experience should emerge in the kingdom of God.

But no man-made authority can establish this; no single social form or institution is granted the right to assume absolute authority over any other. God retains authority over every aspect of life. He does, however, grant limited authority to different social institutions, within their particular spheres. Also, because of sin, God grants human government to us as an institution with the right to take life, a just punishment to evildoers. The state receives its legitimacy only from Him. Its purpose is to dispense justice on His behalf, and it is therefore God's justice that it must dispense, not any person's assumption of what is just. Those in government have the obligation to find from the word of God the behavior He regards as evil and to punish it as He prescribes.

One of the state's primary obligations is to guarantee conditions in which the free play of individual and inter-individual initiative can take place under God. The state should resist any effort on the part of anyone to impose a rigid conformity on the diversity of gifts given by God. The state should protect not only its legitimacy but every valid institutional authority that exists. This is the only way in which the state can serve the greater increase of God's will and kingdom in a world tainted by sin.

As long as Christians seek to advance the ideals of that kingdom, the state must not interfere. If attempts are made to usurp God's rule with man's—if the kingdom of man seeks to displace the kingdom of God—then the state must use its power and authority to prevent that, even acting in a retributive manner to correct that tendency. Which implies that the state ought to be controlled by the same principles that obtain in the kingdom of God. The rebellious spirit, when it wants to achieve the ideals of the kingdom of man, does not need much coaxing to understand that the state, first, must come under its control.

Finally, some notion of what the moral perspective should be in the relationship between you and your neighbor, in a truly Christian ethic, must be laid down. Since we know that for the individual, the emphasis is self-realization, perhaps the ethical foundation for social relationships might be called, in parallelism, *other-realization*. This would leave us with the obligation to develop not only our own potential but, equally and at the same time, oblige us to enable another to develop his or hers. How do we do this?

Above all by fostering conditions that make it possible to be obedient to God's revealed will, and especially His law. And the best way to comprehend this is to consider what Reformed thought has referred to as the "positive intent" of the law; that is, we should not view the law in negative terms, as purely prohibitive. We should learn from the law what we should *do*, not merely not do. By this submission we truly serve our neighbor's needs, and never have to wonder what our ethical responsibilities are. We are not misled by vague notions of love of neighbor, which leave it to us to fill in the content. And we will not distort true justice for something called a "sense of justice."

The law of God, in its broad meaning, is *righteousness*. That defines the nature of our social relationships and sets limits on everybody's other-realization. An adage from Calvin is appropriate here: "If this pleases God, the opposite displeases him; if this displeases, the opposite pleases him; if he commands this, he forbids the opposite; if he forbids this, he enjoins the opposite."[26] Jesus affirms that by our conscientious adherence to God's law, both love for God and love for one's neighbor has been dutifully fulfilled (Mt 22.37-40).

Anything less is not love of God or of our neighbor.

26 *Institutes*, Bk II, Ch 8, p 375.

PART II

CAPITALISM

Without the industry of men there could have been no curing of sickness, no seamanship, no cultivation of fields, no harvesting and storage of grains and other crops. And unless men performed such services, there would certainly be no export of those products of which we have a surplus, no import of those products of which we lack.

. . . Whatever benefits and advantages we may derive from inanimate objects, we could not possibly possess them without the skill and industry of man...by giving and exchanging resources and advantages, none of us lack anything.

Cicero

FIVE

CAPITALISM & PROGRESS

IN AN ESSAY entitled "History and the Idea of Progress" Gertrude Himmelfarb writes, "The idea of Progress—Progress with a capital P—has been in disrepute for a long time now... At every point we are confronted with shattered promises, blighted hopes, irreconcilable dilemmas, good intentions gone astray, a choice between evils, a world perched on the brink of disaster—all the familiar clichés, which are all too true and which seem to give the lie to the idea of progress."[1] Her words are not so much personal sentiment as a proffered explanation for the despair in which contemporary thinkers find themselves mired. These intellectuals, who place their faith in man and his rational intelligence, and in the relativist doctrine of good and evil that accompanies it, and who believe in salvation through social change, are now disturbed by the course civilization has taken as a result of their thought. The world appears to be falling into chaos; and worse, they can do nothing about it.

So a profound pessimism has set in, a pervasive despair

1 Gertrude Himmelfarb, *The New History and the Old: Critical Essays and Reappraisals* (Cambridge: Belknap Press, 1987), p 155.

that permeates the minds of those who claim to be the guardians and the standard bearers of our cultural agenda. Rather than accept any blame, however, intellectuals have simply turned against the culture from which they arose. They hate the West and all it has meant historically.

To a considerable degree "faith in progress" fashioned the outlook of the modern Western world. That faith was sustainable as long as it remained attached to the Christian ethic, its foundation. But as people turned from their Christian past, civilization began to go awry. As Himmelfarb notes, everything gives the lie to the idea of progress. The modern world has let the genie out of the bottle and is now at the mercy of a power it no longer controls. If anything can be pointed to as the primary culprit in all this, some say, it is capitalism. Capitalism unleashed a system of economic and social behavior that sooner or later, they assert, was bound to result in cultural self-destruction; capitalism sprang from a misguided "faith in progress."

My central concern in this chapter is a work by a Christian author, Bob Goudzwaard, one who echoes the pessimism of contemporary secular thinkers. Goudzwaard's *Capitalism and Progress*, mentioned in the introduction, is a denunciation of capitalism. The entire book mentions scarcely a single benefit of capitalism. If it does acknowledge one, it is with grudging reluctance. The author's purpose, falling in line with secularists, is to explain the hated system of capitalism as the product of "faith in progress." And faith in progress is, to Goudzwaard's mind, a secular motif; it has nothing to do with Christianity. Naturally, then, neither does capitalism.

Since capitalism is a product of the Christian ethic, to my view, and socialism the outcome of a secular ethic, I must respond to the central ideas in *Capitalism and Progress*. I first call in question the assumption that "faith in progress," or adherence to capitalism, is not innately a Christian view. I won't argue, however, with Goudzwaard's conception of capitalist practices from an *economic* point of view. I want to focus my attention on the philosophic and moral assumptions that form the foundation of his thought, and I'll start where he does and follow the contours of his work.

Progress & the Middle Ages

Any attempt to trace the roots of an economic doctrine, or to offer an explanation for the economic behavior and condition of people in previous ages, runs into nearly insurmountable difficulties. Economics is an attempt to define the daily, the mundane in human experience, and evidence for such behavior in remote times isn't easy to come by—particularly before the invention of printing. It becomes easy, therefore, to adopt the philosopher's stance and define entire historical epochs in abstract generalizations.

Both the work of research and mental energy are enormously conserved if, for instance, you simply declare, "Medieval society believed..."or "The Middle Ages stood for..." And if you want to get into denigration, it's easier to set the supposed disposition of one age against another. This approach eases the defense of a philosopher's moral stance and simplifies the task of analysis. It also becomes difficult for critics to find fault, since the hypothesis advanced by the philosopher is, in this way, hardly subject to verification; you believe it or you don't.

This is the attitude you encounter in Goudzwaard's explanation of the differences between the outlook of the Middle Ages and the outlook of our capitalist society—which he takes to be its opposite. The image he conjures of the Middle Ages has the effect of forming a moral truncheon with which to beat capitalist society. He doesn't offer real insight into the economic conditions of the Middle Ages. Nor does he explain the way in which the methods of capitalism transformed the far less productive medieval economies, improving the brutal living conditions of that time. By taking a philosophical shortcut, Goudzwaard instead creates prejudices that will prevent readers from understanding the truth about life in the Middle Ages.

The same for capitalism. Goudzwaard's explanations of it are likely to foster a state of mind predisposed to condemn and vilify rather than understand and appreciate.

Every anticapitalist position requires the rigging up of a moral high ground from which to look down on capitalism. Socialists are aware that they have lost the case in the trial of performance; they can't claim the superiority of socialism by an appeal to any socialist reality, and can't say that socialism is of greater *economic* benefit than capitalism. They must instead resort to moral posturing to oppose capitalist economics. They will, claims Mises, "consider it supererogatory to examine the economic problems involved," and instead will insist that we "shift the discussion of pros and cons of the market economy from the field of economic analysis to what they call a higher sphere."[2] So Goudzwaard tells us that our investigation must take place on the level of capitalism's "cultural matrix." He won't discuss performance. He seems to want to make sure we oppose capitalism before we understand it.

Socialism's proponents, from their exalted moral perspective, in a general sense bewail the *dehumanization* of man under capitalist production methods. They speak of capitalism's "cultural structure" as demeaning to human dignity; they refer to the impersonal relationships within it. Capitalism, they say, has exchanged genuine human relationships for the cold and calculating practices of the marketplace. In a similar way, Goudzwaard declares, "the market is ultimately nothing but a mechanism." Capitalism "does not view the market primarily as a meetingplace for people, but rather as a meetingplace for each separate individual with a given price."[3] Our problems begin with our having callously exchanged human relationships for relationships with *things*. Socialists denounce capitalism, in addition, for its avarice and materialism. They indignantly say that capitalism has released the acquisitive spirit and

2 Ludwig von Mises, *Theory and History: An Interpretation of Social and Economic Evolution* (Westport: Arlington House, 1969), p 341.
3 Goudzwaard, p 25.

permitted it to run riot. Before capitalism came along, people were seemingly innocent of any wish for material betterment.

This moralistic disparagement has been the stock-in-trade for some time, and unquestionably it has been effective. Those who oppose capitalism do not believe that their moral position has to conform to an argument based on economics. Economics seems not sufficiently spiritual; it is too concerned with mundane matters like the effects of wages and prices, taxes and tariffs, incentives and the like. Economics emphasizes *property*, whereas morality deals with *people*.

Goudzwaard's antipathy to capitalism contains the same posturing epitomized by the socialists. He, too, takes a superior moral position from which he gazes down on the turpitude of capitalist practices. Scholarly thinkers respect this, and consider it a reasoned position, when it's actually dogmatic. Goudzwaard attempts to demonstrate that his thesis is one that can be rationally accepted, shared by minds that look at matters with an unjaundiced gaze. *Capitalism and Progress* is indeed an intricate argument, I grant that; but a specific motive is at work.

Goudzwaard wants his moral thesis to appear Christian, and capitalism anti-Christian. To make his case, he begins with the outlook of the Middle Ages, because that age, it is generally conceded, was a time when Christianity was pervasive and accepted. May we not suppose, then, that the perspective offered by the Middle Ages was, *ipso facto*, one that was Christian? What was the outlook of the Middle Ages? What view did it express that, according to Goudzwaard, made it morally superior to modern capitalist society?

It is not always easy to come to grips with him on these questions. His remarks are often misleading enough to discourage accurate understanding, and he always leaves himself room to maneuver. We read for example, that "in the Middle Ages we encounter a certain apprehension toward technological change, especially if it could substantially affect the social order and its inherent power relationships."[4] In the first place, in any age, at any period of history—our modern capitalist age included—there is more than a mere apprehension toward technological change. Usually it is a rigid and systematic opposition to change of any kind. Every age wants to preserve the status quo. Change is viewed as unsettling; it takes getting used to, and people cling to familiar ways. What Goudzwaard should have told us is what the peculiar nature of that resistance to change in the Middle Ages meant for different strata of that society: who stood to lose and who to gain by resisting it? Change, in history, is almost always a matter of a particular group's expectation of loss or gain as a result.

Goudzwaard might have mentioned how medieval society was a top-down structure and resistance to change came most strongly from the vested interests at the top, who had the most to lose by it. These people—in both church and state—felt it essential to guard against any threat to the disintegration of feudal society. It meant the loss of their privileged position and its attendant benefits. The power of the nobles rested on economic power, which was rooted in the land—tended by serfs and villeins. One can well imagine why the nobles would resist change. The burdens of that society fell most heavily on the lower orders; their subjugation was necessary in order to sustain the topmost privileges.

For a cogent analysis of the concept of hierarchy and the way in which it was expressed and defended, the reader might look into the French writer, Duby, who notes: "Men of war living on the land, bleeding it white, forcing the peasants, free or not, to produce ever greater quantities, in order to obtain from their labor the pleasures of life never

4 Goudzwaard, p 2.

renounced by the professional soldiers, in order to satisfy the aristocratic taste for luxury and waste, which could no longer find its fill in foreign razzias: this was the economic aspect."[5]

But Goudzwaard is reluctant to admit that the social order that did prevail throughout most of the Middle Ages was primarily, if not exclusively, beneficial to the powerful minority at the top. That would affect the moral image of the era he hopes to portray. Understandably, he would not want us to look too closely at its deficiencies; we might not then see its superiority over capitalist society.

There is, of course, little doubt that to the extent that it was not hindered, capitalism demolished a social order based on privilege. And while some undoubtedly lost in this exchange, millions reaped great benefits. Capitalist society does not mean the breakdown of order, but the end of an order based on privilege. This is disturbing to those who want to shape the cultural agenda, since they understand that their own interests are best suited to a society based on status. They suggest, therefore, that capitalism implies the loss of order; they insinuate that unless a hierarchy of privilege is set in place, then social and moral disintegration is unavoidable. Those who tout this view, however, seldom expect to shoulder the burden of the underprivileged. They anticipate being mandarins at the top, deciding what the rest of society shall do in order to maintain justice and morality.

What is the real moral difference between medieval society and capitalist society, as Goudzwaard wants us to see it? For him it is a difference of "orientation." Medieval society was oriented *vertically*; capitalist society is oriented *horizontally*.

What do these designations imply? Are they legitimate and helpful in describing the ethical outlook of either medieval or capitalist society? I suggest they enable us to understand only the moral outlook of the person uttering them. They

5 Georges Duby, *The Three Orders: Feudal Society Imagined*, trans Arthur Goldhammer (Chicago: Univ of Chicago Press, 1982), p 152.

certainly seem of little use for understanding either feudal or capitalist economics.

By using these designations Goudzwaard doesn't tell us that medieval society was a hierarchically ordered society that sought to preserve status and privilege. He does not say that benefits for those high up were gained at a cost to those beneath. Nor does he demonstrate that the hierarchical arrangement of medieval society tended to breed sycophancy at court more than industriousness at home; that it encouraged a greater interest in the fame of martial exploits than in peaceful and productive occupations.

From capitalism people began to learn that prosperous conditions were possible on a sustained basis, overcoming cycles of famine, pestilence, and the violent plundering prevalent in the Middle Ages. Goudzwaard doesn't illustrate any of the gains of capitalism; he wants us to see its drawbacks only. As Mises has pointed out, "The technique of the historicists' indictment of capitalism is simple indeed. They take all its achievements for granted, but blame it for the disappearance of some of the enjoyments that are incompatible with it and for some imperfections which disfigure its products."[6] So we should understand that "horizontal" is a term of abuse.

Both horizontal and vertical imply, to some degree, approbation as well as disapprobation. A vertically oriented society is one concerned primarily with God and the afterlife; it has little inclination to improve the material conditions of this one. A horizontally oriented society, on the other hand, relegates God to the background. Capitalism, Goudzwaard says, far from having any spiritual values, strives to reach perfection in this life; its goal is to achieve paradise on earth. Mankind's material well-being is all that matters. And as if making this claim were not enough, when Goudzwaard comments on capitalist behavior he employs patronizing

6 *Theory and History*, p 219.

terms like "unadulterated," "unbridled," and "unobstructed." This repeated use of hyperbolic adjectives promotes the portrayal of capitalism as an order of greed and unscrupulousness: a destroyer of civilized values. And this in fact is Goudzwaard's case against it.

Mises has an appropriate riposte: "It is justifiable if ethics and religion tell people that they ought to make better use of the well-being that capitalism brings them; if they try to induce the faithful to substitute better ways of spending for the objectionable habits of feasting, drinking, and gambling; if they condemn lying and cheating and praise the moral values implied in purity of family relations and in charity to those in need. But it is irresponsible to condemn one social system and to recommend its replacement by another system without having fully investigated the economic consequences of each."[7] While Goudzwaard does not specifically recommend the system of economics of the Middle Ages, he ignores the differences between that system and capitalism. In this respect there should be no doubt that capitalism is superior.

Goudzwaard never offers a recognizably Christian outlook by which we may evaluate medieval and capitalist society. He assumes that the vertical orientation of medieval society (as he depicts it) is largely Christian, while the horizontal orientation (in his view) of capitalist society is not Christian. From this assumption arise notions that he neither defends nor critiques. It's as if they're so obvious they require no justification. For example, with regard to medieval society, Goudzwaard says, "Everything in it was ordered and related in such a manner as to ascend from the realm of nature to that which alone can ultimately provide meaning to earthly existence—the realm of grace."[8]

The reader is left to wonder whether this is supposed to represent a Christian viewpoint. What is a realm of nature?

7 *Theory and History*, p 343.
8 Goudzwaard, p 1.

A realm of grace? What does it mean to ascend from one to the other, or to say that this ascent "alone can ultimately provide meaning to earthly existence?" Furthermore, what is Christian in this allegation: "Earthly, natural life had no meaning in itself. It was doomed to eternal sinfulness unless it was lifted, ordered, and directed to heaven and the realm of grace."[9] In both, no discernible biblical view is apparent, and it is the biblical view that determines what is Christian—not philosophical platitudes meant to denounce capitalism. How can Goudzwaard accuse capitalism of representing a horizontal outlook on life if he isn't himself in agreement with what he calls the vertical outlook of the Middle Ages? For Goudzwaard, capitalism is principally a negation of an earlier surpassing moral view; it has no merit on its own.

One may admit that, with the advent of the Middle Ages, Christians, as Latouche asserts, "appear to have lived not so much apart from the world as on the fringe of it..."[10] The belief was widely held that "for these Christians worldly pursuits were of secondary importance."[11] By the third century, the monastic ideal, with its penchant for isolation and contemplation, had gained widespread appeal and permeated society as the accepted Christian way of life. Although this ideal met with failures and setbacks, and underwent modifications throughout the millennium that roughly constitutes the Middle Ages, its moral imperative remained. "The stern teaching of the early Church, that earth was a place of exile and testing, was in no way modified."[12]

For centuries the Church insisted that the acquisition of worldly riches was an objective unworthy of human beings. It "feared that an excessive preoccupation with temporal

9 Goudzwaard, p 10.
10 Robert Latouche, *The Birth of Western Economy*, trans E. M. Wilkinson (New York: Harper, 1966), p 50.
11 *Ibid.*
12 *Ibid.*

things was an obstacle to the attainment of the only true good—the Kingdom of God."[13] We should not assume that this attitude is scriptural.

It is inexcusable to typify the outlook of the Middle Ages as wholly Christian. The real issue for a genuine Christian does not lie in some supposed difference between nature and grace, earth and heaven, horizontal and vertical, and capitalism is not inherently the triumph of the former over the latter. In fact, as history vividly reminds us, when the kingdom of man gains headway, we get socialism in one of its variants. Capitalism—not the false portrayals of it in humanist propaganda—can exist only when God's authority and dominion over our life takes precedence. Capitalism ceases to exist when faithfulness to God's word (and therefore to His precepts for life and prosperity) is exchanged for a substitute set of values.

The Christian faith does not hold that an improvement in the material conditions of life—achieved by capitalistic methods—leads inevitably to moral decline. If moral decline does set in, it is not the fault of capitalism per se. The modern academy, however, thinks it is; and Goudzwaard is, it appears, of the academy.

Progress & the Enlightenment

According to Goudzwaard, the transformation of the medieval vertical society into the modern horizontal one was not a normal historical development. It occurred when modern Western civilization self-consciously and systematically destroyed the "barriers" that were erected in the medieval era to safeguard the religious and moral scheme of things. That is, in one fell swoop, civilization substituted the wholly secular view of the "modern" for the "Christian" view of the Middle Ages. In general, Goudzwaard sees nothing in the modern age that constitutes an improvement over the

13 Latouche, p 53.

conditions of life in the Middle Ages. This would mean that Goudzwaard would have to introduce the economic question on its own merits, and this he cannot do.

Capitalism is exclusively the product of change from the vertical to the horizontal, he says. Without this change capitalism would not have begun. Of course, we would still have had all the *benefits* of capitalism, he supposes, though not the system itself. Capitalism represents a purely earthly outlook on life for him—the desire for material comfort and happiness, the recovery of a lost paradise. From the pursuit of capitalist ideals, all the ills of the present have emerged: pollution, overcrowding, poverty, injustice, war, famine (with some recognition of factors beyond our control), psychological loneliness, boredom, and the rest. The horizontal quality of life is the disease; capitalism is the symptom.

It is true that certain empirical changes took place in the late Middle Ages that, quite beside the moral assumptions in question, helped bring about the transition to capitalism. Tremendous economic and geographic expansion, for instance, took place nearly simultaneously, due to the discovery and exploration of new continents. These opened new markets; appetites were stimulated for novel wares—especially new foods, spices, and other delectations. And these discoveries further spurred an interest in commerce and trade, gradually transferring the center of economic life from the feudal countryside to the dynamically growing towns and cities. Uniting these developments was a single factor that played the most significant role, perhaps, of all: the rapid advance of the natural sciences. This intellectual revolution, more than anything else, demolished the base and foundation of the medieval world.

These and other factors were present in late medieval Europe. At what point does Goudzwaard's change in orientation occur? Did it happen as a result of these late medieval activities, or did it result in them? It's hard to say. At this juncture Goudzwaard glosses over matters quickly. We must simply accept that at some point the horizontal mindset replaced the vertical. Whether this replacement was the result of a change of faith, or resulted in a change of faith, doesn't matter. What does matter is that the "new faith" was directed solely toward the possibility of *limitless progress* in the improvement of mankind's material conditions.

Goudzwaard styles this new faith of horizontality as a belief in the recovery of a lost paradise on earth, through our emancipation from church and heaven, providence and fate. People no longer saw themselves bound by circumstance and limitations beyond their control but, with Promethean self-confidence, set out to attain the perfect future by sheer human endeavor. One's rational destination, as proclaimed by the new enlightened mentality, was to conquer nature and subdue the world for the betterment of all. From this new faith, according to Goudzwaard, capitalism emerged as the cultural superstructure.

Capitalism here is clearly the product of a strictly secular faith in earthly progress. Goudzwaard wants us to believe that capitalism and Christianity had at the outset, and continue to have, nothing in common. Viewed through the lenses of the medieval vertical perspective, Christianity seems opposed to capitalism. Apart from the change of orientation, which was at the same time a change of faith, capitalism would not have appeared. Capitalism feeds off this new faith in earthly and material progress and negates the Christian ethic.

There is a certain amount in Goudzwaard's discussion of the ethical and religious outlook of early modern man that can't be denied. The Enlightenment carried out a fervid and acrimonious assault on Christianity. A new confidence in one's independence and powers of reason, one's essential goodness and perfectibility, displaced an earlier preoccupation with each person's sinfulness and concern for spiritual salvation. We can't doubt that the Enlightenment changed man's attitude toward himself, his world, and his purpose in life, and that a new self-confidence brought about social and political changes that students of history can easily trace.

Of the many intellectual changes that occurred, certainly

one to be included was the belief in progress as a hallmark of society. With the intellectual elite it became the dominant ideal. It is questionable, however, whether such a faith continues to inspire the course of Western civilization today. The intellectual elite no longer believe in Western civilization! The earlier belief in progress at least assumed that Western civilization was more advanced in that respect than any other. One thing is certain: capitalism is no longer granted, if it ever was, the sort of veneration Goudzwaard ascribes to it. The elite of the Enlightenment, the self-appointed guardians of morality, never believed in capitalism but tended always to rail against it—and you could not have found more "horizontal" types than these. This is still true today.

One wonders why Goudzwaard is incapable of seeing that his anticapitalism is at present the reigning faith. Is he unaware of socialism? Not recognize it as the enslavement it is? When he does mention socialism, it is portrayed as a benign humanitarian protest movement against the injustices of capitalism. With respect to the foremost socialists of our age, we read: "Engels was moved by a deeply felt sympathy and seriously wounded sense of justice. The same is true of Marx." Or, "in Marxist socialism we are confronted with the most violent protest against not only the assumptions of the industrial revolution but also against the firm belief in progress which is their foundation."[14]

Socialism is merely the cry of justice against the evils of capitalism, and, in spite of socialism's shortcomings, it is essentially on the right track, he says. Goudzwaard seems blind to the fact that what he pervasively describes as capitalism has, in fact, nothing to do with capitalism. It has far more to do with socialism's intrusions, which have sought all along to hinder capitalism. He could never admit that the Enlightenment faith in progress has resulted in the growth of socialism and in all forms of statism. It would go too much

14 Goudzwaard, p 72.

against the grain of the conventional anticapitalist wisdom.

By the way in which he constructs his moral argument—vertical versus horizontal—Goudzwaard cannot admit that progress is not exclusively, not even originally, a secular faith. He doesn't seem able to accept the idea of a Christian concept of progress. Hasn't he read Augustine?[15] You could even say that the modern secular belief in progress is really a corruption of the Christian view. If a Christian faith in progress had not risen, modern man, like ancient man, might have thought in terms of "movement," or "change," but never in terms of progress.

Man needs an organizing ideal to guide him in building his kingdom. From the scriptural view, that organizing ideal is the Babel principle—the principle that drives the unbeliever in the direction of a greater concentration of power and authority in an earthly (and therefore human) institutional form. The state has proven to be the most adaptable institution for the Babelization of culture. By means of its monopoly of power, unbelievers are able to force every endeavor to conform to a single purpose, which, to be sure, opposes in every respect God and His purpose.

This principle, in its method of organization, erects in our conscience something to symbolize our external, or objective, independence from God. In the modern age, the concept of an autonomous nature suits that goal. It has become the new religious foundation upon which secularists have aroused people to construct an autonomous culture. An autonomous culture can be built only on the base of autonomous existence. Nature, being independent from God, sets man, a product of the evolution of nature, free from God as well. In the modern world, men of reason build culture and society by following the rules, scientifically deduced, that are dictated by nature. And nature claims that socialism is the

15 See, for example, Robert Nisbet, *History of the Idea of Progress* (New York: Basic Books, 1980), Chapter Two.

correct blueprint for the just and good society. Therefore, the state must increase, I and all others must decrease, or else stand in the way of what is "natural" for mankind to accomplish—stand, that is, in the pathway of *progress*.

Who could doubt, then, that attached to autonomous nature (and culture) is something called progress? Here we must not be misled. We can trace the same process of secularization through the idea of progress as elsewhere. It is seen in the way in which modern society came to view the dynamics of nature as the manifestation of a self-operating mechanism, and as forming an immanent continuity of movement—the uniformity of the past seen as the key to the determination of the future. Nature sprang from itself and continues to function by its own means; it is apodictic by reason of its innate laws—no reference must be made to a God above or outside nature. Nature exists and develops inherently and autonomously.

The concept of progress, however, as the necessary unfolding of nature toward a utopian future, is an ethical and religious conception that modern secularists imported from another source: it is not the unavoidable conclusion of the idea of an autonomous nature. As a matter of fact, the idea of progress was not invented by, nor did it originate with, modern secularists. It could not have, for it is not naturally a part of their ethical principles. They have stolen the idea, rather, as they have stolen every one of their ideas from Christianity, and then have perverted it. Yes, Christianity!

Christianity is the original source of the idea of progress; it shaped early modernity. If non-Christians pretend that the idea is the child-genius of their own thought, it is only because they mean to supplant the Christian faith with their cultural agenda. But simply because they have usurped the idea of progress and attached it to their belief in autonomous nature doesn't mean that we should think there is something fundamentally non-Christian at the heart of the idea, as Goudzwaard does. Our responsibility should be to distinguish between them, and to separate the Christian view of progress from the other.

The idea of progress entails more than change or alteration as such; it is not mere activity and movement for its own sake. Most essentially it implies change for the better. It includes the idea of growth or development: of *maturation*.

The task God gave to mankind of bringing the earth under its dominion and lordship can only be achieved over time; it involves improvement. Built into human nature, then, is the need to achieve purposes, and to fulfill inner desires. God meant that we should work, that our work should meet with success, accomplish an end, and receive its reward. All of these are legitimate Christian ideals. The only stipulation is that we should carry out our work under God's authority and direction. Above all, our labor should rise from a deep desire to please God; and in the way in which God desires to be pleased, not the way we desire.

Christians, of course, can't forget that man's fall into sin has changed both the character and outcome of all labor. We live under a curse that robs life of purpose and reduces work to vanity and meaninglessness. If progress is to be achieved, we must come to terms with the sin in our lives and the reasons for that sin. We must see that the problem lies in our own rebellion, not in the corruption of nature or the malign intent of nature's God. We must realize, too, that the solution is found in God's plan of redemption. This is the way to true progress, not in spiritual matters alone, but material ones as well. We must understand that progress in anything is tied to the infinitely more important progress of God's word in our hearts and minds. God has conditioned progress in our lives on covenant faithfulness and obedience to His will. While no inevitable progress exists in this world, we nevertheless should not deny that progress had, and still has, a proper place in God's purposes for us.

The modern secular ideal of progress, on the other hand, believes that nature of itself automatically bestows benefits to us. Secularists should not suppose, however, that nature's blessings remain unconnected to any effort on their part. Their job, as they see it, is to divine nature's secret laws, especially the "law of progress." This gives to sacred science its preeminence; by means of it alone we will learn nature's mysteries and how to master the mechanism of progress, and then guide society by its infallible logic. If we hope to have progress, then, we must cast aside anything that threatens the authority of science. We must rid ourselves and society of bigotry, superstition, dogmatism, and narrow-mindedness. Of Christianity, in other words.

Progress in the mind of the modern secularist means emancipation from the past and from the influence of Christian principles and culture.

When one reads Goudzwaard one seems to read, to be sure, similar things. He appears to be defining the governance of the modern non-Christian. But he does this to convince us that these principles are the religious root of modern capitalism. Did the modern humanist ideal of autonomous nature, then, accompanied as it was by belief in inevitable earthly progress, constitute the religious core of capitalism? On the contrary. When we examine the thinkers of the late-eighteenth and early-nineteenth centuries we see instead a virulent anticapitalism. This is particularly evident in the progressivist visions of Utopia. Utopians were filled with a longing for and a belief in the possibility of the perfect future society. Such a society would be, from top to bottom, controlled by the state and guided by a cultural elite who, through a social science thought to be infallible, would arrange all social relationships and decide what was good and not good for all. This idea of progress in modernity was linked to a vision of salvation through social control.

Mankind was to rest its hopes on the power of the "collective man," a new human type upon which we would erect our perfect society. Rousseau heads the list of devotees to this pagan concept. His thinking has inspired generations of social engineers. He believed in total renunciation of the Christian past and a reconstruction of society in order to achieve human autonomy. One of the chief causes of human misery lay in the chains of social inequality, he said; and inequality was the product of private property.

Like every later humanist, Rousseau blamed faulty institutions—institutions founded on Christian principles. Christianity had diverted humanity from its proper progress, he said, and we must have a new principle on which to build the social future: the General Will. This is to be the new authority over every facet of life. Everyone must, if necessary, be forcibly required to conform to the General Will, as manifested in the state. Therein lay mankind's only salvation.

This idea was accepted and improved upon by every major thinker after Rousseau. From Turgot and Condorcet to Saint-Simon, Comte, and then, at the pinnacle of progressive utopianism in the nineteenth century, Fichte, Hegel, and Marx. Their offspring have been legion.

Progress & The Industrial Revolution

The opponents of capitalism cannot rely only on moralistic and philosophical constructs in order to make their case; they need a tangible, historical reality to point to, one that enables them to say, "Here is capitalism, we have seen it with our own eyes, and it's awful!" The reality most often pointed to is the Industrial Revolution. Here was real capitalism at work; and misery and inhumanity were the result. But anticapitalists seldom look at the Industrial Revolution from any other standpoint than their anticapitalist prejudice. The Industrial Revolution is often made to fit their moralistic presuppositions, apart from any attempt to understand its features.

Needless to say, this is what we find in Goudzwaard. From the start he *assumes* the failure of the Industrial Revolution. His task, then, is to explain that failure. He tells us that the Industrial Revolution failed to live up to something called the "necessary simultaneous realization of norms in society..."[16] He also views the Industrial Revolution as the product of a utilitarian ethic and a deistic religious outlook that, in his words, institutionalized "new forms of production

16 Goudzwaard, p 65.

devoted almost exclusively to technical and economic progress."[17] We may be confident, then, that the Industrial Revolution will be roundly condemned.

Goudzwaard's condemnation of the failure of the Industrial Revolution is a masterpiece of confusion, couched in the incomprehensible patois in which naysayers of capitalism seem to specialize. His use of fashionable metaphysical jargon has the effect of stuffing the Industrial Revolution into an anticapitalist Procrustean bed. As an example of his interpretation of the Industrial Revolution as a whole, we read statements or fragments of statements like the following: "...forces of economic growth and technology... are considered isolated, sufficient, and good in themselves."[18]

It is virtually impossible to know to whom this refers. There were millions of people who participated in the Industrial Revolution. Can we generalize their behavior by a reference to abstract forces to be considered? I doubt that ordinary people, for whom the Industrial Revolution came to mean opportunity and prosperity, thought that economic growth and technology were isolated, sufficient, and good in themselves. Whoever this is supposed to mean!

Goudzwaard's interests run to making summary moral judgments of the forest without stopping to examine the trees. In this way he takes for granted his assumption about "norms of social justice." He claims that by "its" failure to implement those norms the Industrial Revolution was a disgrace. As though by this personification of the Industrial Revolution he can demonstrate its reprehensibility.

He writes: "These norms are consciously viewed as dependent upon and secondary to the force of progress: they are placed in the service of the expansion of technology and the growth of the economy."[19] Once again, consciously viewed by whom? Placed in the service and so on by whom?

17 Goudzwaard, p 66
18 *Ibid.*
19 Goudzwaard, p 66.

Apparently a fellow called "Industrial Revolution" is doing these things, but we can't say how or why. Apart from this, though, note how Goudzwaard takes his idea of *norms* for granted. He summarily passes judgment on the Industrial Revolution in terms of them. But we can't be certain of their source. Goudzwaard seems to assume they came from God, and are inherent in His created order, but doesn't offer a biblical justification of their meaning; you can't be sure they even have a biblical foundation. For Goudzwaard, however, they are moral absolutes, and capitalism their antithesis.

Rather than puzzling over or attempting to decipher Goudzwaard's philosophistical pronunciations against the Industrial Revolution, let me attempt to provide a synopsis of the real Industrial Revolution.[20]

The outstanding feature of the period known as the Industrial Revolution was the rapid growth of population.[21] This growth was due not so much to a change in the birth rate as to a decline in deaths, although an increase in the number of children is documented. The rise in population precedes the date traditionally assigned as the beginning of the Industrial Revolution, so it can't be said that the revolution *caused* the increase in population. All that can truly be said is: "In Britain, in the eighteenth century and later, it so happened that, alongside the increase of population, there was taking place an increase of the other factors of production, and hence it was possible for the standard of life of the people—or of most of them—to rise."[22]

And rise it did, on a remarkable scale. The industrial changes that were occurring proved timely to millions at a crucial juncture in history, when the population began to outstrip traditional ways of providing subsistence. Those who bewail the miseries of the factory system of the time should

20 In preparing this synopsis I have used as a source T. S. Ashton's, *The Industrial Revolution, 1760-1830* (New York: Oxford Univ Press, 1969).
21 Ashton, p 4.
22 Ashton, p 7.

consider that factories became the means by which multitudes were kept from starving. Or perhaps those who prefer the medieval guild system to the factory, as Goudzwaard does, want to ignore the question of how a rapidly increasing population could hope to meet the basic needs of life. It did meet them, and more. The actual standard of living, in every segment of society, slowly began to rise.

One of the peculiar features that detractors of the Industrial Revolution point out in order to condemn it as a period when wealth was concentrated in the hands of a few, while the masses sank deeper into poverty, is the enclosure movement that took place in agriculture. The reduction of the open-field system and the displacement of the yeoman freeholder is viewed as an evil, since many lost their independence on the land and were forced to rely for bare existence, so it is assumed, on the mines and factories springing up. At the same time, their numbers created a surplus of labor, forcing low wages even lower. But this misconstrues what happened.

As Ashton writes, "Enclosure had been taking place almost continuously from at least as early as the thirteenth century [back when the outlook was vertical!]. Its development had been connected with production, not for subsistence, but for the market." We should understand, then, that market forces operated in the Middle Ages, and men were appreciative of this, since their economic success or failure depended on them. What brought about changes in the market? Nothing less than consumer demand. Ashton says, "It was the growing demand for wool and leather, rather than for grain, that provided the incentive."[23]

Anyone with some grasp of the rudiments of economics knows that effective economic demand cannot exist where the means to pay doesn't exist. That men merely want things does not mean they have the means to acquire them. There

23 Ashton, pp 18 & 19.

has to be an increase in purchasing power, beyond what is necessary to meet basic needs; it was not demand for food that produced the change, but demand for less urgent commodities. In accord with market factors, then, a process was set in motion that brought the ownership of land into fewer hands. It was not a simple matter of greed, however, for small freeholders had begun to disappear before the enclosures took place on a large scale.

Those left on the land needed larger holdings in order to compete in the changing market. All this occurred over many centuries, and led up to the Industrial Revolution. It happened without anybody in particular manipulating the process, a truth that anticapitalists find hard to tolerate. The truth, however, is that many yeoman freeholders preferred to sell their small freeholds and use the money for other—and to them more economic—enterprises. No doubt "some transferred their capital and energies to manufacture."[24]

Although enclosure initially took place in response to the demand for leather and wool in the market, it nevertheless "brought about an increase in the productivity of the soil."[25] Ashton even thinks this is the essential fact about enclosure. Instead of leading to a greater impoverishment, it improved the quality of foodstuffs and so improved the health of peasants. It extended life expectancy. A tendency to save, now that there was a surplus, spread more and more, and this in turn augmented available pools of capital for larger industrial enterprise. And with the expansion in production and markets, it became possible for manufacturers to hire

24 Ashton, p 19.
25 Ashton, p 20.

more labor, creating more consumer demand and stimulating even greater changes in market conditions.[26] Ashton, in a positive vein, observes that "the increased mobility of capital was socially beneficial, leading as it did to a substantial fall in the rate of interest."[27] So capital came cheap, and cheap capital is what built "the deep mines, solidly built factories, well-constructed canals, and substantial houses of the industrial revolution..."[28]

Other changes affected people. Entrepreneurship was allowed to expand where outdated regulations and statutes had broken down. Most of these legal enactments, centuries old, were meant to protect privilege and vested interest, rather than encourage economic innovation. It is a tribute to the charity of the inventors and innovators of the period that they refused to protect themselves by the patent system that had been a fixed feature since the days of Elizabeth I.

Many of the Industrial Revolution's great discoveries would not have been possible without the simple principle—decried by anticapitalists—of the division of labor: "Only when division of labor developed, so that men devote themselves to a single product or process, does it [invention] come to harvest. Such division of labor already existed when the eighteenth century began, and the industrial revolution was in part cause, in part effect, of a heightening and extension of the principle of specialization."[29] But what is of greater importance, as Ashton relates, is that "invention is more likely to arise in a community that sets store by the things of the mind than in one that seeks only material ends."[30]

26 Note that it was the increase in the employment of labor that brought an increase in consumer demand. The manufacturers did not produce the demand but merely responded to it. This is a facet of economics that the opponents of capitalism continue to refuse to accept.
27 Ashton, p 8.
28 Ashton, p 10.
29 Ashton, p 12.
30 *Ibid.*

The Industrial Revolution grew out of the *minds of people.* It was the product of the natural energies of the human spirit, of ideas on mechanics and technology, and was in accord with man's obligation, ordained by God, to have dominion. Human beings were exercising their God-given abilities for productive ends. If the general material welfare improved as a result, this shouldn't lead us to suppose that people had been seduced by a horizontal outlook. Incalculable temptations arose at this time. As people achieved prosperity and success, the tendency was to deny their dependence on God. History traces a tragic record in this respect. But it is irresponsible to ignore the benefits received from the accumulation of the technological changes that came about. The Industrial Revolution did not fail; we failed to give proper due to God for His good gifts to us.

One of the benefits of the time was its vertical mobility; a quality unheard of in the Middle Ages. This change was in part a result of the Puritan revolution of the sixteenth and seventeenth centuries. Many of the great industrialists of the period traced their ancestry back to Baptist, Presbyterian, Quaker, or Independent roots. And we should all be aware of the influence of John Wesley and Methodism: "...the effects of Methodism are to be seen less in the quickening of enterprise than in the greater sobriety, diligence and self-discipline of the workers who came under its influence."[31] A major reason that the tradition of the Dissenters (or Nonconformists) proved so productive of people of industry and trade is that they "constituted the better educated section of the middle classes."[32]

At this time education was not principally technical; it was, above all, literary, theological, and moral. Yet it produced men of unique practical minds and initiative, who obviously didn't shun the material world for the vertical outlook of the

31 Ashton, p 14.
32 Ashton, p 15.

cloister. They viewed the world as a place in which to serve God, themselves, their families, and society. Advanced technical schools did exist, true, in particular at Glasgow and Edinburgh, where such subjects as chemistry and experiment were taught and learned with enthusiasm. Other schools in England turned out pioneers in fields such as glassware, metallurgy, and mechanics. And an education did not neglect to include instruction in history, geography, French, and rhetoric. It was a learning intended to expand the mind, not to stifle a full outlook on life.

Well, now, someone will surely say, all of this only evades the issues: what about the overcrowded conditions, the slums, the unsanitary squalor, the long hours, and the employment of children in unsafe workplaces? There were, to be sure, problems that arose alongside the changes taking place. But Hayek notes, "While there is every evidence that great misery existed, there is none that it was greater than or even as great as it had been before."[33] We should keep this in mind when someone writes an idyllic portrait of the Middle Ages. The Romantic reinterpretation of the medieval era is one that rose in the early nineteenth century, as a retreat from the world then coming into existence. Its lenses on the past were, to say the least, narrowly focused. It has been a useful tool in the hands of the opponents of capitalism ever since.

There are many, then, who blame the distortions of the Industrial Revolution on capitalism. But the evils of the time lay in the failure to apply capitalism—indeed in the efforts to prevent it. Hayek writes: "Much that has been blamed on the capitalist system is in fact due to the remnants or revivals of pre-capitalistic features: to monopolistic elements which were either the direct result of ill-conceived state action or the consequences of a failure to understand that a smooth

33 F. A. Hayek, ed, *Capitalism and the Historians* (Chicago: Univ of Chicago Press, 1963), p 18.

working competitive order required an appropriate legal framework."[34]

Trevelyan, in his monumental *English Social History*, observed another disruption: the Napoleonic Wars in Europe were responsible, predictably, for the decline of economic and social life everywhere.[35] There is no question that the years in which Europe was embroiled in war—which had nothing to do with capitalism and everything to do with power-seeking—affected the social and industrial developments taking place. War disrupted supplies of raw materials, drained manpower, created shortages, led to government allocations and controls, caused deaths; increased in every way the misery of the lower classes. It also fostered a fear of social change. And so a reaction against the revolution, and an attempt to halt it, began in Europe in 1789; and began in France, where capitalism did not thrive.

Our problem today is not industrialization; the problem is in our hearts. "Men... have worshipped the power of the machine and have sought to imitate it in their lives. Failing this, they have turned against technology in many quarters."[36] Goudzwaard sympathizes with the secularist rebellion against the modern industrial and technological world. He thinks the future will be assured only when we rid ourselves of capitalism; this system, with its alleged faith in progress, is, for him, the crux of the problem. However: "The future cannot be found by trying to escape from industrialization, but only by a return to the God who created time and all things else, and who commissioned man to exercise dominion through righteousness, work, and knowledge, and to celebrate that dominion in the Sabbath."[37]

34 Hayek, p 28.
35 G. M. Trevelyan (London: Longman, 1978), p 408.
36 Rousas John Rushdoony, *Salvation and Godly Rule* (Vallecito: Ross House, 1983), p 102.
37 *Salvation and Godly Rule*, p 102.

In *From Enlightenment to Revolution*, Voegelin states: "What is sometimes referred to as the crisis of Western civilization is not an event that occurs at a definite point in time. It is a process which extends by now over more than a century and a half. The crisis does not belong to the past, it is a living present. Every day adds to our experience of its extent and profoundness..."[38] Modern Western civilization is, without doubt, in the midst of a monumental and, it would seem, increasingly deepening crisis. But it is a misconception to speak of the crisis of the West, as Goudzwaard does, as "the crisis of capitalism."[39]

If capitalism is in a crisis, it is only because it is caught in the throes of the more serious crisis at the center of Western consciousness. As Voegelin says, the crisis of Western civilization "is a crisis of the spirit..."[40] It is a crisis at the moral and religious center of the whole of Western civilization.

That civilization came into being on the foundation of the Christian faith. Without it, civilization as we know it would not have been possible. As long as that moral order held sway, civilization continued to develop in every cultural aspect. Since the eighteenth century, however, an attempt has been made to jettison the Christian moral heritage and persist in the belief that Western civilization will continue to advance. Because mankind set out to found Western culture not merely on a non-Christian base, but along a distinctly non-Christian bias, this crisis was brought about.

Western civilization can't be built on any other foundation than Christianity, and the attempt to build it in self-conscious opposition to Christianity has led to civilization's demise. Rebellious humankind is encouraged to turn in hatred against the manifestations of Western culture, and to seek a

38 Eric Voegelin, John H. Hallowell, ed (Durham: Duke Univ Press, 1975), p 74.
39 Goudzwaard, p 161.
40 Voegelin, p 74.

new civilization altogether. Instead of repenting and trying to shore up the foundation of Christian moral order, which is God's moral order, mankind has turned to revolution as the answer instead.

Revolution has become the new and demonic spiritual force driving modern society. In the revolutionary mind, humanity has become the Supreme Being. This new god will create a new heaven and a new earth, a new social order on a new moral foundation. To rid itself of its Christian past and every trace of its influence is its ideal. The revolutionary mind seeks a total transformation of the state of the world, including mankind itself, and looks to a life that has not existed in history before.

Modern revolutionaries blame the present order of society, with its economics, its technology and industry, as the cause of our difficulties. We have been dehumanized, they say, transformed into a machine, or even less: the cogs in its mechanism. We are dependent on external forces and social arrangements that prevent the full flowering of each "personality." The fundamental issue for a revolutionary, who is more unswerving than any fundamentalist, is the liberation of the human spirit from its fettered state. This alone, in humanist thought, is the true meaning of history and culture.

The new principle of order for the revolutionary mind—the order that replaces subjection to God with subjection to man—will realize as it premise the autonomy of man's spirit.[41] The ultimate purpose of revolution is to destroy anything that elicits dependence on God. We must be free to create our own order.

In an attempt to fulfill this wish, the revolutionary exhibits a two-fold characteristic. On the one hand, we may speak of it as *revolutionary irrationalism*, which may be expressed as follows: "Let us trust the eternal spirit which destroys and

41 Voegelin, p 197.

annihilates only because it is the unfathomable and eternally creative source of life. The joyful passion of destruction is a creative passion."[42] Every hindrance to the new anti-Christian society must be removed. On the other hand, we encounter *revolutionary rationalism* which, Voegelin notes, "is deeply rooted in the eschatological furor of establishing the final realm on earth."[43]

Something, then, must be put in the place of the Christian order that once supported Western society, and it must be final and permanent. What it will be remains uncertain. It is hoped that the process of destruction will somehow produce an alternative. Destruction is, after all, a "creative passion." So the revolutionary places more stock in what he opposes than in what he desires. And within the frame of the temporal world, he opposes, above all else, capitalism.

The revolutionary, contrary to the Christian, believes in the natural goodness of man. His thinking is therefore involved in "an anthropology which commits the cardinal mistake," Voegelin says, "of projecting the evil in man into his environment."[44] The revolutionary blames external factors for his loss of autonomy. In other words, political and, most especially, "economic institutions have created the dependence of man and thereby have become the source of evil..."[45] Those who think within the framework of the crisis itself are bound to see the problem of man purely on the level of what Voegelin also describes as "intramundane society." They cannot do otherwise, because they have, as matter of fact, deified intramundane society.[46] So the revolutionary's chief purpose is to escape history by attempting to bring it under his sovereign control. He intends to make new history from scratch, and it will conform in every respect to his

42 Vogelin 198. Voegelin quotes here from the anarchist, M. Bakunin.
43 Vogelin, p 168.
44 Vogelin, p 219.
45 Vogelin, p 218.
46 Vogelin, p 176.

amoral vision.

His focus is always to create a new form of community. This new community of "the saints" will replace the detested middle class—the primary form of communal life of Western man to emerge from the Industrial Revolution. But the roots of that form reach farther into the past; it is the Christian ideal of the family extended to greater social participation. The maturation of the middle class in history coincides with the growth of modern capitalism. If that class expects to continue to exist, then some form of capitalistic behavior is necessary. And so the revolutionary plots its demise. To achieve that he must suggest that the very existence of the middle class is morally perverse: it is a community whose ideals extend no farther than the ambition to accumulate material comforts. It epitomizes the triumph of flaccid and unheroic values, and so is viewed with disdain. It is altogether without a proper sense of *justice!* Its continuation, therefore, as a social form, is "unjustifiable."

Goudzwaard to a considerable extent adopts the same attitude. The ideas expressed in *Capitalism and Progress* reveal a mind confined within the crisis: Goudzwaard's concern is with the level of "intramundane society." He shares the revolutionary's attitude that capitalism is responsible for the mess we are in. Again and again there are indications of existentialism, such as: human life has suffered its loss of meaning and dignity as a result of modern economic and industrial developments. When the reader realizes that Goudzwaard is ostensibly speaking for the Christian community, this attitudinizing turns noxious.

A constant refrain indicates his pessimism: we can detect, Goudzwaard says, "a persistent narrowing of human relations and purposes to technical and economic achievements as ends in themselves." "Instead of being the creator of progress man has increasingly become its servant." "As a result of industrial domination man has become one-dimensional." "...the role of technology in modern society...[is] the most serious threat to human personality..."[47] The development of Western civilization, he claims, has been toward self-extinction; "if it wants to survive, [it] will have to learn to control its economic expansion."[48] This is the heart of the issue to Goudzwaard.

For him, the cause of our ills is in the external order of society. Naturally the solution will have to be found there, too. So he offers what he terms a "disclosure of society." We need a disclosure of society, he says, because there has been a "contraction of human freedom."[49] Or the social order of capitalism has diminished the possibility of free human choice. Something in the nature of social revolution is demanded, for he states: "disclosure implies a genuine change in the order of society..."[50]

What that change should amount to is not stated, since Goudzwaard does not pretend that he has in mind any notion of disclosure as an end. "Disclosure is not to be equated with the goal of attaining a disclosed society. It is not a goal; rather, it is a process. It is the opening up and unshackling of a society which has become entangled in the toils of obedience to the autonomous forces of progress."[51] This sort of open-endedness serves the revolutionary well, since it establishes his indispensability to overseeing the process. He will always know better than the herd when the principle of a "simultaneous realization of norms" has been achieved. An expertise is necessary in order to let the rest of us know if and when "human choice" has received its just due.

Goudzwaard wants to provide what he believes is a Christian evaluation of our modern problems, yet not once in his

47 Goudzwaard, pp 112, 119, 164, 165.
48 Goudzwaard, p 142.
49 Goudzwaard, p 205.
50 Goudzwaard, p 188.
51 Goudzwaard, p 186.

book does he affirm that the present crisis stems from our rebellion against God. No mention is made of the authority of God's law or its place in our lives. Nor is any attempt made to call society back to Christ, its only true hope. Goudzwaard does not locate the problem in man and his sinful nature, but in our environment: the social arrangements that have formed in the wake of our industry. And so he sees the Industrial Revolution as a colossal failure; it did not—and does not—meet his ideal of "simultaneous realization of norms" in society. Without God's law as our ethical norm, we begin to imagine a utopia, and are disappointed as soon as it fails to be what we expected.

Some may say I am unfair to Goudzwaard; that he indeed sees the problem as *in* man—in his "faith in progress." And it is true that Goudzwaard tries to locate as the source of our problems a faith in progress that will lead to a material, industrial, and technological paradise on earth. But he takes for granted this faith in progress as a secular ideal. He does not see the issue as a struggle between the kingdom of God and the kingdom of man. Faith in progress may be legitimate in the kingdom of God. So faith in progress is not a sufficient explanation for the crisis of our modern world.

We must penetrate to the spiritual core, where our principles are always pitted against God's, and determine how the concept of progress relates to both sides. We idolize our cultural achievements, including a notion of culture's inevitable progress—a progress based on autonomous morality. We mean to get rid of God and His demands on our lives, yet we shouldn't be led to think that progress as a cultural motive cannot, in God's kingdom, have its rightful place. Goudzwaard seems unable to accept this, because of his distinction between Christian and non-Christian—that vertical and horizontal orientation. In his view, faith in progress defines the outlook of horizontal society alone; and since the vertically oriented world has virtually disappeared, his own faith takes on a profound cultural pessimism.

His anticapitalism colors any actual understanding of real capitalism; his explanation of its features and its historical rise is governed by his pessimism. A few of his indictments of capitalism might merit consideration if we lived in a world in which the capitalist way of production were all that existed. But this is far from true. Socialism also exists, and we have had time enough to evaluate its economic, political, and ethical performance. The failings of capitalism fade into insignificance beside the brutality and destructiveness of socialism in every form. Does Goudzwaard take this into account? Not once.

His examination of capitalism in the West is based on the assumption that capitalism has never been affected by the intrusions of statism, government economic tinkering, welfare programs, or the like. He evades the disrupting influence of totalitarian regimes and the threat that they pose. By his failure to take socialism into account, Goudzwaard to some extent confuses what he thinks is capitalism with its opposite: what is actually the result of malignant socialist ethical ideals.

The central interest in *Capitalism and Progress* is politics, not economics. Goudzwaard means to foster, by way of his moralistic posturing vis-à-vis capitalism, an anticapitalist political activism. And since his ideas fail to increase our economic understanding or spiritual outlook, they only intensify our political indignation.

SIX

THE MARKET ECONOMY & THE MORAL BONDS OF SOCIETY

I DOUBT that it's possible to make an entirely humanistic case for capitalism—not on the premise of mankind's ethical autonomy, anyway. Capitalism does not rise of itself from economic quantifications and statistical abstractions; and any fruitful understanding of economics derives from Christianity. Humanists who defend capitalism borrow their ethical assumptions from Christianity, and those assumptions are what every serious Christian should know.

There are many excellent books to turn to in order to gain a fuller definition of economic behavior.[1] But here I want to confine myself to a single aspect: capitalism as a possibility only when Christian ethical assumptions govern a society. I intend to move through three ethical problems that are inseparable from economic behavior, but whose solutions

1 One might, as a sampling, consult these: *Poverty and Wealth*, Ronald Nash; *Genesis: The Dominion Covenant*, Gary North; *Productive Christians in an Age of Guilt Manipulators*, David Chilton; and, among general authors: *Economics in One Lesson*, Henry Hazlitt; *Essentials of Economics*, Faustino Ballve; and *Human Action*, Ludwig von Mises.

depend upon a Christian explanation: the inviolability of *private property*; a motivation I will term *self-interest;* and, finally, the relationship, if any, between *righteousness and prosperity*.

The Moral Basis of Property

At the outbreak of the Romantic revolution, near the end of the eighteenth century, there was a radical change in attitude toward private property. It lost its moral inviolability for Western society. The Romantics revolted in favor of a new dispensation, accompanied or brought about by a moral change whose influence is still with us. Indeed, the principles of this change appear more acceptable to many today than ever in history. We have hallowed the notion that we are capable of solving mankind's basic problems, mistakenly attributed to poverty, by way of political revolution.

The majority of secular societies today continue to have faith in political revolution, although they may hope to attain it in ways not overtly destructive. But whether they work for abrupt change or a gradual extension of government control over the daily lives of citizens, they believe that the elimination of "thorns and thistles" and the increase of the welfare of humankind can be found only in *political* solutions.

The first historical expression of this sentiment exploded in the violence of the French Revolution. One of its chief rallying cries, besides liberty and fraternity, was equality. At first inequality was denounced on political grounds, but soon came under attack on economic and social bases as well. Inequality of power gave way to inequality of wealth; or, rather, the cause of inequality of power lay in inequality of wealth. The blame at first centered on the artificial social distinctions and privileges that were inherent in the corrupt *ancien regime*. The disparity between the landed rich and the landless poor was too obvious for words. The only tenable solution seemed to be an overthrow of the hated system.

In time, the proclaimers of political utopia saw greater evils rising—capitalism and industrialism. Even more so than the aristocracy, capitalism fattened itself on inequality, they said.

It began to dawn on these messiahs of social revolution that it would be benficial to their own interests to say that the real problem lay in the possession of private property. So private property became the symbol of everything vile. To solve the problem of inequality once and for all, these messiahs had to overturn the institution of private property. And the first act had to be one of destruction, by whatever means, no matter the consequences. As James Billington observes, "Belief in a purely secular salvation leads the modern revolutionary to seek deliverance through human destruction rather than divine redemption."[2]

Here is the point to keep foremost: it was those who hated capitalism who cherished the idea of destruction, and not, as the propagandists of socialism have contended, the other way around. Because socialism, in order to exist, always has to usurp the moral high ground, socialists denounce capitalism as a system of "productive destruction." The propensity to seek salvation through revolutionary destruction did not at first create a replacement for the system of private property. But the revolutionaries quickly came to believe that the state should own, or at least determine, all forms of legitimate (read *just*) property.

From the writings of Karl Marx, a program for the collectivization of the means of production captured the imagination of the revolutionary. In the *Communist Manifesto* of 1848, Marx announced the "abolition of private property" as a central tenet of communism. He believed that property should be held in common and in this way be kept from private exploitation and greed. But property held in common is technically owned by no one. If you believe it is owned by the people collectively, how does the collective express itself? Who makes decisions on the use and distribution of property, and to what ends?

Enter the state. Since the Party would decide in these

2 *Fire in the Minds of Men*, p 25.

matters, naturally the state became the real owner of all property. The Party's line, of course, is that all decisions are in the interest of the people. All will benefit; none will grow rich while others are impoverished. The state will see to it that all receive a just allocation from nature's abundant store. In his advocacy of communism Marx put into words something that continues to capture the modern imagination, even though Marxism itself has been soundly discredited.

Marx did not merely proclaim a new set of principles for economic understanding; he instituted a change at an ethical and religious level. This helps explain his popular appeal, and the common belief that he was somehow deeply touched by societal injustice. In the terms of Marx's ideals, but not necessarily in terms of his programmatic philosophy of revolution, modern man has come to alter his thinking about what is just and right. Marx intended his outlook to replace the ethics of Christianity, particularly its concept of justice.

Many, obviously, have come to agree with Marx. His idea that property should be owned and controlled by the state, and dispensed by its largess, is the dominant ethical view of our day. Wealth, Marx claimed, springs from government (the state's primary institution) and government should guarantee its equal distribution among the citizenry. It ought to micro-manage the economy, and thus raise the status of everybody's well-being in every detail. The alternative, supposedly, would concentrate wealth into fewer and fewer hands, while the masses descended deeper into poverty and oppression. Today even more tenets have been added.

Capitalism, as a system of private ownership, is credited with every conceivable "evil in contemporary society including its greed, materialism, selfishness, the prevalence of fraudulent behavior, the debasement of society's tastes, the pollution of the environment,"[3] and the rest. There is hardly

3 Ronald H. Nash, *Poverty and Wealth: The Christian Debate over Capitalism* (Westchester, IL: Crossway, 1986), p 70.

a country in the present world where people do not believe that government owns, or should own, the property of its citizens. This becomes obvious as soon as we attempt to exchange property with another person. Virtually without exception, the government, by taxation, will claim a part of the exchange. And the larger the economic value involved in that exchange, the larger the portion demanded by the government. When economic theoreticians estimate the Gross National Product, they must take into account the omnipresent and proliferating effect of government. How much belongs to the private sector and how much to the public sector is the expression of that effect.

It is deplorable that private property's ethical importance to economics has received so little attention. But this has been the case since the beginning of modern "classical" economics. In the July 8, 1988 *National Review*, in an article entitled "The Forgotten Right of Privacy," Tom Bethell articulates the ambiguity of this question probably as well as anyone: "The curious thing is that economists, while divided on the question whether private property is essential, are largely united in avoiding discussion of the subject. Some, it seems, think it too obvious to mention; others think it too odious to mention; either way it has remained unmentionable."

Both sides take for granted the issue of property—those who believe it essential, and those who reject it. The latter are more silent, because they despise property on principle, not because they've been able to demonstrate that society can function without it. They *assume* that it can, and so their analysis (based on the model of physics) refuses to take society into consideration. They do not contemplate human beings; they assemble economic data. They assume that humankind is wholly explicable by abstract scientific and mathematical methods.

The differences between the two sides are ethical and religious, and one must understand them at that level before understanding why private property is presumed to be good or bad, useful or harmful, dispensable or not.

First, as Bethell has stated, "Private property is fundamental to economics for the simple reason that exchange of goods is the most basic economic 'act.' But a good cannot be exchanged if it is not owned to begin with." Precisely. But economic theorists actually do ignore ownership as a prerequisite of exchange. They treat exchange as they might treat photosynthesis: as a natural fact. They don't consider exchange a human act that occurs nowhere else in nature, exemplifying our inscrutable interests and concerns. What compels a person, for instance, to exchange something he has for something he doesn't have?

On the surface you might say you do this to satisfy some need. You give up one thing that doesn't satisfy you (or in your estimation is not satisfying) in order to acquire something that will. And you do this to overcome the limitations on your ability to gratify all your needs by yourself; you can't possibly produce everything you need; you can produce only a few things. In order to get the rest you must exchange what you have with somebody else who has what you want, and who wants what you have. Shouldn't we expect economics to have at least this level of common sense at its foundation?

But it is just here that matters become difficult. Men do not desire things by instinct. Nor did they discover the principle of exchange by accident. Here enters the Christian perspective: it says that man was created by God, and that wants and desires are an original part of his created person, as God intended. Though these desires have been affected by the fall, they are not products of it. The principle of exchange, then, was built into the nature of the world that God created. You could claim, with perfect justice, that God intended mankind to build cultures and civilizations and promote His kingdom on earth (at least in part) by economic interdependence.

Man quickly learned that he could get something only by giving something in return, and God meant for each of us to exercise a nurturing dominion in this way. Each would grow morally by learning to make responsible decisions in this regard. The fall has altered matters drastically, of course, by introducing the factor of scarcity, but it has not diminished the need for productive exchange. If anything, it has served to make it more apparent.

The principle of exchange now becomes the most important means for ameliorating the effects of thorns and thistles. In the history of the race, we have sought shortcuts to this end. Guided by the religious ideal of Babel, we once tried to prosper by means of plunder and conquest, violence and revolution. We have, in other words, always looked to political solutions to our problems. Which is to say that we tend to regard the organized power of government—instead of our own labor—as the way to get what we want.

Every attempt in our day to increase the role of government as guarantor of our welfare is a resort to that method. Our moral assumption is that government can be depended upon to satisfy our economic needs. Even when this assumption is disproved in practice, no believing statist ever loses his faith; he cannot abandon the religion of men. We should not be surprised, then, if the majority of economic thinkers essentially bypass the question of private property.

I believe, however, that private property is the moral antecedent of economic behavior. It was not, as the socialists would have us believe, an arbitrary institution of recent invention. It was not conjured up to justify capitalism after the fact. Rather it comes to us from far back in our past, before capitalism even appeared. Yet having said this, I cannot agree with Mises' statement: "Private property was a human device. It is not sacred. It came into existence in early ages of history, when people with their own power and by their own authority appropriated to themselves what had previously not been anybody's property."[4]

Private property, on the contrary, was instituted by God for human use. This is the essential difference between capitalism and socialism. If private property is a human device, then no matter how intricately the argument is put

4 *Human Action*, p 683.

for its usefulness to economic activity, it remains a tool which man, as the true sovereign over his life, may use as he pleases. If it was created by man it can be altered or eliminated at his will. If private property does not have a morally determined meaning and place, we are free to decide on its ultimate right or wrong. And if property isn't morally grounded, it will never be economically or socially secure.

Private property stands in the way of those who wish to become gods over other people's lives. Its origins can't be traced to mankind's experience in the world per se, but must transcend and ethically determine our relationship to the created world.

The central feature of property is conveyed in the concept of ownership. It has a moral relationship because of its ubiquity; it's everywhere. No economic analysis can disregard this. But all of us, and Christians especially, can't merely assume the normative nature of ownership; we must provide an explanation for it. Why do we seek to own things? North states that "a fundamental problem for economic theory [is] the establishment of a point of originating (and therefore final) ownership."[5] Our inclination to own things is involved in this ultimate question. Where does the inclination come from, and why does our ownership of something affect our economic actions with respect to it?

These may seem trivial questions, but in order to set in place a Christian foundation we have to see that the origin of ownership lies in God. I have said that justification of any human behavior is ultimately made possible only by reference to our Creator and Redeemer. God provides the pattern for our life. And so we've seen that man was created *like* God, but on a finite scale; he was meant to be a replica of God's character in all that he says and does in God's world. We should relate to the world in the way God relates to it, and

5 Gary North, *Moses and Pharaoh: Dominion Religion Versus Power Religion* (Tyler, TX: Institute for Christian Economics, 1985), p 120.

the Bible clearly states that God's relationship to the earth is one of ownership. The earth belongs to the Lord. It is His creation and property; He is its owner.

"The earth is the Lord's," the Psalms declare, "and everything in it, the world, and all who live in it" (24.1). God owns not only the inanimate earth but those inhabiting it. Even people are His property. And so, as North has also said, "An individual's personal, private ownership is analogous to God's personal, private ownership of the earth, including the souls of men."[6] If God didn't own the earth and everything in it, we couldn't own a thing. And how could we invent the concept of ownership if He hadn't created us in His image and made us, like Him, owners in the world: joint heirs?

The ownership of property was instituted by God as a concomitant feature of our dominion responsibility. To be sure, we should remember at all times, with thanksgiving, that our ownership of anything is a gift to us in the first place and must be used according to God's commands. And the Scriptures never indicate that we are to have ownership "in common." No provision was made for collective (or state) ownership: it was to be individual, or at least familial. This is because property stands in conjunction with what I have called "self-development." The acquisition of property was meant to serve both as the means and the result of the faithful exercise of kingdom responsibility. It is impossible to have dominion without appropriation; the things of the earth are to belong to us and we're to exercise dominion *through* them.

All. of us should then make our own contributions and receive the fruits of our labors. Property, in this regard, includes not only tangible things, but also skills and talents. Virtually every aspect of our experience connotes some form of ownership.

The relationship between man and woman, for instance, the most basic relationship in Scripture after the one to God

6 *Moses and Pharaoh,* p 118.

Himself, is represented by ownership. In I Corinthians 7.4, we learn that both husband and wife have ownership of the other's body. Only God, however, owns their souls. From the institution of marriage, which is the first form of worldly ownership in Scripture, other forms of ownership derive. No one can contemplate life outside this primary institution.

The institution is used, at the same time, as the first means by which to teach us of the direct and immediate responsibility inherent in ownership. From the distinction between families arises the distinction between *mine* and *thine*. It is understandable, then, why socialists hate the family and want to destroy it. God takes the violation of private property seriously; not only does He forbid theft, but even the desire to steal—covetousness—is abominable to Him.

God's ownership of the world is reflected in His providential care for the world. He values ownership not simply for the sake of possession; it is a means of achievement. Through His creation and care of the world, He intends to increase and magnify His glory. People were created to achieve part of that purpose—build God's kingdom on earth. We are responsible to fulfill this purpose with everything we're given to own. Possession and responsibility are inseparable.

And the moral emphasis falls both ways; we are responsible for what we own, but equally and to the opposite, do not feel responsible for what we don't own. And if we are not responsible, we won't be productive with what we have. In a fallen world, private property is more than ever a moral necessity for teaching responsible behavior. Observing the historical effect of property on moral behavior, John Chamberlain has said: "Private property...has been a powerful instrument for teaching men and women responsibility, and for giving them the leisure to think and freedom to act with prudence."[7]

Only when the moral value in property became the consensus did capitalism emerge as the greatest economic force

7 *The Roots of Capitalism* (Indianapolis: Liberty Press, 1976), p 62.

in the modern world. Contrary to socialist assumptions, capitalism did not emerge as a historical reality that then needed moral justification, which then led men to invent private property. Rather, when the sacredness of private property was secure in the Christian West, free enterprise and market economies began to blossom.

As long as we maintain the relationship between ownership and responsibility, we will benefit from both. Socialism, in jettisoning private property, removes the responsibility that accompanies it. The result is bondage and impoverishment; and with no slackening in greed, materialism, fraudulent behavior, and destruction of the environment.

It's not difficult to understand the importance of private ownership of property to economic behavior when we consider the most basic ecnomonic fact: "The starting point of all modern economics is here: the question of scarcity."[8]

> There is no question that God's curse of the ground created a new environment. From that point on, the earth has resisted man. Thistles that interfere with man's ability to extract what he wants from the ground have grown up to increase man's costs of attaining his goals. Man must sweat in order to eat. His labor is now unpleasant and burdened, or at the very least is often frustrated and discouraging, unlike the labor in the garden. The labor in the garden was entirely pleasant. Man was merely fulfilling his purpose and exercising his God-given talents. "To labor is human," but in the garden, it was without a curse. God added vast new costs to labor, reducing its efficiency, while simultaneously reducing the psychological pleasure and incentive attached to labor. Man would now be *compelled* to labor by his *environment*; no longer would his mere humanity be relied on by God in order to encourage man to fulfill the terms of the covenant of dominion.[9]

In a fallen world poverty is the normal state of affairs; wealth is not. Poverty exists naturally, while wealth has to be produced, faithfully, each day. Unfortunately, the word *wealth* has become a socialist bogeyman. It suggests images of

8 North, *Genesis: The Dominion Covenant*, p 111.
9 *The Dominion Covenant*, p 112-113.

fabulous possessions—houses, cars, clothes, jewelry, high living—and of self-indulgence. The term is now used as abuse by those who have political, not moral or economic, axes to grind, and who regard envy as a normal moral sentiment. There's no reason to load this word with unnecessary meaning. That wealth stands for any condition that contrasts, more or less, with thorns and thistles, is closer to the truth. If we did nothing to relieve the natural condition of penury, we can be certain that life would be short, mean, nasty, and brutish, indeed.[10]

Wealth is present wherever any positive qualities in life have been supplied. When these are present, we can pursue the loftier cultural ideals that enrich life and render it worth living. We shouldn't take these benefits for granted. Wealth may apply differently to different individuals, but there is nothing inherently immoral in even extreme wealth. Many who possess great wealth have gotten it by serving the needs of humanity.

The point is that wealth must be produced *by* somebody, but we don't need to produce poverty; it comes naturally. Like God who created His world, we must recreate ours. The fall may complicate this: to produce wealth in a fallen world entails not only hard work but great risk. We are reluctant to make an effort if we are deprived of any stake in the outcome. If our energies are thwarted, or subject to the dictates of others, poverty quickly falls in place and takes its normal course. "The poor will always be with you," Jesus said. But when we are secure in our property, including the internal property of individual talents, we can be truly productive.

Subjective Value & Objective Value

The second element to consider in understanding how

10 See Thomas Hobbes, *Leviathan* (circa 1650), Chapter XIII: "...and the life of man is solitary, poor, nasty, brutish, and short."

capitalism comports with the Christian view of behavior is the problem, acute in modern economics, of valuation. I stand aside to permit Dr North to clarify this issue: "The problem of value is central to the science of economics. Is value determined objectively or subjectively? Is the value of some scarce economic resource inherent in that resource, or is it derived from the evaluations of acting men? In short, is value *intrinsic* or *imputed?*"[11] Here is a question of ethics that touches at the heart of economic activity. Economics, plainly, includes a striving after ends. Economic activity is meant to produce results that will increase well-being and alleviate the natural poverty. It may require us to choose between numerous means, some of which will be unwise, imprudent, or immoral. Even beyond that, we must evaluate our ends.

Is there an objective basis for determining which goals ought to be achieved and which ought not to be? Or do we decide to accomplish things from subjective motives, because we want them? That is to say, is value relative to one's whims? Is there any standard connected to economic outcomes? Should we assume that economics is essentially selfish—that if some people gain, others must lose? Or we might look at the problem of subjective and objective value from a slightly different angle: Does "economic interest?" have a legitimate place in our behavior in God's world? Did God expect us to act by such motives, or is it sinful to calculate economic self-interest?

If it is legitimate for men to behave in this way, are their judgments strictly subjective? If we say that God intended us to act on the basis of self-interest, are we to assume that we can know what self-interest is, without reference to God? Are we required to separate economics from ethics? Does the valuation of means and ends lie in human autonomy, or are intrinsic and imputed value mutually exclusive?

These are questions asked by modern utilitarians—right-

11 *Genesis*, p 38.

wing humanists who claim that capitalism is possible only on the basis of ethical autonomy. They claim that a completely *subjective* basis of economic value can alone do justice to our striving after economic ends. Are they entirely wrong?

Two works present the utilitarian argument in its clearest light: *The Foundations of Morality*, by Henry Hazlitt, and *Theory and History*, by Ludwig von Mises. Both provide clear and detailed explanations of human behavior, and both are interesting reading. These are the best modern utilitarian thinkers on the subject of ethics. They are entirely humanist in their suppositions, and throughout each I sense a determination to pit the utilitarian outlook against Christianity.

As far as the two are concerned, Christianity represents a non-utilitarian and ascetic viewpoint. As they represent it, the Christian ethic has little concern for the things of this world. Its preoccupations, they imply spitefully, is with the next. So they assume that Christianity has nothing to say about how to arrange our affairs in order to achieve the best in this world. At the very least, they believe, the Christian ethical outlook prepares us to live not in this world but the hereafter. At the heart of the Christian outlook, to them, is a moral renunciation of material things, as if Christianity denies their *value*—or values them as useless.

It teaches, they say, that wealth is a vice and poverty a virtue. This accusation may be true of many Christians; asceticism has a long history in the Christian church. Many today believe that capitalism represents the religion of materialism, and therefore cannot possibly be Christian. Capitalism is pure selfishness, they think. For these high-minded Christians, the extent to which capitalism has been successful in fostering earthly happiness is the extent to which we have lost our sense of the higher, more truly satisfying goals. So although utilitarians are ready to do battle against Christianity, their conception of Christianity is false.

For their part, utilitarians make no pretense of knowing what is good for man beyond the world of immediate experience. Their ethic is based on the assumption that we are a driven animal; we act only to satisfy base desires. By stressing this, however, they have hit on an important point. All of us stand in want of something, whether we need it or not; life seems driven by some dissatisfaction or other that we're trying to set right. One of these desires is for happiness.

One need not think of happiness in strictly materialist terms. For utilitarians, happiness is largely a state of mind, subjective, meaning therefore different things to different people. Even the seeker of religious salvation is one who wishes to achieve a perceived state of happiness. The pursuit of higher goals, utilitarians contend, has a no less utilitarian basis than the pursuit of material gain. The point is that in the end happiness is what each of us desires, regardless of how we define it. Utilitarians do not claim to know what ends we ought to choose, but only the most useful means by which to achieve those ends. That, to them, is what capitalism is all about, and they are not far from wrong.

In utilitarian ethics "...there is no standard available for appraising any mode of acting either of individuals or of groups of individuals but that of the effects produced by such action."[12] In other words, the ends justify—and place value upon—the means. We value those actions that produce happiness, in this view, regardless of what that may be. There is no standard by which to evaluate that outcome in advance.

Why this is important to utilitarians can be seen by their view of its opposite: "All non-utilitarian systems of ethics look upon the moral law as something outside the nexus of means and ends. The moral code has no reference to human well-being and happiness, to expediency, and to the mundane striving after ends. It is heteronomous, i.e., enjoined upon man by an agency that does not depend on human ideas and does not bother about human concerns."[13] On the surface, these words are directed at socialists and absolutists, but

12 Ludwig von Mises, *Theory and History: An Interpretation of Social and Economic Evolution* (Westport: Arlington House, 1981), p 45.
13 Mises, p 82

Christianity falls into the same category. To both Mises and Hazlitt, human experience determines ethics; and absolutists like God do not bother with human experience.

The implications for economics now become apparent. Mises says, "Modern economics traces all human action back to the value judgments of individuals."[14] Clearly, value is subjective. From this assertion Mises draws his conclusion: Since "all judgments of value are personal and subjective... In view of this fact it is useless to talk about absolute and eternal values."[15] As Christians, we may be startled by his conclusion, but we ought to be just as startled by his assertion that value is subjective.

That assertion leaves us at the mercy of relativism: *whatever pleases me is what is right.* Mises attempts to correct the misconception that utilitarianism is an ethic of relativism and anarchy by saying: "This does not mean that every individual draws his valuations from his own mind. The immense majority of people take their valuations from the social environment into which they were born, in which they grew up, that moulded their personality and educated them."[16]

Mises is willing to admit the broader influences of tradition, habits, and taboos; he is aware that these shape the ways in which we evaluate ourselves. Nevertheless, for him, society in general does not value things; the individual does. At best, society represents the sum total of individual values and their effect on one another. This does not detract from valuation taking place at the individual level. Only an individual can say "I prefer, I like better, I wish," Mises would contend. Only an individual can register satisfaction at his preference.

Hazlitt, while sharing a similar view, is more circumspect, willing to recognize that "subjective" and "objective" may be different yet related ways of approaching the same ethical question: "All valuation is *in origin* necessarily subjective.

14 Mises, p 207.
15 Mises, p 22.
16 Mises, p 22.

Value, like beauty, is in the eye of the beholder. All valuation implies a valuer. Valuation expresses a relation between the valuer and the thing valued. This relation depends upon the valuer's own needs, wants, desires, preferences, as well as upon his judgment regarding the extent, if any, to which the object valued will help him to realize his desires."[17] By using the words "in origin," Hazlitt reveals that he does not consider value exclusively subjective.

To begin with, there are literally millions of valuers, and one person's values appear objective to another. Values become external facts that others are forced to deal with. Which leads Hazlitt to conclude that "moral values are subjective from one aspect and objective from another."[18] Though values are largely "instrumental," they may become "intrinsic" if enough people agree on their usefulness. Hazlitt, too, is quick to appreciate the influences of what he terms the "social mind."

In origin, values are principally subjective and relative; they are not properties of things. But because this is so, it is entirely possible that significant numbers will come to see that certain social arrangements (*valuations*) are conducive to what each one values. This produces a type of social cooperation by which it becomes possible for each to gain more easily his or her ends. Without this, in fact, people might achieve nothing. So naturally, in the scale of values, a human being puts the emphasis on social cooperation. By noting that values arrange themselves in a hierarchy, we find an objective basis for value, Hazlitt says. Or rather, we come to see value as relatively subjective and relatively objective.

Utilitarians, then, are not entirely ethical relativists. They value social cooperation, for by it each of us hopes to achieve, they say, what each of us values personally. And because

17 Henry Hazlitt, *The Foundations of Morality* (Los Angeles: Nash, 1972), p 162. My emphasis.
18 Hazlitt, p 165.

social cooperation outweighs other values, it becomes the end of moral behavior. It becomes the *ought* for everyone. But its value is not entirely intrinsic, in the sense that any person can presume to know with certainty what the perfect formula is for social cooperation. It is certainly not something that can be imposed according to a blueprint conjured up in the minds of a group of social high priests.

We cannot confuse social cooperation with an impossible ideal called social justice. Even as a "highest good" it remains an instrumental good: its purpose is to allow each person to increase personal satisfaction. "It is on the implicit if not explicit recognition of this that our codes of morals, our rules of conduct, are ultimately based. 'Justice' itself...consists in observance of the rules or principles that do most, in the long run, to preserve and promote social cooperation."[19]

The utilitarian begins from why and how we act, and claims to understand man. The rules of social cooperation evolve naturally out of the nature of a man who constantly desires, chooses, prefers, or values, they say. This man discovers his moral code by self-interpretation—judging what most aids him in satisfying his desires. "Unless our *oughts* are to be purely arbitrary, purely dogmatic, they must somehow grow out of what *is*. Now the connection between what is and what ought to be is always a *desire* of some kind."[20] From this Hazlitt draws his final conclusion: "Every man, in his cool and rational moments, seeks his own long-run happiness. This is a *fact*; this is an *is*. Mankind has found, over the centuries, that certain rules of action best tend to promote the long-run happiness of both the individual and society. These rules of action have come to be called *moral* rules. Therefore, assuming that one seeks one's long-run happiness, these are the rules one *ought* to follow."[21]

Neither Hazlitt nor Mises ever specifies what those rules

19 Hazlitt, p 13.
20 Hazlitt, p 12.
21 Hazlitt, p 13.

are. That would require them to speak dogmatically—absolutely—and they can't do that. Such rules are the product of results, and the results are always subject to change. The two utilitarians are confident that reason will discover the right rules, when necessary, and seek the application of those rules to social cooperation.

Socrates began with the same confidence in man's autonomous reason. He, too, believed that when consulted in an unprejudiced manner, reason would somehow yield a code of behavior that would bind us into a society to our mutual advantage. But his assumption led to a problem that Plato set himself to resolve. And Plato's solution, as we shall see, promoted the notion that a state-dominated society, with morally superior persons at the top, dictating what others should do, is a necessity. That is the only rational road to take when you begin with the assumption of human autonomy.

Utilitarians will dispute this, and insist that Plato's statist solution is not demanded, not at all, by the premise of ethical autonomy. Socialism is not the inevitable result of ethical self-interpretation. But when we deny our dependence on God's word to guide our valuations, a state-controlled society is all that will hold us together. Otherwise we will impose whatever we believe is in our own best interest. And we can be certain that the more we insist on ethical autonomy, the less likely we are to take a "long-run" view of anything.

We begin to prefer short-term solutions to problems, and this is precisely what makes socialism so appealing. Socialist solutions always appear to cost little or nothing. No level of mankind is entirely reasonable in its purest moments—we disregard long-term costs and seek short-term benefits. We force others to obey rules based on achieving short-sighted gains. All of which is perfectly legitimate in the utilitarian view, so long as the result for those at the top is happiness.

It is a misconception of Christian morality to deny that humanity is designed to make judgments, or choose between ends and select the best means to achieve the end chosen. It is sheer ignorance to denounce Christian morality as ascetic, and claim that it stands for a code of behavior disassociated from human concerns. There is a subjective as well as an objective side to Christian ethics. It is the only ethical viewpoint that contains an objective basis for subjective valuation, providing the possibility of genuine social harmony. "The biblical explanation...affirms that men do have the power to impute economic value. It also affirms that there are absolute, objective standards of value."[22] The biblical viewpoint does not play imputed value off against intrinsic value.

That is the realm of the humanist. The definition of value is found in God. In Scripture we read that after God created the world, He saw that it was good. This is no mere recognition on God's part, it is what He imputed to his handiwork. "God...imputed positive value to His creation, for He created it perfect... The doctrine of *imputation* lies at the heart of the doctrine of *creation*. The creation was good because God created it good and...said it was good. It was good *objectively* because of its inherent conformity to God's decree. It was good *subjectively* because God announced its perfection, indicating its conformity to His standards."[23] Therefore, "God's original subjective...standards served as the sole standard of the creation itself."[24]

Since man is created in God's image, he too possesses the ability to impute value to his world. To impute value means to be designed to act purposefully, according to a plan; we are meant to use our subjective judgment. In order to impute accurately, however, each individual act of imputation must stand or fall "in terms of its correspondence to God's act of imputation."[25] Our imputed value should be in accord with the intrinsic value determined by God. We can know *in advance* which actions are morally right and wrong. We can even know that our real happiness depends upon the activities we choose. We were created to act in terms of God's

22 North, *The Dominion Covenant*, p 42.
23 North, p 37.
24 *Ibid*.
25 North, p 38.

absolute, objective standard, not simply in terms of self-interpreted desire. We ought to value that standard as the surest guarantee of our welfare and prosperity.

Prosperity & Righteousness

David Chilton has written, "Men have always had to choose between two methods of social change: regeneration and revolution."[26] This religious and moral truth isn't apparent to utilitarians. One who seeks to define his moral standard, based on his own interpretation of his desires, becomes revolutionary in outlook. There is no natural disposition in us to limit our passions, since there is nothing to tell us in advance whether our actions are good or evil. And it is a shallow boast to say that we can discover rules of behavior for social cooperation merely because we perceive social cooperation to be in our best self-interest.

The nature of social cooperation is itself an open question. Unless we are regenerated, we can confuse social cooperation with social domination by anyone powerful enough to enforce his agenda upon us. The "rules" in this case simply become the dictates of whoever controls the government. The satisfaction of want is then manipulated by those who, either from idealistic notions or from sheer cynicism, decide who gets what. The principle of revolution and the principle of regeneration are irreconcilable opposites, and determine the moral disposition of all *before* they act. Revolutionaries have always sought to elevate the state above the lives of people; politics becomes the solution to social and economic problems. What government does or does not do will, in this view, be decisive for the well-being of everyone.

Capitalism, on the other hand, has never been the product of socialist methods. Nor has it ever been able to function when politics becomes the chief means to satisfy desires.

26 David Chilton, *Productive Christians in an Age of Guilt Manipulators* (Tyler: Institute for Christian Economics, 1981), p 74.

Where societies have considered state domination to be the highest expression of social cooperation, capitalism has contracted and died. Capitalism thrives where the principle of regeneration rules. This principle asserts that we impute value in terms of God's absolute standard. Our desires and the satisfaction of them are submitted to a transcendent test of right and wrong. We are controlled by a moral outlook that is not of our own devising. Only Christianity represents the principle of regeneration.

Chilton sets down its essential ideal: "The Christian seeks first to discipline *himself* to God's standard. He then publishes the gospel and attempts to peacefully implement the laws of God into the life of his culture, trusting in the Spirit of God for the success of his efforts. He knows that there is not, and never will be, a perfect society in this life. He knows that the Kingdom of God spreads like leaven in bread—not by massive, disrupting explosions, but by gradual permeation. He knows that justice, righteousness and peace result from the outpouring of the Spirit in the hearts of men (Isa 32.15-18); a nation's legal structure is, therefore, an indicator, not a cause, of national character. Law does not save."[27]

Where the principle of regeneration has gained control over people, they have become productive in every sense of the word. And where we become truly productive, there, too, we see and experience authentic prosperity. For regeneration draws out of us behavior that conforms to the purposes of God, and it teaches us to wait upon God for His blessing. Regeneration is not a formula for economic prosperity, but it instills in us the moral values that receive God's approval; and in receiving His approval we receive His reward.

Prosperity is dependent upon righteousness.

27 Chilton, p 74.

PART III

SOCIALISM

The idea of collectivism is government for the good of the people by experts, or officials who know, or think they know, what is good for the people better than either any non-official person or than the mass of people themselves.

A. V. Dicey

SEVEN

THE QUESTION OF SOVEREIGNTY

The Rule of the Best & the Wisest

ERIC A. Havelock has written: "...whenever western man has directed his thinking towards those problems created by his relation to his fellow man, problems of society in general, of the state in particular, of government and law, of rights and responsibilities, of duties, of constitutions, of citizenship, he has consciously or otherwise used the political and often the moral vocabulary supplied to him by the two masters."[1] The two masters are, of course, Plato and Aristotle.

We should understand that Greek philosophy, in both the social and the political realms, as epitomized in the works of these two, has provided perhaps the predominant vision for an ordered society in the West. Referring in particular to Plato, Karl Popper says that he "was one of the first social scientists and undoubtedly by far the most influential."[2] Whenever a scheme has been devised for society, it is Greek

1 Eric A. Havelock, *The Liberal Temper in Greek Politics* (New Haven: Yale Univ Press, 1964), p 12.
2 Karl R. Popper, *The Open Society and Its Enemies*, "The Spell of Plato" (Princeton: Princeton Univ Press, 1971), Vol I, p 35.

philosophy, sadly, that has set the terms of the debate. Greek ideals of life and society retain their influence on social thinkers down to the present. What is disconcerting, however, is that some of these thinkers are confessing Christians.

Why? What are the Greek goals for individuals, society, and the state? Do they square with—or can they be built upon—the Christian ethic? The two outlooks are, I submit, opposite and mutually exclusive. Greek ideals are the ideals of men in rebellion against God. Whatever emerges from those ideals, then, serves to advance the kingdom of man. Greek philosophy is the spirit of Babel attempting to justify itself. Many, certainly, would deny this. Some would even suggest that Christian values can be culled, to a certain extent, from the writings of the two masters.

I'll confine myself to Plato, the more foundational of the two. I realize there are profound differences between Plato and Aristotle, but they pale to insignificance in the light of Christianity, and their differences are largely tactical; they are in perfect agreement on the strategic importance of the kingdom of man.

First, Plato proposes a total program for the individual and society. He has a "kingdom" idea of life that leaves nothing out. What he envisions, then, excludes the possibility of compromise with any alternative or competing point of view. At the center of his philosophy is a principle of authority that demands submission from all. Christians need to understand that their attempts to pour Platonic wine into Christian wineskins would not meet with Plato's approval. His vision is a self-contained whole. And no viewpoint is more clearly antithetical to all that Plato stands for than Christianity. There is no halfway house between them.

The eminent classical scholar Werner Jaeger understood the Greek cultural ideals well. For the Greeks, he said, "the state was a spiritual entity, which assimilated all the loftiest aspects of human life and gave them out as its own gifts."[3] This is particularly true of Plato. He wanted to see the state exercise supreme authority over all facets of society. But who should be in charge of the state? Plato believed that its power and authority ought to rest in the hands of a few individuals who were clearly of marked intellectual superiority: the philosophers. Everybody would have to submit to the supposed wisdom of these few, not only in public affairs, but in private ones as well.

This is Plato's doctrine of the philosopher-king. His efforts to make the doctrine rational and respectable form the nucleus of his philosophy. Whatever other speculations he entertained in seemingly unrelated fields of thought—aesthetics, geometry, metaphysics, epistemology—these actually served his statist agenda. Plato fought for the glorification of man; but not mankind in general; only philosophic man, the one for whom reason alone mattered. With this in mind, we come to something peculiar in the nature of Plato's statist ideal. He did not believe that the state had any power or authority apart from those in charge of it. They *are* the state. Whatever they decide is the will of the state.

Plato was confident that with the "Best and Wisest" at the helm, the ship of state would sail in the direction of a just and well-ordered society. As with most people at present, his faith lay in the expert, the *specialist*, who would guide society into some perfect, overall design. The social, economic, and cultural life of society would function properly, in Plato's vision, when it was caused to function according to a scientific blueprint. At the top of the heap sit the social engineers and elite planners, and the rest of us ignoramuses have to rely on their wisdom and submit to every decision they make.

What Western intellectual tradition has come to value as

3 Werner Jaeger, *Paideia: The Ideals of Greek Culture*, trans Gilbert Highet (New York: Oxford Univ Press, 1945), Vol I, p 108.

Plato's lasting contribution to enshrined ideals is the *manner* in which he made his statist agenda acceptable. His philosophy, therefore, must be seen as one integral unit, not a hodgepodge of disjointed categories. When we attempt to disconnect Plato's metaphysics or epistemology from his ideal of the state, we run the risk of being deceived by his innocuous "idealism." And when Christians succumb to the temptation to read him in this fashion—to pick and choose what they like and disregard the rest—they fall into an attitude that should give them pause, considering this further assertion by Jaeger: "All human effort to reach the truth is ultimately justified for Plato, not by the urge to solve the riddle of the world, but by the necessity of knowledge in maintaining and shaping human life. *His aim was to bring the true society into being* as the proper milieu for the achievement of the highest virtue possible to man."[4]

This highest virtue is obtainable only by means of a "true society." We shouldn't suppose that Plato had in mind any achievement for humankind in general. Jaeger is somewhat disingenuous on this point; plainly, Plato was interested only in the achievement of the highest types—the philosophers. What elevated their virtue was his chief concern.[5]

It is true that Plato's notion of society did not find universal acceptance among the intellectuals of ancient Greece; there is even contemporary debate between Platonic and Sophistic traditions. But we should not assume from this that the cultural tradition of ancient Greece did not reflect a common set of principles, or shared values, on the issue of man's highest good. It was the consensus that the source of highest good was the state—in the classical period, the city-state. Civil government was the center of religion. Greek civilization did

4 *Paideia*, Vol II, pp 84 & 85. Emphasis mine.
5 *The Republic of Plato*, trans Allan Bloom (New York: Basic Books, 1968), Bk V, 473d,e; 474b, pp 153 & 154.

not look to the gods to provide moral direction. The gods cared little for men.[6]

Virtually all the Greeks, rather than seeing the state as an institution for repressing evil and redressing injury and injustice, viewed the state as a repository of moral values, which, apart from the philosophers, the common herd could not be expected to know. The herd, therefore, had no idea of what their true status should be until the state instructed them. It provided moral guidance. It arranged all the details of each person's life in order to insure its own well-being. Without the state's moral guidance, society was liable, Plato would say, to disintegrate.

Not surprisingly, the chief concern of the Greeks, and of Plato especially, was to set in place a political arrangement to protect against moral erosion and social contamination; these resulted in civil wars and revolution, the bane of every society. Plato taught that above everything else, the causes of these convulsions were the impure motives that inspire economic gain. He could conceive of nothing so base and selfish as the quest for commercial success and material gain. To be concerned with such lowly matters testified, for him, to a lack of a communally-minded spirit. He believed that the good of the community should take precedence over the good of any individual. The state was the only instrument capable of making sure that communal interests prevailed over the selfish preoccupations of mere individuals, he said, and if we were left to ourselves, factions, intrigues, violence, and disorder were bound to occur.

Plato divined the central problem: the toleration of private interests. In his specialized jargon Plato would say that the preeminence of private interests in society elevated *matter* over *form*. How to bring about the reverse in the minds of men was Plato's all-absorbing concern. It began with faulty

6 See W.K.C. Guthrie, *The Greeks and Their Gods* (Boston: Beacon Press, 1955), *passism*.

reasoning, he said; wrong thinking and false ideas were what led the masses astray. They had no idea that their true welfare was linked to the welfare of all of society. The state had to stand guard against wrong-headed opinion, in order to preserve the community.

A frequent allegation by scholars fascinated with Plato is that his political philosophy is really only a theoretical proposal for a civil structure; this structure would prevent (or anyway reduce the possibility of) an organized special interest from coercing civil government into implementing that interest's agenda. When material gain is our chief preoccupation, they allege, then distinctions are bound to rise between the haves and have-nots. Each will vie with the other for control of the power of the state apparatus, in order to force policy to comply with personal wishes.

When that happens, the social fabric unravels, communal life suffers, and the likely result is civil war. Plato, it is said, only wanted to prevent the power of the state from falling into the hands of factions whose interest was merely to increase their private welfare. He wanted to promote the common good, they say. And it was out of *this* concern that Plato offered a scientific epistemological theory upon which to erect his ethical and social ideals.

That Plato's epistemology (or method of knowledge) formed the presupposition to his ethical and social theory is without question. But was his epistemology created out of a genuine concern for the common good?

That epistemology brings us face to face with Plato's metaphysics as well: in these he introduces the world of transcendent "forms." These, of course, were Plato's famous *Ideas*, or permanent standards, according to which, in the changing world below, we could pattern our thinking and behavior. Since we live in a world in which changing material and bodily temptations are unavoidable, an absolute authority for life was paramount, he said, and offered us a transcendent world of self-existing Ideas.

But now a problem arises in the humanist interpretation of Plato. For Plato never imagined that just anybody was capable of grasping his lofty ideals. That ability belonged to a select few, specially endowed by nature; they would make sure that life was carried on in terms of his ideas. And Plato saw no reason why those select few should not take charge of the community: thus the philosopher-king.

Plato did not arrive at his elitist model of society without first having passed through the ethical school of Socrates. It was Socrates who defined for Plato the original problem that would require the solution of statism. We must clarify, then, the "Socratic problem."

Socrates made the care of the soul his chief concern. His ethical perspective advises us to suppress every appetite of our bodies in order to engage in the more important cultivation of the soul. The body was material, and matter possesses an inherent evil we must rid ourselves of, Socrates said, to allow the innate goodness of our spirit to triumph. By cultivating the things of the soul, Socrates expected to reveal a realm of absolute and general standards by which to act, and these would allow us to overcome the base and selfish motives that arise from material concerns.

Many are attracted to the Socratic ideal. Isn't it pretty close, after all, to Christian values? Socrates teaches us to concern ourselves less with external wants than with matters of eternal value, no? Isn't that what the Sermon on the Mount is about? Illusory semblances aside, however, where did Socrates imagine that such eternal and spiritual verities would be discovered? Whose authority requires us to submit to their demands? This quintessential point is, quite simply, the ethical basis of the kingdom of man, the beachhead upon which Plato builds his social and political program.

In his writings, Van Til often mentions that for the non-Christian in general it is the "moral consciousness of man" that stands as the final court of appeal for all questions of ethics and conduct. When those questions are specifically about social justice or public policy, we tend not to consult any other source than our infallible consciousness. It is imperative to see in this that fallen man had assumed for himself the right to pronounce, by his own lights, that which is good or evil, right or wrong, just or unjust. "On the Socratic basis man must cast up his own moral ideal, he must seek the way toward the realization of that ideal by the guidance of a criterion within himself, and he must seek the power that leads him onward toward that ideal also in himself."[7]

So when Socrates argues that we ought to dispose of our material interests and tend to the soul—putting spiritual values in contradistinction to bodily values—the argument rises from his belief that the soul is divine, whereas matter, and hence the body, belong to a corruptible and finite world of existence. That corrupt existence is subject to hopeless transitoriness and change, he says—an altogether false basis for ethical wisdom. Nothing summarizes the Socratic ideal better than a comment by Jaeger, whose own sentiments indicate the ideals that inspire the non-Christian: "Socrates became the leader of all modern enlightenment and modern philosophy, the apostle of moral liberty, bound by no dogma, fettered by no tradition, standing free on his own feet, listening only to the inner voice of conscience—preaching the new religion of this world, and a heaven to be found in this life by our own spiritual strength, not through grace but through tireless striving to perfect our own nature."[8]

We should understand, then, that Socrates enjoined us to live by the dictates and prescriptions of our conscience. We must rely neither on the traditions in which we were brought up or the prevailing opinions of the day, he says, and must take nothing outside ourselves as an absolute authority. We must obey only those principles that are dictated to us by that which is supreme in our conscience: reason.

Whenever Socrates mentions the cultivation of the soul, then, he means that reason should become the autonomous and infallible principle to light our lives. By harkening to reason's inner voice, we will know the good, and in knowing

7 Van Til, *Christian Theistic Ethics*, p 184.
8 *Paideia*, Vol II, p 13.

the good will naturally *do* the good. Socrates never doubted that we would obey the "divine spark" of reason in our own souls once we came to appreciate the independence and self-reliance it suggests. Anything less, Socrates contends, amounts to a betrayal of our true destiny.

The Socratic problem isn't entirely apparent until we also consider that Socrates, who insisted that each should live by his own lights, expected at the same time that each individual would adopt a "universal" and "objective" ethical viewpoint that would unify every human relationship. Beginning from a principle autonomous in each of us, we were to arrive at a common view. That principle was reason. It was to be governed by no standard except the individual, yet it was to form a standard on which to base the social relationships of everyone. Socrates firmly believed in the "ultimacy of the moral consciousness of man," and reason was the guiding principle of that consciousness. Reason participated in the divine. Since this was so, according to Socrates, he expected reason to act as the universal-in-man, eliciting from each of us a common set of values. Using any other source to define moral precepts was to Socrates inconceivable. He certainly did not look to God as the authority on our behavior.

While staking all on an ethical individuality, Socrates was nevertheless averse to individualism. His ideal of "inwardness" (belief in the ultimacy of man's moral consciousness) meant that the dictates of a conscience would prove to be wholly objective. Socrates was an optimist.

It has been said that he pondered these questions during a time of utter skepticism, marked by widespread rejection of traditional values—a period, moreover, in which those masterful purveyors of "individualism" and "conventionalism," the Sophists, filled the void. And, to be sure, Socrates was himself a kind of Sophist; he too concerned himself chiefly with the ethical questions of his day; he also wondered whether he could formulate a basis on which to build a permanent community. Like the Sophists, he rejected a common explanation, judged to be naïve: that these were institutions created by some God.

New circumstances require a reevaluation of the old ways, he taught, and the premise of God had sunk from ascendence after the protracted and brutal internecine struggle known as the Peloponnesian War. All that the Greeks had built their view of communal life upon was destroyed. A loss of faith in every established custom of justice and conduct, whether it was handed down by some ancient law-giver (a Solon or a Lycurgus), or derived from the gods themselves, began to sour souls. There was little justice in daily dealings between people in Grecian communities. Authority assumed an arbitrary cast, and power fell to the strong.

Into this turbulent world came the Sophists, who offered society a new ethical outlook. The Sophists claimed that social relationships were wholly conventional; that, in fact, nothing like a universal and objective basis had ever existed; people had simply formed social compacts, agreeing to protect themselves from the encroachments that were inevitable once mankind got entangled in material pursuits. People were, by nature, selfish and egoistic, they said, driven by personal inclinations and whims. It was not natural for them to form social communities; when they did, it was only because people saw these as their only source of long-term benefit and hope. In the final Sophist analysis: "All alike took their stand on the complete absence of absolute values and standards... All human action was regarded...as based on experience alone and dictated by nothing but expediency."[9]

Socrates, to the contrary, insisted on absolute and universal standards; but he would allow only those derived from individual consciences, which would prove them to be the product of inherent reason. On this score, Socrates shared the Sophist's view of "man as the measure of all things." Yet he departed from them on his definition of the way to attain this. The Sophist claimed that subjective factors—personal

9 W. K. C. Guthrie, *The Greek Philosophers: From Thales to Aristotle* (New York: Harper, 1960), p 7.

feelings and experiences—were the basis of moral behavior. But Socrates rightly saw that the feelings and experiences of any individual cannot guarantee a universal point of view.

We must transcend mere sense perception and consult the principle that is universal in us all, he said; we must turn to reason. An ordered society is not possible unless we subjugate the influence of the senses, for the senses will only lead us to motives of a purely selfish kind. Sense perceptions are material and, as such, limit the outlook of the individual on himself. He will not take the social point of view; he will refuse to act on behalf of a community. Consequently, we must not base a social order on personal perceptions; we have to have faith in the inherent powers of the intellect to discover the true principles of justice and community.

But Socrates' appeal to reason is at best merely formal. He cannot say what this universal point of view involves, or what rules require absolute submission. He can't give any specifics on the matter, for fear that one person's perspective will intrude on another's. All he can say is that all of us ought to live in accord with reason, and so by a universally absolute standard of conduct. In each particular circumstance, however, he isn't able to say how that standard should apply, and his inability to do so reveals the flaw in Socrates' thought: his insistence that each ought to live according to the dictates of his own conscience.

With each person's reason as an infallible guide to life and conduct, Socrates said, the consulting of reason alone was sufficient. The irony in this compelled Socrates to allow each individual to follow his private convictions after all; he had to tolerate, in other words, a principle of *self*-interest in human conduct. Anything less would amount to servitude and debasement, to him, because what was at stake was the freedom to live entirely by one's own lights. So Socrates lets each person decide on his or her own behalf, in each situation, which actions are good or bad, just or unjust. To tell somebody else what to do would be to sacrifice that person's independence and depart from the authority of reason. And didn't Socrates see the departure from reason as the root of the problem in the first place?

Instead of relying on the truth within their souls, the Greeks had relied too much on past customs, he thought, or had placed too much faith in the wisdom of their founders. But we are bound to ask, How could Socrates' perspective offer a solution? As it turned out, the discovery of genuine universal principles depended upon each person's private assent to them. Socrates simply *believed* we could live by reason—and therefore absolute standards—if we could be properly persuaded. Reality tends to throw cold water on such naïveté.

So the Socratic problem required an even more pure solution. Could a way be found to maintain the authority of reason, which is also the authority of inner absolutes, and still allow for the autonomy of each person? Enter Plato. His entire philosophy represents his conviction that he had indeed discovered *the way*. So we shouldn't be astonished at his conclusions.

From the start, Plato "shared with Socrates...two fundamental characteristics, a faith in the possibility of knowledge and a conviction of the need for absolute moral standards."[10] He agreed that an objective standard was necessary to insure the compliance of every person to a certain sort of behavior. This ethical authority had to extend to everyone alike, if a genuine community were to be possible. Socrates had failed by not formulating a *state* concept to embody his ideal of authority. Plato set about to rectify this. His resolution of the Socratic problem turned into a political arrangement which would elevate the state to the status of highest importance in both social and ethical realms. The community must take precedence over all, Plato's ultimate maxim might read, *and the state is the community*.

But Plato was no philistine. Far from it! His interest wasn't in simply imposing an undisguised tyranny. His approach

10 Guthrie, p 71.

was too subtle—the approach of one who means to persuade us that what he has in mind is "just" and for the good of all. To achieve his end in the most compelling way, he couched his state program in the language of philosophy, science, knowledge, metaphysics, and epistemology. In short, he tried to persuade others by rational means that they ought to entrust themselves to his vision. They must be prepared, of course, to reorient their thinking from the bottom up, for Plato was persuaded that "No real reform of the fundamentals of political thought could take place without a corresponding reform of men's ideas about the whole nature of reality."[11]

One curse of our sinful nature is a tendency to couch our political ideals in terms of a total vision for all of life. People therefore have to undergo something like a spiritual conversion in order to see the need for the sort of state-ordered society Plato envisioned. He believed that by rationally demonstrating that the good of the state had to become the purpose behind everybody's actions, he could convince them that the state constituted the essence of justice. Once this was accomplished, he could proceed to explain how the best state should be constructed in order to guard it against internal and external threats.

For the most part, Plato presented the substance of his program for man and the state in the *Republic*, a dialogue whose opening confidently declares that it is not only desirable, but altogether possible, to eradicate evil from human life. Its "gospel" proclaims that when each person sees the need to promote the interests of the state, and those absolutely, then his or her life will be made safe and secure, and the communal welfare increased.

Every possible activity one might engage in—painting a picture, starting a school, buying a house, going to church, writing a book—received its justification to the degree that

11 Guthrie, p 84.

it enhanced the good of the state. In the language of humanism, the good of the state means "the common good." But putting Plato's humanist jargon aside, the question of the good of the state devolves to, Who defines it? Plato was not as confident as Socrates that all were, at least potentially, capable of rising, by rational persuasion, to *his* level of universal ethical conduct. So where could you expect to discover the truth?

Plato was as convinced as Socrates that reason was the only infallibly divine source of truth and righteousness. He, too, believed that by the powers of unaided reason we could come to a knowledge of goodness and justice. He accepted the essential divinity of the soul, which we need only tend in order to have a lamp for our feet and a light to our paths.

But if he was in agreement with Socrates on this point (yet on the whole less sanguine about human nature), where did Plato expect to find an answer to the question of who should decide the good of the state? Undaunted, Plato thought in purely aristocratic, which is to say, elitist terms. Only those special natures, equipped with the requisite intellectual abilities, as well as the requisite and proper training (the *Republic* is largely a treatise on education), would be placed in positions of absolute authority. These men, properly endowed by nature and conditioning, according to the Platonic ideal—fit vessels, as it were—should be the ones to determine the common good, as well as exercise the power to achieve that good in life.

Plato's ideal state reflects his hope of having superior intellects, like himself, decide for everyone what is just or unjust, good or evil, solely by their supposed intellectual superiority. At bottom in Plato, then, is an ethical and political ideal that gives total sovereignty to government experts and social planners who know better than others how to achieve the good of society. The moral vision of socialism always begins with the assumption of the "ultimacy of the moral consciousness of man," and ends with a few men controlling others absolutely—and then speaks of the whole setup as justice!

Plato's central purpose in the *Republic* is to persuade us to believe that unless we accept his prescription of sovereignty we won't be able to prevent society's degeneration. He skillfully arranges each argument, masterfully contorts each tidbit of reasoning, to pressure us to give way. It is for our own good, his chief spokesman Socrates intimates, to embrace rigid class distinctions, and obey all authority, ethical as well as political, descending from superior reason at the top. Plato tries to con us into believing that those rulers will exercise their responsibilities with perfect justice, since they will be guided at all times by infallible insight into the highest ethical obligation—the "idea of the Good."

We have to suppose that his elite will get its principles for ruling from a superior grasp of the "forms" that serve as universal and objective standards. Then they supposedly won't exercise their authority for selfish ends, or motives of personal gain, but by reasoned insight into the Good as such. It would be disastrous, of course, to hinder the application of their insight by constitutional guarantees or other legal niceties designed to protect the governed from misrule. To fetter the elite with anything like the "rule of law" would only limit their potential. They must be free to act according to their insights, and so lead social policy in whatever direction they deem necessary. Finally, then, we reach the apex of Plato's concept of sovereignty: the will of man.

Only totalitarians recognize no authority for human conduct beyond one's conscience. Plato may have believed that he had found an objective principle of authority in the "idea of the Good," but it was, in fact, an entirely formal authority; and entirely empty. The Good was itself a product of the mind of man, for men supply the actual substance (Universal Form) of what is to be Good. In application, then, Plato's concept of sovereignty relies on the discretionary will of *greater* minds at the top. And as those minds change, so can the definition of good.

For Christians, good must be the will of God. They must confess that His will is their ultimate authority. The will of God should be no less applicable to politics and social policy than to personal behavior. Anything less leaves us at the mercy of the will of sinful inventions of men. It is the arrogant assumption of socialist thinkers, everywhere and always, that their view alone presents a realistic option; Christianity is forever pie-in-the-sky, they complain.

The extent in our day to which Christians have accepted this assumption is the extent to which Platonic ideals still hold sway in society.

The Rule of Law & Tradition

The ideal of Plato's sovereignty, while pervasive throughout Western history, has never been received in the pure form in which Plato envisioned it. The acceptance or rejection of Plato's social program has always depended on whether men were willing to accept his entire philosophical outlook, including its metaphysics and epistemology. It is probably fair to say that these last gained little headway with serious thinkers beyond the ancient world, at least on the surface of things. And a good number of his socio-ethical expostulations about establishing philosopher-kings have been regarded as hare-brained, if not downright immoral. You need merely think of his thesis on the community of wives, or on the communistic ownership of goods,[12] to get an idea of where his philosophy ends.

Yet Plato's central thought—that certain superior men ought to have charge of all others for the good of society—has never slackened in its appeal to intellectuals and social revolutionaries. His idea that some men should rule absolutely is based on the fatuous concept that since nature has endowed some men with greater insight into what is good for everybody, these men don't need the approval of those they rule. In the words of Leo Strauss, a latter-day defender

12 *Cf* Frank E. and Fritzie P. Manuel, *Utopian Thought in the Western World* (Cambridge: Belknap Press, 1979), pp 104-114.

of Plato's thesis, "...the wise rulers ought not to be responsible to their unwise subjects. To make the rule of the wise dependent on election by the unwise or consent of the unwise would mean to subject what is by nature higher to control by what is by nature lower, i.e., to act against nature."[13]

Because Plato can't conceive of any higher source of authority than what is generated from the interior self, he assumes that the "highest human type"—the one with fully developed reason—should be given the authority to direct not only society, but the totality of life within every level of it. He takes it for granted that putting power in the hands of specialists will not lead to tyranny or arbitrary authority, since this elite will always perceive and enact the Good.

Modern socialism derives from these suppositions of Plato. Though the socialist may not accept every plank in Plato's platform, most contemporary non-Christians believe in the essential ultimacy and infallibility of Plato's "moral consciousness of man." So it is still a common belief that the good society is possible if a scientific blueprint is applied to it by superior intellects. The ethical assumptions are the same for modern socialism as for Plato: that we need only look within ourselves to find the source for whatever behavior we declare to be good or evil, right or wrong. Plato believed that a society could a priori be planned and constructed so that in the end the epithet "just" would describe it exactly. With the proper elite in charge, that would be accomplished. What we have, then, is a set of beliefs based on the ideals that rise from Babel—a man-centered and man-glorifying culture.

An altogether different tradition from Plato's creation took hold in the West: the rule of the law. This tradition gained supremacy because of the spread and triumph in the West of Christian doctrine. That the ideal of the rule of law still finds adherents among modern humanists only demonstrates the

13 Leo Strauss, *Natural Right and History* (Chicago: Univ of Chicago Press, 1953), p 141.

extent to which their thinking has been influenced by Christian morality. From that morality rose the concept of the equality in sin of all men; it destroyed the notion that some few possess a natural ethical superiority over others, and so should rule. When Christianity spread in the West, it set in place the foundation of true justice: every specific human authority is subject to God's absolute authority. In particular, "the principle of justice for all...[was] based on the principle of God's final judgment on all"[14]

This new concept of justice was based on the universal law-order of God; that His law alone is the unchanging stability on which civilization can be built. True justice is effective only when it is applied universally; Socrates understood that much. But he believed reason to be a divine guide that would lead him toward universal justice. Under Christian influence, however, the rule of law claims that human beings have no such capacity in themselves, and need the authority of revelation to instruct them in the truth. Naturally, this alters the pagan notion of sovereignty. Sovereignty resides in God alone, and each person must give a separate account to Him.

At the heart of the rule of law, then, is the understanding that law does not rise from within human beings, but from without: from Holy Scripture, which supplies a truly objective principle of conduct. It alone promises to unite the interests of all of us with our neighbor, for its covenant framework is inclusive of all of life. It does not separate material life from moral obligations and spirituality. To insure complete obedience, the Lord God promised complete blessings. Further, the biblical command of obedience includes *self-control* within each person's conscience. It demands, in the first place, self-government.

But we aren't permitted to suppose that this is a private

14 North, *Moses and Pharaoh*, p 196.

affair. As North points out: "Self-government under God's law is the primary form of government in every sphere: civil government, family government, church government, economic government."[15] So the motive of the Christian ideal of law originally meant self-government in every aspect of social and cultural life. This reinforces the rule of law as a restraining influence over human authority, including authority over one's self, or autonomy. Its concept of justice contains the inextricable feature of righteousness; this is the justice of God above all else. It denies us the right to exercise our sinful inclinations under any circumstance, whether public or private. For Christians, injustice is a direct result of rebellion against God; His sovereign authority is the final arbiter of every delegated authority given to man. In all respects, then, we should act in accordance with what God says, and not by what we suppose to be good for ourselves.

The Christian law-ideal provides the religious foundation for the western concept of the rule of law. Beginning with the rise of modern science, however, when thinkers tended to believe in an autonomous *reason* freed from the framework of the Christian religion, submitting to no authority outside the mind of man, the concept of the rule of law was gradually emptied of its Christian presuppositions, and men scurried to find a source for it other than divine revelation.

By the time of the Enlightenment, the concept of human law per se was dissociated from any higher law structure, even though "natural law" continued to serve as a formal idea of the origin of law. Nature became emptied of moral substance until all that remained was a concept of *legality*. God's law as the transcendent source of law had been rejected, and justice no longer stood for righteousness in the biblical sense.

The rule of law was no longer attributed to God. It was viewed instead as a natural principle that evolved, as man evolved, from the state of nature, through tribes, then into

15 *Moses and Pharaoh*, p 204.

modern, diversified society. Law was thought to rise from the perception that one's quality of life would be enhanced by it. So the rule of law began to take on a definition supplied wholly by man. The result was an exclusively utilitarian ethic, though there was one absolute to which it did do service—individual liberty! The exercise of this "moral absolute" of liberty came to define the nature of truth itself. At the same time, though, its entire premise was opposed to authority. The natural outcome of this trend reduced the rule of law to mere instrumental status, the tool of every ideology climbing toward power.

I won't trace in detail the development of the modern secular doctrine of law, but want to examine one of its latest models in the thought of F. A. Hayek, who is probably this century's best interpreter of that law's original "liberal" concept. Hayek, however, doesn't merely recount its original formulation; he recasts that formulation in the light of modern sociological and economic hypotheses, and so renders the rule of law compatible with twentieth century civilization. That at least is his ostensible purpose, but there are a number of crucial questions. Can his essentially secular doctrine of law, for instance, provide an alternative to the socialist morass into which popular culture has descended? Does it rest on a moral foundation sufficient to challenge the humanist belief in the ultimacy of the moral consciousness of man? Or is it just another form of stones for bread?

What is perhaps most appealing about the kind of liberalism we find in Hayek is his conviction that socialism, in virtually whatever guise it takes on, is not merely a mistaken policy but will quite simply end civilization as we know it. It is not surprising, then, that Christians turn to him as an ally in their struggle against the Babelization of culture that socialism portends. And there is much in Hayek that is amenable to a Christian point of view; most especially, he rejects the notion that some people are ethically and intellectually superior to others, and ought therefore to regulate them. He believes that all should be governed by the rule of law; government, that is, should be limited by law. It should be bounded by known and general principles that are agreed upon by all, and to which all equally submit, including those who administer government.

Every person should be free to act as he sees fit, restricted only by regulations that apply to each alike and without prejudice. In Hayek's view, "It is...of the essence of the rule of law that the private citizen and his property should not...be means at the disposal of government."[16] He knew that socialism threatens the sanctity of property, and consequently threatens entrepreneurial initiative, which is the only basis of what he, following Adam Smith, termed the "Great Society."

Nevertheless, in Hayek's explanation of how the consciousness of obedience to the law arose in the first place, we see serious differences between his and the Christian point of view. We have to recognize that in the original analysis, Hayek does not really begin on a different premise from Plato: the ultimacy of the moral consciousness of man. And so his view stands feeble-kneed against humanist ambition, with its statist religion, in spite of his masterful confutations of every humanist argument.

If we consider his essential criticism of socialism, or the reason for its failure, we immediately become aware of his secularism: "All the totalitarian doctrines, of which socialism is merely the noblest and most influential...are false, not because of the values on which they are based, but because of a misconception of the forces which have made the Great Society and civilization possible."[17] The widespread acceptance of socialism's central tenets, he says, should be seen as a failure in the reasoning process of deciphering and explaining the forces that have shaped modern, complex society. The problem of those attracted to socialism is not moral, he says,

16 Friederich A. Hayek, *The Constitution of Liberty* (Chicago: Univ of Chicago Press, 1960), p 214.

17 Friederich A. Hayek, *Law, Legislation and Liberty* (Chicago: Univ of Chicago Press, 1973), Vol I, "Rules and Order," p 6.

but rational. Or, rather, irrational. Socialism's success is not due to the great numbers of people who believe in its ethical premise, but from conclusions incorrectly drawn from scientific analyses of social processes.

Nowhere does he say that socialism derives from an ethos that presupposes a set of assumptions about what is good or evil, just or unjust. He would be loathe to admit that socialism rises from the spirit of Babel that fills every covenant breaker with the motivation to build towers of the kingdom of man—socialism being only the latest manifestation. We may agree that socialists are ignorant of the way in which economics works, but their ignorance is the fruit of a religious rejection of the God who created them. Any misconceptions of how societal life is meant to function are due to the values socialists have adopted. They believe that no actual God exists, and that the world is certainly not dependent on His will. Human creatures, then, are to create their own world.

The acceptance of socialism's ideals can't be attributed simply to a failure in reason to recognize the forces at work, but to self-conscious *religious* assumptions that define the nature of man, society, the world, its purpose, and the ultimate ends of all human behavior.

We need, however, to understand the difference between Hayek's explanation for the formation of modern societies and the explanations of socialist dogma. Hayek feels obliged, because of the basic misunderstanding in the socialist mind, to explain how ancient society—the society of tribe and chieftain—evolved into the modern industrial, Great Society. Here is the crucial fulcrum to his thinking. An explanation of how modern, complex societies have emerged will influence one's view of the central and primary role that reason has played, and may continue to play, in its further unfolding. And it is the issue of reason's role that sets Hayek's view against that of socialism. From this confrontation, Hayek means to demonstrate the misplaced confidence we have in supposing that science, unaided, can mastermind social reality. He believes that the underlying misconception of socialist theory stems, in part, from its presumption that modern society is the deliberate result of a conceptual design.

Socialist theorizers have more or less explicitly assumed the basic infallibility of man in knowing every detail of societal life from beginning to end, and our capability of tailoring those details to achieve a desired outcome. This is what Plato believed. There's no doubt that socialist reasoning begins from the same conviction: society has been generated from a blueprint in the minds of superior intelligences who, with obvious prescience, foresaw every specific factor of life, and so were enabled to construct "perfect," or near perfect, social relationships. This conviction rests on the faith that others know what is good for you better than you, and must take charge in engineering an overall outcome. Hayek refers to this presumption as the constructivist fallacy.

He brings his logical powers to bear against this. He calls it the presumption of omniscience. It proceeds on the assumption that every fact can be known in advance, and it is therefore possible to arrange them in accordance with a predetermined plan. In veiled terms, he charges the socialist theorizer with playing at God. So Christians certainly should empathize with Hayek's statement: "The chief reason why modern man has become so unwilling to admit that the constitutional limitations of his knowledge form a permanent barrier to the possibility of a rational construction of the whole of society is his unbounded confidence in the power of science."[18] But how does one account for this unbounded confidence in the power of science, one might ask, apart from the system of values every secularist holds? There is no real scientific explanation for the attitude, nor does Hayek provide one; he simply denies its validity.

It is the religious disposition of constructivists which leads them to believe that no limitations should be placed on reason. That religious disposition is the urge of all rebels everywhere to replace God's design for life with a construc-

18 *Law, Legislation and Liberty*, p 15.

tion of their own. It is, further, an expression of assumed divinity to submit yourself to a moral order of your own design. For this reason, secularists always believe "that human reason is so powerful that it allows us to soar above our civilization and to judge our rules and values in some 'scientific' or objective way, and that we can produce a better civilization by completely redesigning them."[19] The citizens of Babel wanted to instigate their own civilization, and that same spirit lives in the constructivism of modern socialists.

Hayek's chief concern with this faith has to do with what a constructed society inevitably becomes. When planners fabricate a society to achieve certain results, the society always comes to rest on a "relation of command and obedience, or a hierarchical structure of the whole of society in which the will of superiors, and ultimately of some single supreme authority, determines what each individual must do."[20] Constructivism, to be blunt, leads to totalitarianism, because when a society comes to rest on the sovereign will of man, soon it will rest on the will of the strongest one. Hayek rightly deplores this oppressive state of affairs. Those who preach its virtues haven't a single historical example to point to.

Predestined societies permit only the few to have unlimited power over the lives of all the rest. Hayek knows from history what Christians should know on principle: that unchecked power in the hands of sinful and willful people only fosters an illusion of righteousness and omnipotence. His solution is to establish the rule of law to limit the arbitrary exercise of power and coercion. But his humanistic explanation of the emergence of the rule of law can't sufficiently counter our innate, sinful desire for arbitrary power and control. To get to this you have to examine fully Hayek's theory of the origins and development of modern society.

19 Eamon Butler, *Hayek: His Contribution to the Political and Economic Thought of our Time* (New York: Universe Books, 1985), p 34.
20 *Law, Legislation and Liberty*, p 36.

He plainly rejects the assumption that social order is capable of being *made*. It is the result, he says, of spontaneous and impersonal evolutionary forces whose overall outcome could not have been predicted by anyone, let alone orchestrated. It seems obvious to him that the achievement of modern society involved complexities impossible to fathom, much less devise. Hayek argues for order that he says has *grown*. Stated differently, modern society is the product of "individual elements adapting themselves to circumstances which directly affect only some of them, and in which their totality need not be known to anyone..."[21]

If, in the course of time, the actions of some tended to have repercussions on the actions of others, neither could know exactly what the total effect would be. The inherent limitations of our knowledge about the outcome of our actions, which issue from the different goals each person pursues, require that we all work together if we wish to further our purposes, Hayek supposes. And so human civilization becomes possible with the observance of rules of conduct that everyone gradually accepts, but which no one especially thought up. We don't need to know the results of our actions, only the rules that everyone agreed should govern the way those results were to be achieved. It wasn't so much the outcome that mattered, then, as how we played the game. A rules-oriented behavior allows everyone to plan his own life and pursue his own interests, rather than to submit to what somebody else demands.

In Hayek's explanation, this rules-oriented behavior came about as a result of "natural selection." Men learned the value of actions by trial and error. Like any animal, man discovered methods that worked to his advantage, and when he did, he didn't hesitate to adopt them. If certain arrangements proved disadvantageous, they were discarded. So the idea that rules

21 *Law, Legislation and Liberty*, p 41.

should regulate behavior and determine what is just is the product "of the evolutionary selection of different groups of men with different systems of rules, and exists because they help particular groups to survive and prosper better than others, not because they have been decreed by anyone."[22] Or, in Hayek's own words, "These rules of conduct have thus not developed as the recognized conditions for the achievement of a known purpose, but have evolved because the groups who practiced them were more successful and displaced others."[23]

What we learn, then, from Hayek's theory of the origins of modern society is that the evolutionary process is our ultimate social fact; it is, at the same time, our ultimate ethical fact. The evolutionary process is our only environment, the source of all values. Our most essential need is to come to terms with this, Hayek says, and we must realize that our life and the society in which we were born are simply artifacts of randomly evolving cultural and social forces. We can change things to a certain extent, but only in a highly limited sphere—our own. Although choices and decisions are made by millions of people at every moment, affecting the overall picture, the complete environment itself is *impersonal.* The social evolutionary process is indeterminate, indeterminable, with no set of values, no foundation on which to rest. "The maxims of morality in no way presuppose an authority, human or divine, from which they emanate..."[24] Our values issue from the evolutionary process, according to Hayek, and are therefore subject to permanent transience.

Does this mean we are somehow helpless in the situation, at the mercy of relativism? To Hayek, not at all. We have been endowed with a wonderful gift for adapting to constantly changing social configurations. "The Great Society," he

22 Butler, p 30.
23 *Law, Legislation and Liberty*, p 18.
24 John Gray, *Hayek on Liberty*, p 33.

says, "and the civilization it has made possible is the product of man's growing capacity to communicate abstract thought; and when we say that what all men have in common is their reason we mean their common capacity for abstract thought."[25] Because of this "common capacity," this reason, Hayek believes that we can build self-regulating social structures to give form to changing experience, whether in language, statutes, or moral norms. With our capacity for abstract thought, we can integrate the social behavior of millions, even if no agreed-upon purpose governs our actions. Hayek's rules do not connote explicit commands; but since they are a product of our common capacity for abstract thought, we submit to them as "universal" norms.

Can this Hayekian liberal scheme deliver the goods? It isn't Hayek's belief in the superiority of regulated behavior that troubles me, nor his insistence that law alone liberates us from those who wish to manufacture a society that conforms to their vision of what is good for us; it's his explanation of the basis of law and of obedience. In human behavior, especially when it affects others, Hayek believes that principle should take precedence over arbitrariness and expediency. He believes that society requires an ideal of justice to live by, if people don't want to find themselves at the mercy of manipulators of power. And he believes he has found that ideal in the rule of law. Yet by his own admission, the social evolutionary process cannot come up with anything like an overarching moral norm.

Whatever ethical values arise are mere conventions, meant to meet the needs of the moment. When those needs change, a new set of norms will be necessary. Usefulness determines legitimacy. Hayek and all liberals are utilitarian. Hayek holds what one might call an indirect or consequent concept of utility; that is, we adopt rules of behavior for their welfare-

25 *Law, Legislation and Liberty*, p 33.

enhancing effect. So to test for a specific set of norms, we decide whether or not the effect "maximizes an individual's chance of achieving his unknown purpose."[26] Social order à la Hayek, then, does not depend on absolutes that stipulate how we ought to act from the outset.

He would like to see a respect for law in our modern social attitude, but will not accept a transcendent source of law. The substance of law must be entirely subjective in nature for him, because it derives solely from that welfare-maximizing function. The trouble here is that the perception of one's welfare is just that—one's perception. No law exists to define a person's welfare from the start. There is no standard by which to judge the actions or interests we pursue, and nothing to distinguish righteous law from unrighteous law. So if we adopt rules of behavior entirely on the basis of their utility, what is to prevent us, in the words of Frederic Bastiat, from making "the conversion of the law into an instrument of plunder?"[27] If law itself isn't rooted in an absolute and transcendent standard of justice, what will hinder constructivist designers from using it for their utility?

I'm certain that Hayek would call constructivist law the antithesis of justice, but by what right does he do that, if it maximizes constructivists' welfare? They can excuse themselves by claiming to adhere to the rule of law when they are actually redefining justice to mean whatever they want. As Bastiat says, "There is in all of us a strong disposition to believe that anything lawful is also legitimate. This belief is so widespread that many persons have erroneously held that things are 'just' because law makes them so."[28]

The observance of law certainly must be useful, but it cannot be the product of usefulness per se without its becoming an instrument for promoting whatever anyone takes to

26 Gray, p 60.
27 Frederic Bastiat, *The Law* (New York: Foundation for Economic Education, 1984), p 12.
28 *The Law*, p 13.

be useful. There has to be a distinction between righteous and unrighteous use. Christians must accept God's definition of what is useful in terms of absolute principles of good and evil, just and unjust. What's more, Christians should never countenance the notion that sinful people will ever come up with anything but self-serving principles. God's law provides the only sufficient foundation for law; it applies universally and is therefore able to unite the behavior of all on the base of a common ideal. God's law tells us what is *useful*, and so what is *lawful*. And since it is His law, it is enforced with His sanction—a far more powerful inducement to obey than any offered by a utilitarian concept of law. And adherence to God's law frees us from the dictates of those who think their vision of justice is the one required by society.

If Hayek wants to see a universal norm applied to social behavior, he has to affirm the objectivity of law. In this respect, there is one ethical presupposition that he does accept—individual liberty. But because he will not accept any universal principle that transcends mankind, his concept of liberty is merely negative. What it really means is freedom from coercion by others. And since that law lacks positive moral content, we can be sure that fallen sinners will soon be pouring that content in.

Anything can be justified in the name of liberty. Even tyranny, if you make truth relative to what you want. Here, too, then, Hayek stands for the ultimacy of the moral consciousness of man. To achieve liberty, he says, the best we can do is to apply the "Kantian universalizability test." That is, we should act "only on that maxim through which one can at the same time will that it should become a universal law."[29] Act, In other words, *as if* your actions were to become, through your will, a universal law.

Could the humanist ethic be better stated? Hayek thought

29 Immanuel Kant, *Foundation of the Metaphysics of Morals*, trans Lewis White Beck (Indianapolis: Bobbs-Merrill, 1976), p 39.

the above meant that you should do your duty regardless of the outcome. He didn't want to attribute justice or injustice to social ends; he would say, rather, that certain rules of just behavior delimit social action, but benefit no one in particular. Justice stands indifferent "to the inequalities in men's initial endowments and material fortunes."[30] He correctly observes that government otherwise has too much discretionary power to determine whatever social outcomes some may want on their own behalf. To put it plainly, government can produce socialism. And yet Hayek's only objection to socialism is that it is a detriment to economic efficiency and the liberty to increase one's welfare. So economic efficiency becomes the sole criterion of what is just. But without the word of God, economic efficiency can mean anything anyone wants it to mean.

The result is always an economic inefficiency that parades as justice: a few men seeking to manipulate others for their own selfish gain.

30 Gray, p 72.

EIGHT

THE QUESTION OF THE PUBLIC GOOD

MOST OF US are quite certain we know where true happiness lies and how to get it. This certainty distinguishes our ethics as belonging either to the kingdom of man or to the kingdom of God. Another facet of the ethics of socialism, in its pursuit of economics (and jurisprudence as well), is the question of The Public Good. Just as the question of sovereignty pits the ultimacy of the moral consciousness of man against God's law as the highest authority, so in considering the public good, we tend to suppose that the basis of our happiness is exempt from God's covenant requirement that we seek *His* kingdom first. Transforming a Christian state into a modern "care" state requires finding an ethical substitute to replace God's revealed will, and we begin to rely on our own ethical wisdom.

As the modern world forged an increasingly secular outlook on life, that ethical substitute came sharply into focus. In the eighteenth century, the era of the Enlightenment, utilitarianism was widely welcomed. It inaugurated a new ideal of social and public justice—one that today is taken for granted, and has become the conventional wisdom of intellectuals and others who scramble for positions of power. The ethical doctrine of *utility* has become not only the implied but the stated frame of reference by which we view any concern for the welfare of humankind. All that remains, then, according to utilitarians, is to manipulate the machinery of politics to insure its successful dictates.

At the beginning of this book, I quoted Mises, who said that socialism is the watchword and catchword of our day, and that "the socialist idea dominates the modern spirit." In one sense he was merely paying tribute to the obvious: an ethical change had gained such general acceptance it hardly gave pause for reflection. Mises is saying that a transformation so thorough has come about in the moral sensibilities of our society that we've almost ceased to be aware of it. What is now orthodoxy was at one time, of course, heresy. Capitalism and socialism have switched places. Capitalism, it is now believed, cannot possibly deliver happiness or well-being, nor self-esteem, while socialism produces equality, eliminates poverty, and promotes peace for all. This change in popular belief requires an explanation.

Though it may seem ironic, the roots of our national conversion to socialism were prepared in the past, in the soil that secular historical scholarship alleges to be the seedbed of capitalism itself. This is a remarkable confusion. The doctrine of utilitarianism, which came into being alongside what we know as the Industrial Revolution (credited with the beginnings of capitalism), is said to be the ideological corollary of that revolution. Its ethical premises supposedly nurtured the dogma of laissez-faire, with its dog-eat-dog individualism and self-aggrandizement.

Adam Smith's theory of the "invisible hand" takes its cue, these scholars theorize, from this ethical system. And we can see, they say, the result: capitalism at that stage engendered widespread poverty and social unrest. A handful acquired great riches, and did this by exploiting impoverished masses. Utilitarianism, as the ideological justification of capitalism, bred cold and heartless economic practices. Every social evil of the present day descends from it. We may be thankful, they say, that we have outgrown utilitarianism's brand of thinking and reached a better ethical basis upon which to build culture. Their argument goes on something like that.

As an ethical theory, however, utilitarianism was the fox in the hen house. Its appearance in the minds of many of that day demonstrates an already incipient anticapitalism, which in the long run produced the outlook on government and society that destroyed capitalism. Even more, utilitarianism didn't begin as the ethics of downtrodden classes, or the proletariat, but as the social ethic of an intelligentsia. Which is why it is often seen, mistakenly, as the ethic of capitalism.

At its heart is a secularism at war with Christianity. It exudes hatred for any social, economic, or political order that cannot be justified in terms of *self*-defined wants—an order fashioned, in other words, with the specific purpose of augmenting our happiness in the here and now, without reference to God. Utilitarians said that it was possible to increase material well-being by dissociation from everything to do with "higher" ends. Utilitarianism encouraged a belief in the things of this world alone, and feigned indifference to a transcendent basis for moral behavior.

The church retreated from this advancing system of secular values. One may indeed point to pietistic revivals during this period, but their cumulative effect did nothing to turn society from its secular course. In fact, it was during this period that the church itself, by its capitulation to higher criticism and philosophical rationalism, adopted a humanist stance. With some study you will find that the assault on historic Christianity was carried on as virulently from within the church as without, and more so: her trained clergy did more damage than the entire scientific community. The church lost faith in the doctrine written down for all the saints, and came to accept instead the ethics of humanism; and humanism was dominated by the utilitarian outlook.

Today matters are, if anything, worse. Few Christians feel any compunction to call in question the humanist assumptions that govern our ideas of society and public justice. The church has surrendered its territorial obligations to a modern god-state. The gargantuan control the state has usurped over the lives of its citizens is hardly ever disputed in principle. For most, the problem is simply to get government to become more *responsible.*

But the problem runs deeper, because an entirely secular engine is driving it. To understand exactly what this means for the Christian, he or she must examine the foundations of utilitarianism, and the best way is to begin with the cornerstone of the modern liberal state—the philosophy of John Locke (1632-1704)—to view the process of secularization that has produced socialist values.

John Locke

In the prefatory remarks to his outstanding book, *The European Mind*, the French historian Paul Hazard writes of a phenomenal transformation in western civilization:

> Never was there a greater contrast, never a more sudden transition than this! An hierarchical system ensured by authority; life firmly based on dogmatic principle—such were the things held dear by the people of the seventeenth century; but these—controls, authority, dogmas, and the like—were the very things that their immediate successors of the eighteenth held in cordial detestation. The former were upholders of Christianity; the latter were its foes. The former believed in the laws of God; the latter in the laws of Nature; the former lived contentedly enough in a world composed of unequal social grades; of the latter the one absorbing dream was Equality.[1]

The turn from seventeenth to eighteenth century brought an upheaval to the ideals of Western culture. The medieval world had been in decline; its Christian values-system was assailed everywhere by anti-Christian attitudes. The complete Christianity Hazard describes was lumped with the ancients into a category of principles that had outlived their usefulness, not to mention credibility. Philosopher-kings attempted to replace Christianity with a new ethos, one they could justify by principles deduced from human experience

1 Paul Hazard, *The European Mind, 1680-1715* (New York: World Publishing, 1969), p xv.

alone. At the center of life, man replaced God—this far in advance of the theory of evolution, which came along later to minds prepared for it. The change was no minor affair, no mere modification; it was rather a revolution. It elicited a vehemence and vituperation toward Christianity unlike any since ancient Rome attempted to prevent the Christian view from undermining its own.

It is surely right to begin with Locke; more than anyone, he clarified the parameters of the modern liberal state. Other thinkers, notably Montesquieu and Rousseau, deserve credit here as well, but their ideas did not express, as well as those of Locke, liberalism in its purest form. It is largely overlooked that significant portions of the writings of this trio, especially Rousseau, fit into the pattern of socialism. And a thinker like Hobbes does not properly belong to this coterie; if anything he represents a precursor. His thinking was too imbued with the absolutist notions of the middle seventeenth century.[2] For the full development of liberal doctrine to take place it took the pen of a ready and waiting writer, John Locke.

Better than any thinker of his day, he devised a theory of the liberal state that also contained a definition of Public Good. This definition has had more lasting effect than any in Western civilization. Locke also stands athwart the great divide that, as Hazard depicts, separates the seventeenth century from the eighteenth. And because of his position at the onset of the modern age, Locke's thinking represents the amalgam of two contrary worlds: the older world of Christianity now coming under attack, and the newly emerging world of the eighteenth century. When Locke's ideas are misinterpreted, as they often are, it is due to a failure to take his commingling of two world views into account.

Locke customarily uses the newer language of rationalist thought, but his assumptions usually cling to the not yet extinct Christian view. Hazard appreciates this. On the one

2 See his *Leviathan*, for example.

hand, he observes, "The masters and friends of John Locke in England, France, and Holland were Calvinists; his ideas, his arguments are all the products of his Calvinistic studies, and, of course, he supports them with frequent quotations from the Bible." At the same time, Locke's thinking matured under the tutelage of Descartes, as Hazard notes: "Locke made no secret of the debt he owed him..."[3]

Descartes had taught a generation of thinkers to consider nature a closed system in which the pure application of mathematics, a model for "clear and distinct ideas," would unlock all secrets. Nature is a self-governing mechanism, in other words, whose knowledge reason could pierce, beginning at zero and moving ahead on the basis of its autonomous authority. And, of course, to know nature was to control her. But Locke hardly needed Descartes to tell him that; he had already been nourished on the pabulum of Francis Bacon.

Christianity is most pervasive in Locke's monumental *Second Treatise on Civil Government*. The secular dimension is present, to be sure, and that is what a later generation drew from him—and is the only dimension modern scholars ever see. We should focus on the Christian elements.

Locke drafted the *Treatise* in 1680, during the reign of Charles II—a faithful if somewhat cowed Stuart absolutist—primarily as a response to Robert Filmer's *Patriarcha*, a ridiculous defense of monarchical absolutism. Locke's treatise was not published until 1689, after the Glorious Revolution had brought William and Mary to the throne, and it stands as the culmination of Locke's thinking on the origin, nature, and extent of government. Locke felt an obligation to provide the definitive Whig justification for a limited state—one in which law rules above every power, including the monarch. The jurisdiction of government power must not be the arbitrary exercise of any man's discretion, he argues. Government is not a private possession, but

3 *The European Mind*, pp 91 & 130.

a possession of the public, and so must use its legitimate authority only in conjunction with known and stated laws, in the interest of the Public Good. To ground his argument, Locke sets its base on the "nature of things." He makes civil order subservient to the "order of Nature."

And here we have to penetrate the surface to see that Locke was using Christian antecedents to substantiate his concept of the order of nature. The order of nature, for Locke, is created; it is God's order, not some contrivance of human ingenuity. As a created entity, nature takes priority over every civil society; the structure and obligations of society are based on nature's external order. When Locke moves on to the existence and behavior of man in the state of nature, he makes plain that our duties and responsibilities do not derive from the moral authority of government but the preexisting order of nature, which is God's order.

Locke has no special fascination for nature as such, or as an idyllic state despoiled by civil society. His concept of nature is set down to define the extent of government, and one would be mistaken to suppose that he entertains a romantic or simple optimism about nature per se. He views it as an order of things that predetermines human obligations and takes logical precedence over civil associations. He fully expects everybody to form these associations; they, too, derive from the obligations of nature.

But humankind cannot form civil orders in any way it pleases, he would say; it has to base them on the prior demands of the order in creation established by God. When this order is properly established, government becomes our servant and not our lord and master. The order of nature prescribes the *ends* of civil government and defines its powers and responsibilities. And since, by implication, Nature was ordered by God, the obligation of government is to preserve that order in God's interest, not mankind's. Stated broadly, the state is not our ultimate environment; it is part of a larger design created by God.

What responsibilities, then, does nature impose on us? Does it prescribe the basis for the possibility of our welfare?

To understand Locke's view of the public good we have to address these questions, and it is necessary to keep in mind that Locke's idea of nature does not presuppose the secular version of it that arrived later. The premise of nature for him *is* God, the Creator and Ruler of nature. If he didn't always state this with clarity, it nevertheless is his basic assumption.

Locke's idea of nature has been noted for its mildness as well as its harshness. Unlike Hobbes, who held nature to be in a state of unmitigated war, Locke gives cause for optimism as well as pessimism. Nature presents neither a condition of unhindered goodness nor abject evil; it has the potential for both. One great weakness in Locke's thinking was his failure to give any reason why nature should be understood in this way. On one hand, he assumes that nature is fitted for human habitation; its purpose is to benefit mankind. Yet he never rests his reasoning on biblical evidence. He probably supposed, rightly, that most people of his day would agree that the world is the way it is because its architect was God.

On the other hand, it doesn't seem necessary to him to explain why, in the state of nature, societies tend to encroach aggressively on one another. For him this is a fact of life. If he takes sin to be the root of all evil, he doesn't say so. He assumes the people of his day will concur that man is by nature aggressive and prone to plunder his neighbor, and that government must therefore hold every evil propensity in check, so culture can develop in a tolerable fashion.

The order of nature is an order of *reason* and *freedom*. It is a condition of "perfect freedom," Locke says, because in it man can order his actions and dispose of his possessions as he wishes, free of compulsion. It is a state of equality, in Locke's view, but not of license. "The State of Nature has a law of Nature to govern it which obliges everyone—reason is that law..."[4] In Locke's context this means that we are not

4 John Locke, *Two Treatises of Government*, Thomas J. Cook, ed (New York: Harper, 1947), p 123.

merely animals in the state of nature, but are under a law that gives our lives more dimension than mere materiality. Obedience to a higher law gives us purpose, Locke says, and by adding "reason is that law," he is saying that the law of nature is something we can clearly perceive and act on with rational intelligence. We are not simply creatures of impulse or instinct to Locke; we have the capacity to set concrete and practical goals for life and act on them with foresight and purposefulness.

Here is an obvious indication of Locke's high regard for us as God's creatures. This is the indelible imprint of Christianity on his mind. There is a nature in us, Locke believes, that causes us to act as human beings, not beasts. The governing principle of our existence is spiritual, not material. As a transcendent authority, the law of nature teaches us that we ought to attend to our own preservation. Nor does Locke mean by this merely existence, but the preservation of everything that makes life fully human. Which teaches us to attend to the building of culture, for the law of nature informs us that our entire welfare is at stake unless we take intelligent steps to secure it.

And now Locke introduces two essentials of the state of nature that urge us, he says, to act for self-preservation. First he speaks of man in the state of nature as prone to attack his fellow man. Men desire to control their fellow men and the fruits of their labor. Locke does not proceed, as moderns fashionably do, to attempt to psychoanalyze why we behave this way. He is not particularly interested in psychological or sociological causes for such apparently "anti-social" behavior. For him it is a given of life. He seems prepared to accept, as an inherent aspect of human nature, our propensity to violate the laws of nature and reason, and to enter what he calls a state of war. His thought in this regard presupposes the older Christian view in which evil and the hatred of one's neighbor are embedded in our consciousness. For Locke, this adds a considerable urgency to the necessity for our own preservation.

The second feature of the state of nature that compels us

to act, Locke says, is nature's natural scarcity. Any existence in the state of nature is one of poverty; nature has resources but no finished products. There is one method to achieve prosperity: work will sustain life. The pathway to prosperity is in production, not plunder.

It is primarily this first feature—natural aggression and war—that suggests to Locke the need for civil government. He states: "To avoid the state of war...is one great reason of men's putting themselves into society and quitting the state of nature; for where there is an authority, a power on earth from which relief can be had by appeal, there the continuance of the state of war is excluded..." Elsewhere Locke is more emphatic: "Were it not for the corruption and viciousness of degenerate men, there would be no need of any other, no necessity that men should separate from this great and natural community and by positive agreements combine into smaller and divided associations."[5]

Locke never supposes the natural penury of the state of nature to be the cause for combining into civil society; nor does he consider government necessary to enable us to overcome our poverty. For him, the solution to that is in labor! Only intelligent and productive labor can increase the bounty of nature, and thus guarantee the preservation of life. What government can do—indeed, must do—is establish the conditions that make it possible for us to employ our skills and ingenuity in fruitful labor. Any actual good that we achieve never derives directly from government. Government assists indirectly, by providing the social stability within which we, with whatever abilities we possess, gain a greater or lesser degree of prosperity. Civil government is to hinder our natural predilection to rob and plunder. As to this, Locke entertains little doubt that nature will prove obliging.

From this Locke develops his famous (and presently hated) theory of property. Property, for him, is a natural and

5 *Two Treatises*, pp 131 & 185.

inviolable right; a legitimate concomitant of people laboring to surmount nature's penury. Locke does not see property as merely material possessions. We have property in our own person; our labor is our property. Further, "Whatever then [one] removes out of the state that nature hath provided and left it in, he hath mixed his labor with, and joined something that is his own, and thereby makes it his property."[6] So Locke sees interest in one's own welfare as wholesome and natural, not selfish in a pejorative sense.

We labor with the desire to possess the product of our efforts, he would say. If we accumulate possessions, it is because these enable us to preserve our life. In turn, possessions become the means to further effort, for no one can cease his labor and not expect to slip back into the impoverished condition of nature. To threaten us with the loss of property is to threaten us with a serious deprivation of our *person*. Nature provides no other means by which we can increase our well-being. So if we rob someone of his property, we violate not only his estate, but his life and liberty as well. And because of the corruption of human nature, the State of Nature leaves all of us "uncertain and constantly exposed to the invasions of others."[7]

Political society and its attendant controls, then, are formed with a view to the mutual preservation of Life, Liberty, and Estate. A new "social power" must guarantee this mutual preservation. This, for Locke, is finally *The Public Good*. The power of government has only one purpose: to make certain no one's labor is unnaturally impeded, or the fruits of one's labor denied anyone. Social justice is not so much a positive value as the negation of what threatens nature's order. The state of nature may not be a condition of opulence, but it may bring about the relief of poverty. Locke is unable to conceive that, if we apply ourselves diligently,

6 *Two Treatises*, p 134.
7 *Two Treatises*, p 184.

nature will always disappoint us in this regard. He expects, too, that as long as government holds to its proper role, the normal industry of all of us will achieve prosperity.

But before long, as a more secular climate of opinion began to prevail, the view of the role of government in our welfare began to change dramatically, shifting from the view of Locke. We shouldn't wonder that the ground for this was prepared to a considerable extent by Locke himself. Here we observe the non-Christian or eighteenth-century aspect of his thinking. In the *Second Treatise* Locke reasons from the standpoint of the "law of Nature"—a necessary, universal rule of obligation imposed on every man. In his *Essay Concerning Human Understanding*, while Locke tries to retain that absolutist perspective, you will find that, in fact, the groundwork has been laid for a subjective ethic. Perhaps without intending it, Locke seems to have substituted for the order-of-nature outlook in his *Treatise* a relativistic test for human conduct in his *Essay*. And the *Essay*, turning on the philosophy of utility, hands us utilitarianism.

The welfare of all comes to mean what each individual, in response to stimuli of pleasure or pain, regards as advancing his "happiness." In the *Treatise*, Locke subordinates this principle of self-interest to transcendent values: life, liberty, and estate. Our self-interest will not be served, he says, if these are denied us. "Happiness" means the maintenance of these values on each person's behalf; or, in his words, "mutual preservation." In the *Essay*, happiness is isolated from the higher principles governing The Public Good. The only universal principles behind conduct, he says, are pleasure and pain. We are moved by a feeling of "uneasiness." It presses on the psyche, and somehow informs the conscience that what it needs, to achieve some satisfaction or other, is sorely lacking. This urge of uneasiness arouses our desires, and these goad us into action, to get hold of what we lack.

Locke sees this sense of uneasiness as entirely natural to human beings. He doesn't find it necessary to admit that the impulses of desire may have been blackened and corrupted by sin, and therefore may not be trustworthy guides for human conduct. He appears to take for granted that we will act on our desires in a wholly righteous manner. Has he backed from his assumption of the natural degeneracy of man as he proclaimed it in the *Treatise*? Certainly that work contains some of this perspective. The penury of nature awakens an uneasiness in us, inducing in us the desire to relieve our condition. Poverty, as well as our natural corruption, will be experienced by all. It will have the effect of motivating us to seek our own preservation. And Locke would certainly associate the remedy that brings satisfaction with a state of happiness.

Still, it isn't happiness per se that compels us to action, to his mind, but the necessity of nature. And those transcendent values of life, liberty, and estate are viewed as the true goals of conduct to which happiness attaches itself as a by-product. In the *Essay*, happiness is detached from every value but itself. It does not appear there, however, as a positive force: rather it is the removal of whatever causes uneasiness. *Uneasiness*, then, is the compelling urge that drives our consciousness to act in this way or that. The desire to displace or remove unhappiness is the fountainhead of all our labors. As here, according to Locke:

> But that which immediately determines the will, from time to time, to every voluntary action, is the uneasiness of desire, fixed on some absent good...
>
> For we constantly desire happiness; and whatever we feel of uneasiness, so much it is certain we want of happiness...
>
> If it be further asked—What it is moves desire? I answer,—happiness, and that alone.
>
> Happiness, then, in its full extent, is the utmost pleasure we are capable of, and misery the utmost pain...[8]

Indeed, the concern for happiness became the dominant theme of the eighteenth century. And so, in every respect,

8 John Locke, *An Essay Concerning Human Understanding* (New York: Dover, 1959), Vol I, pp 334, 339, 340.

the desire for happiness redirected society's moral disposition. People felt little need to govern their affairs by principles that were sacred, universal, and inviolable. A loyalty to duties that transcended the self in order to further the Public Good, as Locke conceived it, gave way to a concern for purely personal satisfaction. "In short, man had but one moral duty, and that was to live a happy life. The Quest for Happiness...[has become] the Grail of the modern world."[9]

What is worse, the sort of happiness that was being hawked by the self-appointed pontiffs of reason had nothing to do with eternal happiness. It was strictly an earthly brand of happiness, concerned with the here and now. To suppose that happiness was in any way connected to God, the soul, sin, or redemption was a woeful mistake. Religious matters were viewed as obstacles to *real* happiness, which we should have right now! Why wait till later? And so whatever didn't bring personal happiness was disregarded, as at the present. A moral revolution had penetrated to the center of Western civilization, and with it came two relevant consequences: the first was that our perspective on culture underwent a reorientation. Since, in the new understanding, "happiness was not something freely bestowed, it was something you had to win by your own exertions,"[10] people became mere pragmatists; principle no longer governed them.

Everyone's energy went into the improvement of his or her material lot. Society became preoccupied with a "use-value" of means and ends. Its labors ceased to have any connection with the concept of *truth*. The long-run implications of this became apparent when a ruthless anti-intellectualism began to emerge.

Through the nineteenth century this anti-intellectualism ascended and in the twentieth reached its peak—what I *feel*

9 Paul Hazard, *European Thought in the Eighteenth Century: From Montesquieu to Lessing* (New Haven: Yale Univ Press, 1954), p 15.
10 Hazard, p 18.

is right. People came to see themselves less as rational and intelligent moral agents with the capacity to act with foresight and deliberation, and came to put more store, instead, in lower impulses. They tended to regard the satisfaction of every inner desire to be of utmost importance. Knowledge of the truth and a defense of absolute standards gave way to the pursuit of a temporal standard of well-being. This is the hallmark of our day.

How do we reconcile this, then, with today's relatively monstrous academy, and the proliferation of enshrined and often off-base intellectuals? For we have handed our future generations over to their sometimes sincere but sincerely misguided intellectual governance. The answer is quite simple: they, too, reject principle and are guided according to happiness and *feeling*. The rule of what arouses the most emotion, particularly in the area of advocacy of arcane causes (also known as political correctness) now holds sway in the modern academy; and consensus of feeling, not principled justice or a disciplined search for truth, is the law.

The second consequence, which branches out of a growing interest in the first, causes us not only to strive for earthly happiness, but to demand it as our inalienable right. Few describe this sentiment quite as well as Hazard:

> The upshot was that happiness became a right, something to which we were entitled, an idea that superseded the idea of duty. Inasmuch as it was the aim and object of all intelligent beings, the center on which all their activities were focused; inasmuch as it was the primary object of desire; inasmuch as the statement 'I want to be happy' was the first article of a code far older than any written law, than any religious creed, people now gave up asking themselves whether they deserved happiness; they asked whether they were getting the happiness to which they were entitled. The question now was not, 'Am I a good man?' It was, 'Am I a happy man?'[11]

This disposition altered all understanding of the public good. A change was inevitable, because a new rationale was

11 *The European Mind*, p 24.

needed to adjudicate whether the happiness of one person conformed to the happiness of all. What is to prevent the happiness of one from clashing with, and perhaps decreasing, that of another? Keep in mind that happiness is now every person's right. Might not one's pleasure cause another's pain? And how can we be certain that what is increased is general happiness and what is decreased is miserableness? It is significant that while a more relativistic ethic was being forged, its forgers immediately found a new absolute principle on which to base it: utilitarianism now spoke of the happiness of *society as a whole*. This was the goal toward which every person's actions were to tend.

Again, society's needs would take precedence over whatever purposes people set for themselves, in order to avoid the inevitable consequences of purely selfish motives. So with the triumph of utilitarian morality in the eighteenth century, as Himmelfarb astutely observes, "the test of individual conduct was found in the welfare of society, and the warrant of individual happiness in social utility."[12] Is it possible, considering this, to believe that utilitarianism provided the ethical basis for capitalism?

Utilitarianism has only led to welfare and socialism, which is indeed all it can do, once you consider specifically its essential tenets.

Utilitarianism

Utilitarianism is that doctrine which states, "Nature has placed mankind under the governance of two sovereign masters, pain and pleasure. It is for them alone to point out what we ought to do, as well as to determine what we shall do."[13] With these words we come face to face with *natural*

12 Gertrude Himmelfarb, *Darwin and the Darwinian Revolution* (New York: Norton, 1962), p 401.

13 Jeremy Bentham, *A Fragment on Government and An Introduction to the Principles of Morals and Legislation*, Wilfrid Harrison, ed (New York: Macmillan, 1948), p 125.

man, as the apostle Paul would define him. Cornelius Van Til, a more recent teacher, explains that these are the sentiments of "would-be autonomous man." This moral premise generated a school of philosophical thought, primarily in England, formed by the likes of Bentham and the Mills, James and John Stuart.

The moral assumptions of this school are the assumptions of every covenant breaker, whether he reflects on this or not. They are normal for every person whose religious disposition is of the kingdom of man. From any vantage, these assumptions are entirely man-centered. They teach that each ought to think of himself as his own highest duty. Utilitarianism is often regarded as the moral and intellectual (even ideological) defense of the Industrial Revolution. It accompanied that revolution in the course of history, as I have said, but it is maintained nowadays that self-interest is the only philosophical justification capitalism has ever had. Looking closer at history, it is clear that utilitarianism's result is not capitalism but the rise of socialism. Could it be that capitalism can't function in the context of a selfish pursuit of earthly happiness? Or that an exclusive attention to happiness in the here and now saps the moral strength that makes genuine capitalism possible?

Capitalism thrives only in a moral world in which people distinguish and follow absolute values, placing eternal happiness above its earthly counterpart. Another conclusion is equally inevitable: preoccupation with earthly happiness has always and only nurtured the inexorable growth of statism and socialism.

We shouldn't suppose that intellectual utilitarianism reduces every pleasure or pain to the lowest form of vulgar sensualism. There is, to be sure, a scale on which its proponents arranged pleasure and pain in a kind of hierarchical relationship. Mill *fils*, for example, was aghast that anyone would presume otherwise. He claims that "it is quite compatible with the principle of utility to recognize the fact, that some kinds of pleasure are more desirable and more valuable than others...in estimating all other things, quality is considered as well as quantity."[14]

Pleasure, then, means more than the pleasure of animals. Utilitarians strenuously maintain that there are higher and lower pleasures. There is a difference, for example, between mental pleasures and mere *bodily* pleasures. Mill certainly had little doubt that the mental sort were superior to, and ought to take precedence over, those of the body—the common schizophrenia of the antinomian intellect that remains untouched or made one by Christ.

Mill's view is merely his conviction; in the true utilitarian outlook, there is no way to decide whether some pleasures are better than others. For Mill to arrive at his conclusion, he has to abandon his utilitarian position and become an absolutist. If a person should prefer bodily pleasures over mental ones, who is to say that person has chosen a lesser good? If it gives him happiness, why, bodily pleasure is best! Mill would, of course, deny he had abandoned his position; he would insist that nobody would choose the lower pleasures over the higher, because a utilitarian hates to think of our will as having anything to do with moral consequences.

If some prefer the lower to the higher, it's naturally due either to circumstances, ignorance, or a bit of both. Those who *recognize* the higher and the lower will always choose the higher, he says. From this, utilitarians came to view education, or the lack of it, as man's basic problem, and we see where that got education. Like Plato, who taught that his elite, once knowing the good, would naturally do it, utilitarians extend the same moral assumption to all men. Remedy man's ignorance, gentlemen, and he will choose the higher pleasure every time.

Remarkably, however, the actual choice between one sort of pleasure or another, utilitarians say, has nothing to do with moral preference. Naturally! Since no actual distinction

14 John Stuart Mill, *Utilitarianism, Liberty and Representative Government* (New York: Dutton, 1951), p 10.

exists between higher and lower, except as one's happiness is enhanced thereby, why should the choice of one or the other involve morals? The choice resides solely in the pleasurable qualities elicited by "feelings" when any decision is made. How, then, can there be a difference in kind if everything boils down to a matter of one's private feelings?

The only moral criterion allowed is *the greatest happiness for the greatest number*. The principle of utility maintains that when a greater number of human beings are enabled to enjoy happiness, then, morally speaking, that is good; but when the opposite is the case, when a lesser number enjoy happiness, well, then, evil lurks at one's door. No other moral consideration is allowed to govern the pursuits of mankind.

But utilitarianism has yet another twist. It is not so much the achievement of some positive pleasure—a dubious product at best—that is desired; the removal of pain, rather, is uppermost to the utilitarian. One can't expect to be happy when burdened by pain, they say, while at the same time they claim that we would all be happy, naturally, if it weren't for the presence of pain. Remove it, and happiness reigns.

Removing it means removing its causes, and this is the utilitarian's single ethical purpose, this is what utilitarianism comes down to: if, say, poverty causes pain, poverty must be removed, and so on ad infinitum. Nothing is permitted to stand in the way of earthly happiness. Utilitarians believe, then, that mankind's ills are expungable. One should strive for one purpose—to remove as much pain as possible from the lives of as many as possible. To act from any other motive is, to the utilitarian, base and selfish.

Once you understand this, you will appreciate why utilitarians are driven by a spirit of *social reform*. Nothing occupies them more than the desire to change society, to enforce its conformity to their moral goal of achieving the greatest happiness for the greatest number. Utilitarians are incurably self-anointed to improve the lives of others. Or so it might appear. They don't mean, however, simply to inform us of our duty; they intend to organize society through the power of government to make sure we do what we ought to.

What we ought to do, of course, is what they say we ought to.

So the utilitarian strives for a political agenda that will control the life of every citizen. Referring in particular to Bentham, Halevy points out that he "appealed to the legislator to solve, by means of a well-regulated application of punishments, the great problem of morals, to identify the interests of the individual *with the interests of the community*."[15]

The interests of community take precedence over the interests of individuals. Personal pleasure and pain were originally individual preferences, utilitarians recognize, but they are persuaded they can use that individual view to foster genuine social ends. They have unbounded confidence in the wisdom of legislators and governors to apply "scientific" utilitarian principles. As far as they're concerned, morality is identical to legislation. "It is by means of good laws alone that virtuous men can be made; the whole art of the legislator consists in forcing men, through their feeling of self-love, to be always just to one another."[16]

I appreciate that *forcing*. And what lies behind this optimistic assumption is the belief that human nature is a blank sheet of paper on which can be written, by legal means, any moral code the legislator of the moment feels it necessary to imprint. Because human nature, to the mind of the utilitarian, is transformable without limits, it is possible to shape it by government control. The ghost of Plato then emerges as a reality. Only elect or, better, set in place enlightened experts, and they will engineer a just society. No ethical principles exist higher than those of the legislator, with nothing to curb or dictate his actions but his sense of the interests of society.

To "identify the interests of the individual with the interests of society" becomes the chief moral problem, then, of utilitarian reformers. It could be compared to the order-of-

15 Elie Halevy, *The Growth of Philosophic Radicalism*, pp 17-18. My emphasis.
16 Halevy, p 20.

nature outlook mentioned earlier. Utilitarianism only substitutes an order-of-government as its highest moral imperative. I refer not merely to Locke, but also to Locke's successor, Adam Smith, who coincides with the rise of utilitarianism, and so provides a fitting historical contrast.

I mentioned earlier that Locke sought to define the powers and responsibilities of government by an ethic preceding it: the order of nature. Locke summarized the transcendent obligation of nature as the duty to preserve life, liberty, and estate; this is to be the government's sole purpose. It neither creates this sense of duty in us, nor has the right to deny it, and it may not protect these in arbitrary fashion but only by written laws that bind government as well as the governed. Government, therefore, has no ethical agenda other than the one that preceding it, the author of which, Locke maintained, is none other than the Lord God. So the acts of government, its law-making and judicial powers, must be used to enforce a system of values that transcend government's ends.

When government, in Locke's view, departs from this, it can be said to have entered into a state of war with its citizens. For Locke feared not only aggression between individuals; he knew that some would attempt to seize the organized power of government and employ it, by seemingly legitimate means, for aggressive purposes. To prevent this, the role of government was to be carefully circumscribed. That done, people would engage themselves in the duties imposed on them by nature with little difficulty.

Taking this same perspective, Adam Smith went one further and affirmed that, by reason of the order of nature, each one's pursuit would form a "natural identity of interest" with all others. The order of nature could be counted on to guarantee a natural harmony between the activities of each person. Like Locke, Adam Smith remained ruled by the belief that nature's order was upheld by divine providence and a higher moral purpose than self gratification.

Utilitarians, of course, begin from an entirely different set of assumptions. Bentham, for example, denied that anything like a "natural identity of interests" could exist. He rejected the idea of an a priori order of nature. He therefore denied that there was something called "human nature" that rested permanently on higher ethical obligations. There was no absolute moral basis on which to found anything. The only moral duty we have is to be happy, and if a moral order does exist, it is because government creates it.

To the utilitarian mind, we do not institute government because we recognize an ethical obligation and need government to ensure compliance with it, but because we're without morality altogether. Every person is an incorrigible egoist, controlled by feelings of pleasure or pain, and if the interest of one is not to collide with that of another, government must generate an "artificial identity of interests" to give moral direction to our otherwise animal behavior. Commenting on Bentham, Halevy says, "...the interest of the individual must be identified with the general interest, and...it is the business of the legislator to bring about this identification."[17]

There is no moral order, then, that creates and limits government. Government *is* moral authority. The order-of-government then constitutes our ultimate ethical environment. "The legislator is the great dispenser of pleasures and pains in society. It is he who creates the moral order, the equilibrium of interests. Society is the work of his artifices."[18] So for utilitarians there are no such things as "natural rights." All rights are conferred by government, and all are measured by the extent to which they promote the interests of society. Society is the only moral necessity utilitarians are inclined to accept. Legislators are ruled by no imperatives but this one. Just as they are not bound by any prior order-of-nature obligation, let's not think of binding them by conventional limitations: no written constitutions!

To put into practice this ethical—or unethical—program, utilitarians believe that government should *make* law, and

17 *Growth of Philosophic Radicalism*, p 17.
18 Halevy, p 487.

control education. Utilitarians have always been great rationalists, with unbounded confidence in the power of science: "Just as science guarantees to man the power to transform physical nature at will and without limits, so also, if it be true to its word, it should guarantee him the possibility of transforming human nature without limits."[19] The legislator is a man of science, and government is his instrument for the scientific formation of a just society. Since human nature is a product of habit, by controlling the education of our habits, legislators can mould society into whatever shape they wish.

The Welfare State

From these assumptions it was only one step forward to the welfare state. The shift to its brand of socialism was scarcely perceptible, yet it was guaranteed, once the morality of utilitarianism was accepted. But one slight development had to occur before the idea of state-dispensed welfare could arrive in full bloom: the concept of a *positive* society. Utilitarians had thought too much in contrasting terms, it was concurred: on one hand, they recognized the happiness of the abstract individual, while on the other they upheld their concept of order-of-government. Now they needed a positive society to bond the two together in a way that would involve more than the "greatest number."

The idea of the greatest number was too impersonal, too demeaning to be a positive moral ideal for governance. At the same time, the new thinking could not simply posit a new society; in keeping with earlier liberal principles, it had to create a sense of social relationships from the stuff of personal, or individual, experience—such stuff as dreams are made on. The continuity must remain unbroken.

In his book *Liberalism*, L. T. Hobhouse offers us the sort of new liberalism that links the older form, beginning with

19 Halevy, p 53.

Locke, to the social liberalism on which the modern welfare state is founded. Hobhouse finds it necessary to substitute something called "social freedom" for "personal freedom." He hopes to show that personal freedom provides a framework in which social freedom can be attained. To guarantee this, he proposes a new foundation for liberty—not one which, after the fashion of Locke, seeks merely to prevent the encroachment of one person upon another, but one which fosters, in a more optimistic vein, the growth of the entire human personality.

Hobhouse believed this should be the goal of all moral striving, the very purpose of our lives. The growth of personality, the development of will and character, and the achievement of self-control should, in order to bring about positive social harmony, be the real goals of liberalism.

He believed we had two options: either social freedom or unsocial freedom. If we follow in the steps of Locke, he said, we arrive at unsocial freedom. Hobhouse was motivated by high hopes: one "harmonious society." In the new liberalism, social harmony is the driving moral ideal. The route to that is character development. But character development is possible only so long as it is extended to all alike, on an equal basis. So the state has to ensure character development by enforcing equality of *conditions*. It must prevent any disruption in the process of uniformity, and now has the responsibility to act as a positive agent for the maintenance and improvement of life.

But that improvement is not now to be in the life of the individual. It is to go the way of social harmony and social freedom. The state has the awesome task, Hobhouse says, of guaranteeing to everyone a "civilized standard of life." How wonderful it sounds—if anyone could define exactly what it means. In fact, we have come to learn that it means whatever anyone powerful enough to manipulate government wants that standard to mean.

When we examine Hobhouse's view of "economic liberalism," we see even more clearly into his mind. Every economic benefit we enjoy in his system is to have a socially redeeming value: otherwise it is unjustifiable. The welfare of any person must have the approval of society or it will be taken as an unfair advantage over others. In this respect, Hobhouse holds property to be social in nature; that is, legitimate only because the organized forces of society maintain the rights of the owners by protecting them against theft and destruction. Since this is the case, any use of property is justifiable only when it benefits the whole of society. Hear Hobhouse pontificate on this:

> An individualism which ignores the social factor in wealth will deplete the national resources, deprive the community of its just share in the fruits of industry and so result in a one-sided and inequitable distribution of wealth. Economic justice is to render what is due not only to each individual but to each function, social or personal, that is engaged in the performance of useful service, and this due is measured by the amount necessary to stimulate and maintain the efficient exercise of that useful function.[20]

Circular reasoning of this sort offers a moralism which, once it's taken seriously and believed, makes people prey to the machinations of socialist utopians. There is no objective way to tell what constitutes an "inequitable distribution of wealth." The charge can be made on the basis of sheer envy. To render each one his due can easily come to mean what anyone takes to be *his* due. If that is the measure of "economic justice," it's not a standard to which all would give assent. It becomes necessary to extract consent from them, then, by the coercive arm of government.

And what, pray tell, can Hobhouse possibly mean by *useful service*? A useful service, in any economic sense, is a service useful to someone else. If any service ceases to be useful to those who at first found it useful, then on what grounds should wealth be distributed to render the service continuous? Hobhouse can't conceive that a market order, or the orderly demand for services and labor and products on the

20 L. T. Hobhouse, *Liberalism* (Westport: Greenwood Press, 1980), p 99.

basis of market trade, can operate as a dependable gauge by which a useful service receives its due.

For Hobhouse, society has a rightful claim on all the wealth that is produced; and the collective progress of society is of greater importance than the progress of any member. Society is the owner of the property of all its citizens, since it is society that makes ownership possible in the first place—another circle devolving upon the mere question of ownership. Beginning with this assumption, Hobhouse arrives at two significant conclusions. First, it is necessary to impose a graduated tax on all wealth, including inherited wealth, so that society, to lay claim to its rightful due, can "shift taxation step by step from wealth due to individual enterprise to the wealth that depends on its own collective progress, thus by degrees regaining the ownership of the fruits of its own collective work." Again, "On the face of the facts inherited wealth stands on a different footing from acquired wealth, and Liberal policy is on the right lines in beginning the discrimination of earned from unearned income."[21] This is the liberalism that now lives with us.

Second: "The central point of Liberal economics, then, is the equation of social service and reward. This is the principle that every function of social value requires such remuneration as serves to stimulate and maintain its effective performance; that every one who performs such a function has the right, in the strict ethical sense of that term, to such remuneration and to no more; that the residue of existing wealth should be at the disposal of the community for social purposes."[22]

The morality resident in these words can only result in socialism. And who will decide when and where "social service" and "reward" are equated? Who will know when his or her "effective performance" receives the "remuneration"

21 *Liberalism*, pp 100 & 102.
22 Hobhouse, pp 107 & 108.

that is ours by *right*? What measuring device will tell us when wealth becomes residual? Who will say what our "social purpose" really is?

You know the answer to that as well as I: *It is government that will have the say.*

CONCLUSION

THE theologian Herman Bavinck said "that the destiny of man and humanity must bear an ethical character, and that that ethical character must take the first place..."[1]

In this book I have tried to indicate that the ethical character of capitalism and socialism derive from opposite sources, and thus teach contrasting ideals. The ethic that forms the basis of capitalism, including the societal behavior that issues from capitalism, is first and foremost a Christian ethic, while the ethic that is the basis of socialism is, without equivocation, anti-Christian to its core. Each forms the foundation of an antithetical kingdom; each has its own outlook on the life of the people within society. So each represents the basis of differing principles of authority and behavior.

In our day, people are terribly confused about the ethical roots of the two socioeconomic systems. This confusion stems in large part from the decline of Christianity as the undergirding ethical foundation of Western culture, and the acceptance in its place of a moral relativism that increasingly fuels the interests and purposes of socialism.

As the members of Western society have turned away in hatred from the rule of God over their lives, they more and more have looked to the state to engineer solutions to their problems. People now assume that politics is the only means by which to achieve justice and prosperity. The state, in turn, has taken on supreme ethical authority over every aspect of human life.

1 Herman Bavinck, *The Philosophy of Revelation* (Grand Rapids: Baker, 1979), p 259.

Many Christians—far too many, in fact—have lost sight of their own ethic, and have been seduced by the reigning relativism in ethics. As a consequence, they, too, have fallen prey to the seeming glamor of socialist ideals and statist agendas. Like their secular counterparts, they revile and denigrate capitalism as selfish, as materialism personified, and often vilify capitalism with the same emotion found in the high priests of socialism. If modern life has become sterile and impersonal, they place the blame, like their socialist counterparts, on the economic system of capitalism. Many are unaware of the religious and ethical suppositions of socialism, and the man-centered society it intends to build.

The crisis of today is a crisis of ethical authority, and it is at the center of every consciousness. The humanist view teaches the independence of every person from any moral authority except the one that emerges from man himself, in the form of an oligarchy of the elite. The Christian view claims that God's authority alone must dominate and crown our activity in every area of life. The Christian view also recognizes that the authority of God is not external to humankind; it plainly teaches that "good must be the inner inclination of man."[2] This good is whatever God says it is. The good of God will not become engaged in the cultural and economic realms, however, if it does not in the first place engage our souls. This is because human beings are not by nature good in themselves, but bent on rebellion against God.

In order for us to do good, we must first receive good as a gift of God's grace. Our inner natures must be changed so that we will want to do the good He commands. Cultural efforts or works in themselves are powerless to renew us in the inner man. They will only make manifest our innate disposition to be a law unto ourselves. And so "the true, and the good, and the beautiful, which ethical culture means and

2 Bavinck, p 262.

seeks, can only come to perfection when the absolute good is at the same time the almighty, divine will, which not only prescribes the good in the moral law, but also works it effectually in man himself. The heteronomy of the law and the autonomy of man are reconciled only by this *theonomy*."[3] To state it finally, "man must first become again a son of God before he can be, in a genuine sense, a cultured being."[4]

Capitalism, for all its faults, presupposes this ethical perspective. Any deviation from that perspective is a deviation from capitalism itself. Those who denigrate capitalism, claiming that its sole concern is for money and possessions, are not aware that they are using capitalism to describe other ethical phenomena. Capitalism cannot exist without the moral responsibility before God that Christianity teaches. Anything less is not capitalism.

The time has come for Christians to cease to allow humanist propaganda to define the nature of capitalist behavior. It is in the sphere of ethics that the real battles must be fought.

It is questionable, however, whether the Christian church of today is itself doctrinally and ethically prepared to do battle on this most important and compelling, most relevant, and most necessary front.

3 Bavinck, p 263. Emphasis mine.
4 Bavinck, p 266.